Industrialization in the Gulf

In recent years we have witnessed huge economic and sociopolitical changes in the Arab-Persian Gulf region. This book examines the rapid industrialization of the region and how local economies are starting to diversify away from petroleum, exploring how this transformative process is beginning to impact the region's economy and social make-up.

Some of the top scholars and practitioners in the area take on this topic, discussing such issues as economic development, relations with Iran, foreign labor, and women's education and work outside the home. Chapters explore how the massive growth in investments and products such as oil, gas, chemicals, metals, and cement has triggered numerous societal changes.

Covering in detail a broad range of issues, this book will appeal not only to Middle East experts, particularly those with an interest in the Arab-Persian Gulf, but also to development experts and political scientists.

Jean-François Seznec is Visiting Professor at the Center for Contemporary Arab Studies, Georgetown University, and is Senior Advisor to PFC Energy in Washington, D.C. His research centers on the influence of the Arab-Persian Gulf's political and social variables on the financial and oil markets in the region, with a focus on industrialization of the Gulf and, in particular, the growth of the petrochemical industry.

Mimi Kirk is Multimedia and Publications Editor at the Center for Contemporary Arab Studies, Georgetown University. She has a B.A. in anthropology from Haverford College and an M.A. in cultural studies from Emory University, where she focused her research on Islamic and French colonial architecture in the city of Fès, Morocco.

Routledge studies in middle eastern economies

This series provides up to date overviews and analysis of the region's economies. The approaches taken are not confined to a particular approach and include
analysis of growth and future development, individual country studies, oil, multinational enterprises, government policy, financial markets, and the region's role
in the world economy.

The Egyptian Economy
Performance policies and issues
Khalid Ikram

The Turkish Economy
The real economy, corporate governance and reform
Edited by Sumru G. Altug and Alpay Filiztekin

Economic Co-operation in the Gulf
Issues in the economies of the Arab Gulf co-operation council states
Badr El Din A. Ibrahim

Turkish Accession to the EU
Satisfying the Copenhagen criteria
Eric Faucompret and Joep Konings

Turkey and the Global Economy
Neo-liberal restructuring and integration in the post-crisis era
Edited by Ziya Öniş and Fikret Şenses

Industrialization in the Gulf
A socioeconomic revolution
Edited by Jean-François Seznec and Mimi Kirk

Industrialization in the Gulf

A socioeconomic revolution

Edited by
Jean-François Seznec and Mimi Kirk

Published in Association with the Center for
Contemporary Arab Studies, Georgetown
University

Routledge
Taylor & Francis Group

LONDON AND NEW YORK

First published 2011
by Routledge
2 Park Square, Milton Park, Abingdon, Oxon OX14 4RN

Simultaneously published in the USA and Canada by Routledge
711 Third Ave, New York, NY 10017

Routledge is an imprint of the Taylor & Francis Group, an Informa business

First issued in paperback 2012

Typeset in by Times New Roman by Glyph International Ltd.

British Library Cataloguing in Publication Data
A catalogue record for this book is available from the British Library

Library of Congress Cataloguing in Publication Data
Industrialization in the Gulf : a socioeconomic revolution / edited by
Jean-François Seznec and Mimi Kirk.
    p. cm. — (Routledge studies in middle eastern economies)
"Published in Association with the Center for Contemporary Arab Studies,
Georgetown University."
Includes bibliographical references and index.
1. Industrialization—Persian Gulf Region—Economic aspects.
2. Industrialization—Persian Gulf Region—Social aspects.
3. Diversification in industry—Persian Gulf Region—Economic aspects.
4. Diversification in industry—Persian Gulf Region—Social aspects.
I. Seznec, Jean-François. II. Kirk, Mimi.
HC415.3.I53 2011
330.953—dc22   2010004036

ISBN 978-0-415-78035-3 (hbk)
ISBN 978-0-203-84665-0 (ebk)
ISBN 978-0-415-65666-5 (pbk)

Contents

Tables and figures

Tables

Figures

Notes on contributors

Paul Aarts is Senior Lecturer in international relations at the Department of Political Science, University of Amsterdam. He has published widely on Middle East politics and economics. His most recent publications are P. Aarts and G. Nonneman (eds.), *Saudi Arabia in the Balance: Political Economy, Society, Foreign Affairs* (Hurst/New York University Press, 2005/2006); with Joris van Duijne, "Saudi Arabia after U.S.-Iranian Détente: Left in the Lurch?," *Middle East Policy*, 16 (3) (Fall 2009); and, also with Joris Van Duijne, "The Saudi Security Environment: Plus Ça Change ...," in: L. Guazzone and D. Pioppi (eds.), *The Arab State and Neo-Liberal Globalization: The Restructuring of State Power in the Middle East* (Reading: Ithaca Press, 2009).

John Duke Anthony is the founding president and CEO of the National Council on U.S.–Arab Relations; founder of the Arab–U.S. policymakers conferences; founding president of the Middle East Educational Trust; co-founder and first president of the Society for Gulf Arab Studies; and a co-founder and board member of the National Commission to Commemorate the 14th Centennial of Islam. For the past 36 years, Dr. Anthony has been a consultant and regular lecturer on the Arabian Peninsula and the Gulf for the U.S. Departments of Defense and State. He has taught at the Johns Hopkins School of Advanced International Studies, the Defense Intelligence College, the Woodrow Wilson School of Government and Foreign Affairs at the University of Virginia, the Universities of Pennsylvania and Texas, and the U.S. Naval Postgraduate School. He has received the Distinguished Achievement Award of the U.S. Department of Defense's Institute for Security Assistance Management, the U.S. Department of State's Distinguished Visiting Lecturer Award, the Stevens Award for Outstanding Contributions to American-Arab Understanding, and the Medal of the Order of Ouissam Alaouite, the nation of Morocco's highest award for excellence. From 2006 to the present, he has served as an adjunct professor at the School of Foreign Service, Center for Contemporary Arab Studies, Georgetown University. Dr. Anthony holds a B.A. in history from the Virginia Military Institute, a Master of Science in Foreign Service (with distinction) from the Edmund A. Walsh School of Foreign Service at Georgetown University, and a Ph.D. in International Relations and Middle East Studies from the Johns Hopkins School of Advanced International Studies.

Hazem El Beblawi is Advisor and Acting Director of the Legal Department at the Arab Monetary Fund in Abu Dhabi. He previously served as Under Secretary General for the UN and as Executive Secretary for the United Nations Economic and Social Commission for Western Asia (ESCWA). He was also chairman of the Export Development Bank of Egypt. Dr. Beblawi started his career at the University of Alexandria in 1965, and he became Professor of Economics in 1976. He is now Professor Emeritus there. He also taught at Cairo University, Ein Chams University, the American University in Cairo, Kuwait University, UCLA, and the Ecole Pratique des Hautes Etudes (Sorbonne, Paris). Dr. Beblawi has published several books and articles on money and banking, international trade, finance, and development. He also has a newspaper column in the Egyptian paper *Al Ahram*. He holds the titles of Chevalier de la Légion d'Honneur from France, Commandeur de l'Ordre de Leopold II from Belgium, and Grand Officier de l'Ordre National du Cèdre du Liban from Lebanon.

Frances Cook is a former U.S. ambassador to Burundi, Cameroon, and the Sultanate of Oman. She also held numerous senior positions in the Department of State, including Deputy Assistant Secretary of State for Refugee Programs, Deputy Assistant Secretary of State for Political-Military Affairs, Consul General in Alexandria, Egypt, and Director for West Africa. She transitioned to the private sector in May 1999, where she runs an international business consulting firm, The Ballard Group LLC. Ambassador Cook currently serves on the boards of Alliant Techsystems (NYSE), the Global Options Group (NASDAQ), the Corporate Council on Africa, and LONRHO (AIM-London). She is a senior fellow at the Center for Naval Analyses, a member of the board of the Middle East Policy Council, and a member of both the American Academy of Diplomacy and the Council on Foreign Relations. She was educated at the University of Virginia and Harvard University.

Joris van Duijne holds an M.A. in international relations from the University of Amsterdam and has recently published several articles on Gulf politics, including, with Paul Aarts, "Saudi Arabia after U.S.-Iranian Détente: Left in the Lurch?," *Middle East Policy*, 16 (3) (Fall 2009), and "The Saudi Security Environment: Plus Ça Change...," in L. Guazzone and D. Pioppi (eds.) *The Arab State and Neo-Liberal Globalization: The Restructuring of State Power in the Middle East* (Reading: Ithaca Press, 2009). He also works at Free Voice.

Munira Fakhro is a former associate professor at the University of Bahrain, having received her doctorate in social policy, planning, and administration from Columbia University, where she has served as a visiting scholar since 1997. She has conducted research on gender, citizenship, and civil society in the Gulf states at the Center for Middle East Studies at Harvard University, and has published works on Bahrain, including issues related to women, civil society, and democratization. Dr. Fakhro is currently a board member of the

Bahrain Academic Society and the Supreme Council for Women. She was a member of the advisory board for the Arab Human Development Reports of 2004 and 2008. Dr. Fakhro also serves as the general coordinator of the Gulf Development Forum and is a member of the Expert Advisory Panel for the Club of Madrid's Shared Societies Project.

Hatoon al-Fassi, originally from Makkah, teaches in the Department of History at King Saud University in Riyadh, Saudi Arabia, and is a visiting professor in the Department of International Affairs at Qatar University. She received her Ph.D. from the Middle Eastern studies department at the University of Manchester. Her research covers ancient and Islamic women's history, modern women's issues and Islamic rights, women's religious rights, history of the Arabian Peninsula, heritage preservation, and human rights. She is an advocate for reform, particularly in her homeland, where she was one of the main promoters of women's participation in the municipal elections of 2004. She also led a campaign for equal participation for women in areas of worship in the holy cities of Makkah and Madinah in 2006. She currently writes a column for the Saudi newspaper *Al-Riyadh*. In 2008 France decorated her as a Knight in the Order of Academic Palms (Chevalier dans l'Ordre des Palmes Académiques). Dr. al-Fassi's latest scholarly publication is *Women in Pre-Islamic Arabia: Nabataea* (Oxford: Archaeopress, 2007). She is the mother of two: a five-year old son, Ajwaad, and a three-year old daughter, Zein al-Sharaf.

Steffen Hertog is currently Kuwait Professor at Sciences Po Paris and a lecturer in political economy at the University of Durham. His research interests include the political economy of the Arabian Peninsula, Islamic political violence, and structures of authoritarianism in the Middle East. He has published in journals such as *World Politics, Comparative Studies in Society and History, International Journal of Middle East Studies,* and *Review of International Political Economy.* His book about Saudi state-building, *Princes, Brokers, and Bureaucrats: Oil and the State in Saudi Arabia,* has recently been published by Cornell University Press.

Alastair Hirst is a member of the English bar and a Fellow of the Chartered Institute of Arbitrators. He has practiced business law in the Gulf region for the past 30 years, with periods of residence in Bahrain, the Sultanate of Oman, and the United Arab Emirates. In addition to capital markets work, he has been involved in many technology transfer and infrastructure development projects, including the establishment and operation of special zones and industrial estates. Much of his current work is in Arabic language areas, such as legislative drafting and administrative law, as well as in commercial arbitration. He is a visiting lecturer in business law at Sultan Qaboos University in Muscat.

Karen Nielson graduated from Weber State University in 2007 with a degree in political science and art history. She is currently based in New York City.

Matteo Legrenzi is Assistant Professor at the Graduate School of Public and International Affairs at the University of Ottawa. He has published several scholarly articles on the GCC and on international politics of the Gulf. He recently co-edited *Beyond Regionalism? Regional Cooperation, Regionalism and Regionalization in the Middle East* (Ashgate, 2008) and guest-edited a special issue of the *British Journal of Middle Eastern Studies* devoted to Gulf security. He is also the author of the forthcoming *The GCC and the International Relations of the Gulf: Diplomacy, Security and Economy Coordination in a Changing Middle East* from I.B.Tauris. His current research deals with mutual threat perceptions in the Gulf and the feasibility of establishing an alternative security architecture there.

Gwenn Okruhlik is a visiting scholar in the Department of Political Science at Trinity University. She received her Ph.D. from the University of Texas at Austin in 1992. Dr. Okruhlik specializes in the politics of the Middle East with a focus on the Arabian Peninsula. She has worked in Egypt, Lebanon, the UAE and, primarily, in Saudi Arabia. She is the recipient of two Fulbright awards to Saudi Arabia, where she has conducted extensive fieldwork. Her research is largely at the intersection of political economy and social movements. Dr. Okruhlik's work covers a wide array of issues, such as networks of Islamist dissent; oil wealth and the rise of opposition; labor migration and industrialization; regional border disputes; tourism and narrative; struggles over the rights of citizenship; and relations between the government and the private sector. Her work appears in *Comparative Politics*, the *Middle East Journal*, *Middle East Policy*, and the *Middle East Report*, as well as numerous edited volumes.

Mary Ann Tétreault is the Una Chapman Cox Distinguished Professor of International Affairs at Trinity University in San Antonio, Texas, where she teaches courses in world politics, the Middle East, international political economy, and feminist theory. Her recent books include the second edition of *Global Politics as if People Mattered*, co-authored with Ronnie Lipschutz (Rowman and Littlefield, 2009), *Stories of Democracy: Politics and Society in Contemporary Kuwait* (Columbia University Press, 2000), and *The Kuwait Petroleum Corporation and the Economics of the New World Order* (Quorum, 1995). Presently, she is editing a volume on contemporary Gulf politics, and she continues to write regularly about politics and society in Kuwait.

Editors

Jean-François Seznec is Visiting Associate Professor at Georgetown University's Center for Contemporary Arab Studies. His research centers on the influence of the Arab-Persian Gulf's political and social variables on the financial and oil markets in the region. He focuses on industrialization of the Gulf and, in particular, the growth of the petrochemical industry. He is Senior Advisor to PFC

Energy in Washington, D.C. He holds an M.I.A. from Columbia University (1963) and an M.A. and Ph.D. from Yale University (1994). He has published and lectured extensively on the importance of the Gulf's petrochemicals and energy-based industries in world trade. He is interviewed regularly on American television and radio and in newspapers, as well as by the foreign media. Dr. Seznec has 25 years of experience in international banking and finance, of which 10 years were spent in the Middle East, including two years in Riyadh at SIDF and six years in Bahrain covering Saudi Arabia. Dr. Seznec is a founding member and managing partner of the Lafayette Group LLC, a U.S.-based private investment company.

Mimi Kirk is Multimedia and Publications Editor at the Center for Contemporary Arab Studies at Georgetown University. She has held editorial positions at the Institute for Advanced Study in Princeton, *Smithsonian* magazine, and *AARP The Magazine*. She has a B.A. in cultural anthropology from Haverford College, an M.A. in cultural studies from Emory University, and an M.A. in creative nonfiction writing from Johns Hopkins University.

Foreword

Shaykh Mohammed bin Isa al-Khalifa, Chairman of the Economic Development Board of Bahrain, is in charge of economic reform in the Kingdom. He delivered the keynote address at Georgetown University's Center for Contemporary Arab Studies' 2008 symposium, "Industrialization in the Gulf: A Socioeconomic Revolution," upon which this volume is based.

I know many of you have already had firsthand experience and knowledge of the Arabian Gulf and of my home country of Bahrain. Those of you who do will know of the unprecedented growth that is taking place across the region. In just a few short years we have seen our economies transformed through industrialization and diversification. This growth and change in the Gulf Cooperation Council nations—Bahrain, Kuwait, Oman, Qatar, Saudi Arabia, and the United Arab Emirates—is being referred to during this symposium as a "socioeconomic revolution." And although the word "revolution" is sometimes misappropriated, I can assure you that in this instance, it is an apt description of the pace and extent of the current activity and development in the region.

For those of you who have yet to visit the Arabian Gulf, it may be difficult to grasp the scope of this seismic shift. Let me try and give you a brief idea: We have seen small fishing and trading towns in the desert transformed into international centers of commerce and industry in the space of just one generation. Cutting-edge architecture is springing up from the sands, and dynamic city skylines are being shaped and changed daily. What were not long ago small and sleepy airstrips have now expanded into huge international terminals as leisure and business visitors flock to the region, and our airlines have become some of the most respected carriers in the world. We have seen our population multiply as those from the East and the West come to the region seeking employment and opportunity. Our own national populations are growing too, and are better educated, more productive, and longer-lived than ever before. For the economists among you, there is a wealth of hard data relating to this growth.

The economies of the Gulf Cooperation Council (GCC) have grown steadily and sustainably over the last decade, and now have a combined wealth of about three-quarters of a trillion U.S. dollars as well as infrastructure projects underway totaling more than one and a half trillion dollars. Between 2001 and 2005 foreign direct investment (FDI) in the region increased fivefold. Gross domestic product has increased by more than 6 percent each year since 2000, both in Bahrain and across the region. And in 2006 it increased by 7 percent in real terms, according to a recent McKenzie report.

Of course, we cannot ignore the impact of oil on this transformation. The GCC economies have gained substantially from the recent influx of petro dollars, and based on current and future global energy demands, will continue to benefit for the foreseeable future. Indeed, Goldman Sachs estimates a cumulative of between four and five trillion dollars from sales of our energy. Our national energy resources will be enriching Gulf economies over the coming 25 years, above and beyond income stemming from other non-oil revenue streams.

But this is where, for me and for business people the world over, the real interest lies: in those non-oil streams in our diversification—in our post-oil futures. There are a number of people, including some here in the United States, who are somewhat skeptical about our region's ability to achieve success beyond the petroleum sector and develop balanced, productive, and globally competitive economies. These doubts are not totally unfounded, as previous booms saw little impact on our economies beyond our immediate energy sectors.

But what is happening now is a world apart from what we saw in the 1970s. What we are witnessing across the GCC states is a program of real and sustained investment in a post-oil future, in the region, and in its people. The Arabian Gulf is looking to the long term and responding to the need to move from an unearned income model toward an earned income model, one that extends far beyond mineral wealth into a post-oil economy that is real and productive.

With this economic step comes economic opportunity for Gulf nationals, for those immigrating to the region for work, and for businesses looking to tap into what is not only lucrative in key markets in its own right, but also a strategically balanced business center placed midway between the established European and Asian markets—a key growth market that is, in part, helping to stabilize and regulate global business interests at a time when some other markets are sadly suffering downturns.

So business and industry have never looked brighter in the GCC. More people are employed in more businesses across more sectors than ever before in our history. We have seen not only a huge upshift in FDI, as I've mentioned, but also in intra-regional development.

But it is essential that we are honest and open about the challenges that face us today. Over the coming decades, if we are to achieve lasting success, we need to examine and address our economic realities—our flaws, our failings—and do so with a level of openness that we have not done in previous generations. Our oil wealth gives us a valuable window of opportunity to invest in the long-term success of the region, and we must focus on the employment and income challenges we now face, the first and most pressing of which is our changing demographic.

In the Middle East, we have a thriving, young population. Almost 20 percent of the region's population is between 15 and 24 today—one in five people, compared to just one in 10 in the United States. This, on the one hand, presents a significant opportunity. We have been blessed with an amazing and still largely untapped resource of youth, enthusiasm, and vitality—global citizens ready and able to embrace technology and play their role in a knowledge-based future economy.

However, it also presents us with a very real and immediate challenge. We must create the employment opportunities needed to ensure that these people do not find themselves disenfranchised from society, that they are not faced with the evils of unemployment—or worse, underemployment, which has the potential to create dissatisfaction, instability, and political unrest, eroding the very fabric of the communities and wasting the lives and talents of individuals.

In the past the region has tended to create jobs within the public sector or to impose quotas in the private sector to ensure nationals are employed. But these measures are neither effective nor sustainable solutions for a modern and competitive global economy, and indeed act as a hindrance to today's global businesses. In order to rise to the challenge, we need to tackle the issue from more than one angle.

First, we must attract investors and industries that will be able to provide the type of opportunity our citizens deserve, with the longevity needed to sustain and stabilize our growth and development. For this reason we are targeting investors across service- and knowledge-based industries. These will help us build our middle classes and create more diverse, more prosperous, and more balanced societies throughout the region.

Second, we must ensure that our young people leave schools and colleges with the knowledge and skills that these industries demand so that they are able to adapt to the needs of the workplace and at the same time provide a clear benefit for employers in terms of increasing productivity, creativity, and innovation, creating a virtual circle of development and stimulating future growth.

Third, while we need to reduce our dependence on low-skilled overseas workers, we will continue to welcome overseas employees and employers to the Gulf. But our present reliance on a large volume of low- and unskilled workers is neither desirable nor sustainable—not for the region, and not for the countries from which these working men and women originate. The good news is that solving this problem is not rocket science. Many of the tasks currently undertaken by this imported workforce can be mechanized and modernized and replaced with higher-skilled, higher-waged employees from within the Gulf and from other places. What is needed for this to happen is simply a mindset shift. This is something we believe can be changed within the space of a generation if we are willing as a region to embrace it.

I've mentioned the need to attract international businesses and industries to the region, but we also need to stimulate the growth of businesses and products *from* the region. That is why we are now seeing a huge upshift in investment to foster productivity, to increase and broaden access to capital, and to stimulate entrepreneurship and innovation on all levels. The success of our home-grown small businesses, which may well develop into home-grown big businesses, is essential to our long-term development and global presence. For we are now looking outward as a region as never before. We have begun telling the world about what we have to offer as artists, as designers, as business people, and as global citizens.

Part of this outward-looking process is about moving toward greater transparency and accountability. We cannot and should not underestimate the impact global technology and communication is having on this process. Change is inevitable. Although each nation within the GCC is moving at its own pace, and in its own way, there is, and will continue to be, change.

So we are increasingly aware of our status as global citizens, and in keeping with global concerns, we realize that a post-oil future is not just about the depletion of our natural resources, but about the creation of a global community that is no longer dependent on fossil fuels. In the Gulf we have a clear opportunity to explore the promise that exists in alternative energy. We are perfectly placed to utilize and to build on years of experience in the traditional industries of oil and gas. In particular, we see huge potential in the new fields of solar and wind as sources of alternative energy, and we are focusing on investment and research development in these sectors. We are also looking closely at nuclear power and the potential to harness an energy source with partners not regionally, but internationally. Of course, we will not pretend that nuclear power can present us with an immediate, simple, or risk-free energy solution. But we fully appreciate the need to explore the possibilities it offers.

This isn't the only opportunity for future Gulf growth. We know that there is the potential to continue to expand our position as a new, dynamic world business center. In recent years economists have often spoken of the rise of India and China as the new economic superpowers. While we may not be there yet, I expect a day in the not-too-far-away future when the same economists talk about India, China, and the GCC as future rising economic superpowers.

Stretching forward, we predict strong and sustainable futures for business services, professional services, logistics, tourism, health care, and the future knowledge-based industries that we have yet to develop. What is transparently clear is that we of the Gulf, like those of you here in the United States, cannot afford to invest in low-skilled, low-wage employment. Our people deserve more. Instead, the Gulf economies must harness knowledge and innovation and move up the world value chain ladder, increasing the value-added elements to our services for local and global consumption. This essentially means more demand for skills that will be rewarded by higher wages and a healthy private sector, building our middle classes and, in turn, contributing to the stability of the region.

Economic growth is about far more than simply increased opportunities for global business. This symposium is equally focused on social and economic impacts of regional industrialization—and for very good reason. As Chief Executive of the Bahrain Economic Development Board, I am of course interested in forging new business relationships, thus increasing the levels of overseas investors within our shores and fostering new trade links and relationships that contribute to mutually beneficial growth. But what is of real importance to me and my organization is that economic development cannot and should not simply be about building businesses. What really matters is the positive effect our policies and behaviors have across private and public sectors on the lives and well being of our citizens, providing opportunities for businesses and opportunities for the people working in them. Developing the region's new economies is about each of our nations addressing the reality that our true wealth is not, and should never have been considered to be, oil and gas, but rather in the talents and strengths of our peoples and our communities.

We have before us the chance to forge a future that is not hampered with the outdated, outmoded systems of the developing world. We have the people and talent that can help us forge dynamic partnerships, harness technologies, drive innovation, and develop new industries. We are also lucky enough to have the revenue stream that will allow us, if we continue to invest wisely and prudently, to benefit not just the region and our citizens, but the world as a whole.

Acknowledgments

This book compiles a number of papers that were written for a two-day symposium on industrialization in the Gulf in March 2008 at Georgetown University. The Center for Contemporary Arab Studies (CCAS) under the leadership of Dr. Michael Hudson organized the symposium, and experts and practitioners from the United States as well as Bahrain, Saudi Arabia, England, Canada, France, and Germany participated in the event. The Center is grateful to the speakers for making the symposium possible and for delivering challenging talks that gave rise to exciting dialogue with the audience. Unfortunately, not all the participants were able to provide a paper for this volume; among those not included, we would like to particularly thank Ms. Sarah Leah Whitson of Human Rights Watch for an engaging presentation on labor conditions in the Gulf.

The symposium, which gathered participants from at least 24 different universities and organizations, took a staggering amount of work to organize. The staff of CCAS bore the brunt of this work and was extremely successful in bringing about the event. Margaret Daher, Public Affairs Coordinator for CCAS, worked tirelessly to make sure the symposium appeared effortless. She deserves our heartfelt thanks for her efforts and organizational skills. Many larger institutions would not have been able to pull off what she did.

My colleagues at CCAS were extremely helpful in suggesting panels and participants, and I am grateful for their assistance. Of course, Georgetown's School of Foreign Service (SFS), as usual, gave CCAS its full cooperation in this endeavor. Indeed, we were honored to have Dr. Robert Gallucci, Dean of SFS, deliver the opening remarks and introduce our keynote speaker, Shaykh Mohammed bin Isa al-Khalifa, Chairman of the Economic Development Board of the Kingdom of Bahrain. Finally, I would like to thank my co-editor, Ms. Mimi Kirk, for husbanding the papers and editing them to a most admirable level of academic standard.

Jean-François Seznec

I began working as the editor for CCAS in March of 2008, and one of my first days on the job coincided with the Center's symposium on industrialization in the Gulf. I was lucky to be present for the event and to hear the papers in their original form, as well as to meet a good number of the presenters. Little did I know how closely we would work together in the coming months!

It has been a great pleasure working on this volume with my co-editor, Dr. Jean-François Seznec, and I thank him for his collegial partnership on the project. I also thank the contributors for all their hard work and good humor as we honed their chapters. I am particularly grateful to CCAS Director Dr. Michael Hudson, CCAS Associate Director Ms. Rania Kiblawi, and CCAS Director of Educational Outreach Ms. Zeina Azzam Seikaly for their encouragement and for being some of the best colleagues I have encountered. I also thank the rest of the CCAS staff: Ms. Margaret Daher, Ms. Catherine Parker, Ms. Liliane Salimi, Ms. Kelli Harris, and Ms. Marina Krikorian for their continued support and friendship. Special thanks goes to my editorial assistant on the volume, Mr. Robert Duffley, who diligently formatted the manuscript and ensured the bibliographies and endnotes were complete. Joe Whiting and Suzanne Richardson of Routledge continue to be wonderful to work with, and I thank them for their guidance and professionalism.

Mimi Kirk

Introduction

Jean-François Seznec

The Center for Contemporary Arab Studies at Georgetown University (CCAS) organizes yearly symposia on issues of importance to the Arab world. In 2007 and 2008, it became obvious to many observers of the Arab-Persian Gulf that major changes were taking place in the GCC countries. Indeed, it seemed that the region was growing at a pace unseen elsewhere in modern days. The growth of Dubai, the boom in high technology industrial plants in Saudi Arabia and Qatar, and the regional explosion of such enterprises as housing, roads, airports, and harbors were nothing short of mindboggling. Industry was taking hold of the region via massive investments by both states and private individuals, or even more often by joint investments between the private sector and the states. Not reflected in the mere listing of investments and products such as oil, gas, chemicals, metals, and cement are the numerous societal changes, such as labor migration, educational reforms, declining natality, and shifting gender roles, that this growth has triggered.

Furthermore, it occurred to many academics, politicians, and business leaders alike that the changes taking place were not temporary nor merely of local importance. In short, we had been witnessing a tectonic economic and sociopolitical change. For example, it has become apparent that the GCC states, particularly Saudi Arabia, will be the largest producers of chemicals in the world by 2015. This may sound too business-oriented for the political analyst, but such changes in economic power imply a substantial shift in the relations between states.

The emergence of a socioeconomic revolution

Until the end of the twentieth century, the Gulf countries were locked in a "North-South" dynamic, in which richer countries sold goods and military hardware to the Gulf in exchange for large shipments of crude oil. This made the GCC countries completely dependent on the vagaries of raw commodities pricing. The international oil companies, mainly the "seven sisters,"[1] made most decisions on volume of production and pricing without involving the states. Locals were employed and trained by the oil companies, but the numbers were quite small.

After the nationalization of oil began in 1972—suddenly for some (e.g., Libya or Iraq), and slowly for others (e.g., Saudi Arabia)—the local states took over the ownership and management of the industry. Nevertheless, even a locally control-led oil extractive industry requires only a minimal number of laborers. Saudi Arabia, which boasts the largest oil company in the world, Saudi Aramco, only employs 40,000 people, while the country needs to create at least 200,000 jobs per year to keep up with its population. Even adding service jobs to the oil industry does not come close to providing the employment levels necessary to satisfy 19 million locals, 50 percent of whom are below the age of 18.

It occurred to Gulf technocrats as early as 1975 that the countries had to build economies that could provide good jobs at good wages. These technocrats, particularly in Bahrain and Saudi Arabia, began to establish industrial develop-ment programs that could provide this type of employment. It was obvious that because the region's geography does not permit much growth in agricultural jobs, service jobs would be the solution. However, service jobs need something to service. Much effort was placed into developing industry, which would create manufacturing jobs and in turn many times more service jobs.

The initial efforts were slow and halting. In the late 1970s, development policies were based primarily on import substitution. This approach was not entirely successful, as the local economy is fundamentally a trading one. If local industry were to displace imports, the goods produced would either have to be competitive with high-quality and low-cost Asian and European products or protected by very high tariff barriers. This would have decimated the merchant class, which controls all imports, and would have lowered the standard of living of the local population.

Each trading family maintains hundreds of family members and associates. These families are also staunch supporters of the present political systems, which have greatly favored them. Prior to the 1950s, the trading families of the smaller Gulf states were the main source of funding of the local royal families. Even in Saudi Arabia today, the merchant families carry a lot of weight—albeit unofficial—in the political system, effectively lobbying senior princes and the King to preserve their privileges. If the states had pushed for high barriers to protect fledgling industry productions, many merchants and their allies and reti-nues would have lost their basic source of income. As such, high tariffs were a nonstarter in the development equation.

And indeed, how could one expect Saudi-made televisions to compete with Sony or Toshiba? Futhermore, the disastrous example of the backward Syrian and Iraqi economies, which had developed import substituting factories and implemented high protective tariffs, were enough to encourage the Gulf countries to seek another model.

While some Gulf import substitution industries were developed in the late 1970s and early 1980s, they were sensitive to high transportation costs. Factories began to produce cement to provide the booming local construction industry with fresh building material—a necessity for quality construction standards. Various materials based on cement or clay, such as red brick and extrusion for windows, also replaced imported products. However, very few consumer products were manufactured in the region, which increasingly spent its oil money on imports from Asia, Western Europe, and the United States. And while the new cement industries grew and prospered, they did not create enough jobs for the almost 10 million youths.

The effort to create new industries and the services to go with them was then pushed as fast as possible, though skilled labor had to be brought from other countries. As a result, not only did the new industries not create enough jobs for local Gulf citizens, but the countries became dependent on a large expatriate workforce. Further, the merchants, who developed the service industries and competed for service contracts with manufacturers and government entities, also became forced to use cheap foreign labor. Today, close to 95 percent of jobs in the private sector go to foreign workers. The Ministry of Labor has tried forcing the merchants to hire locals, but this has provoked significant tension between the merchants, who feel that their livelihood (read profit margin) is threatened, and the civil service, who believes that the merchants only want slave-like labor that can be easily controlled in order to pocket oil money downstream from the government.

These developments forced the technocrats in the civil service to find a means of boosting the economy within the framework of merchants and foreign labor. In light of the success of the construction supply industries, it occurred to them that the Gulf should manufacture products with which it has a natural advantage. Indeed, a successful cement industry requires low-cost fuel, limestone, and capital, three items in plentiful supply in the Gulf that allowed for large-scale development of cement and its numerous downstream products. It was not hard to see that the main advantages of the region—low-cost energy and a large amount of capital—could facilitate the creation of downstream products from oil and natural gas, both those derived directly and those created further down the transformation chain, such as polypropelene and acrylic products. With tens of billions of dollars, these enterprises could lead the region in a quest to become the world's largest producer of chemicals.

In 1982 the Gulf began establishing large manufacturing plants in joint venture with technologically advanced partners such as Mitsubishi and Exxon (now ExxonMobil). Little by little, Saudi Basic Industries Corporation (SABIC), the Gulf's main petrochemical company, became one of the leading world chemical companies. Today, SABIC does not call on foreign partners to acquire new technology and marketing skills; rather, it develops its own and acquires foreign companies to gain markets and technology when needed.[2] In turn, Saudi Aramco is also going into the chemicals business. It has partnered with Sumitomo in a $10 billion venture called PetroRabigh on the west coast of the Kingdom, and has signed a Memorandum of Understanding (MoU) for a similar, but bigger, venture with Dow Chemicals on the east coast. In Kuwait, Dow is also a partner in Equate, a large petrochemical concern. In the UAE, the state is partnering with OMV, the large Austrian chemical concern, and Borealis, the leading Norwegian chemical manufacturer, to produce ethylene and downstream products.

Qatar, for its part, is developing a large chemical industry in venture with some of the largest Western firms, such as Chevron Phillips.

The growth of the chemical industry is only a small part of the present development. The region is also becoming a major producer of aluminum, a metal whose cost comes significantly from energy (around 50 percent). Hence its manufacturers have traditionally placed aluminum smelters close to sources of electricity. The region is also growing rapidly as a center of direct reduction steel (DRS), particularly in Saudi Arabia and Qatar. Like aluminum, DRS requires large amounts of low-cost electricity and benefits from a location near those sources.

Such industries provide many more jobs than the mere production of oil and natural gas, but still not enough for the numbers demanded by the Gulf's youth bulge. However, each investment requires services, construction, and transport, which in turn create large numbers of jobs, initiating the virtuous cycle of jobs to industry to jobs.

Gulf industrialization has made its mark in Asia. Most of the region's exports go to China. Further, Chinese exports to the United States, Japan, and Europe would not be as efficient were it not for the plastics sold to China by Gulf suppliers. We are witnessing the growth of a new Silk Route, one that could perhaps be deemed the "rayon route," in which plastics replace silk.

The societies of the Gulf are evolving with this modern industrial revolution. The over 15 million expatriates, still outnumbered three to one by the local citizens in Saudi Arabia but outnumbering locals ten to one in the UAE and Qatar,[3] are creating huge problems for planners and political elites. Suddenly the traditional control of society by conservative religious establishments has come into question, and debates about whether to keep local women out of the workforce or allow them to replace foreign workers are on the table. In Saudi Arabia, this debate has centered on whether to let women drive, which would put the hundreds of thousands of mainly Indonesian drivers on whom they depend for transportation out of work. The whole concept of gender segregation has been called into question. In addition, the expatriates are draining capital from the region by sending tens of billions of dollars overseas in the form of remittances. This may not be a major issue when oil income is based on prices at $147/barrel, but when such income declines to $40/barrel or even lower, such as between $10 and $20/barrel as in 1999, it is an issue that cannot be ignored.

Pursuing an industrial revolution and competing in the world based on local technology is feasible, but it requires huge efforts to modernize the educational system. In Saudi Arabia, King Abdullah, his immediate entourage, the civil service, and the merchants are making every effort to develop a new educational system based on exact sciences, research, and the scientific method. Though not officially announced, this new system implies a decline in the amount of *Wahhabi* religious courses taught in school—a major keystone of the *Sahwa*'s[4] control of Saudi society.

Between questioning the role of women and the modernization of education, the *Sahwa* is now under extreme pressure. King Abdullah's economic policies and industrialization efforts show a leader seeking to bring his Kingdom into the twenty-first century, where it will soon be a leader of the world economy. These efforts, which are currently bearing some fruit, will undoubtedly marginalize the *Sahwa*. Whether the King himself is bringing this about or the *Sahwa*'s decline is simply a consequence of modernization policies, the fact is that this movement may become obsolete.

Similar patterns can be seen in other Gulf countries. Bahrain is not blessed with an oil bounty similar to that of the Saudis, and as a result, the al-Khalifas do not have the large sums needed to develop industry and co-opt the various religious establishments that may not support their rule. However, like in Saudi Arabia, some members of the Bahraini leadership are seeking to change the economic system by creating employment for all citizens and limiting dependence on foreign workers. But unlike Saudi Arabia, where the oldest members of the royal family seek to modernize the country, in Bahrain it is the younger generation of princes, technocrats, and community leaders whose aim is to break with tradition and open the economic system to foreign and local investments and modernize labor practices.

The downturn in the world economy and the changes in the Gulf since March 2008

When our symposium was held in Washington in March 2008, the economy of the Gulf seemed to be on the rise. The price of oil on the New York Mercantile Exchange (NYMEX) was hovering at around $98/barrel. This was far from its peak of $147/barrel in July of the same year, yet eight months earlier the price had been around $70/barrel (Lou 2009), not far from the level at this writing. In early 2008, the expectation in the Gulf was that a price between $60 and $80/barrel was likely to continue for the foreseeable future, and that $100/barrel was not going to last. The price did fall, but not before the spike in July 2008 that created the expectation that the Gulf would become enormously wealthy. Even so, the socioeconomic plans of the region's main states were based on income from oil at $60 to $80/barrel. Thus, the future income and expenses expected in March 2008 were in fact not substantially different than those we find today. As a result, the socioeconomic plans currently being developed are not unlike those referred to by most of the symposium participants. In other words, many of the papers presented in March 2008, which would have been somewhat obsolete later in 2008, are turning out to be quite relevant to the situation in 2009.

The difference compared to the situation in 2009 is that the conference was held in an atmosphere of general optimism. Prices were known to be at peaks but expectations were positive, and most participants in the conference saw the future in relatively rosy terms. Today, after a cut in price and income by a factor of more than two, the glass is half empty. This change in perception has altered economic expectations. And, even though the Gulf is suffering less from the downturn than the rest of the world, some tensions have arisen vis-à-vis the development of the region and its effect on world markets.

The SWFs

Perhaps the most dramatic change has been the realization by Western institutions that the wealth of the Gulf is not limitless. 2008 saw numerous articles about Sovereign Wealth Funds (SWFs), with an emphasis on AbuDhabi's ADIA fund, which was reported to have $850 billion in assets that would quickly reach $1 trillion before the year's end.[5] Many reported that the Saudi SWF was over $500 billion. SWFs of Kuwait, Qatar, Dubai, and others in the region were also seen as growing exponentially, with more than $450 billion in assets. All the reports were highly exaggerated. Most of the funds never released a value of their assets, and the figures were the creation of overzealous consultants eager for employment.

In fact, it could easily be argued that the UAE could not have had more than $450 billion in assets. As for Saudi Arabia, it does not technically have a SWF, as most of its funds are managed directly by the Saudi Arabian Monetary Agency (SAMA), the country's central bank, and are invested in U.S. treasuries.[6] Since mid-2008 most SWF investments have decreased sharply along with the value of the bank shares they bought, such as Citibank or United Bank of Switzerland shares. A number of SWFs, including those of the Gulf, irretrievably lost their investments in hedge funds that were liquidated.

In short, the Western financial and political analysts who predicted Armageddon in the West because all the money was going to the Arabs can now predict Armageddon in the Gulf, because the Arabs have no money. The reality is much more stable. The funds did lose capital, but the main ones still have money, and their future income is similar to what was expected in March 2008.

The Dubai debacle

Yet one major effect of the economic downturn is the serious hit taken by Dubai. While the Gulf is not suffering as much as most, the expectations of a downturn in addition to the actual decline in GNP in the rest of the world pricked the Dubai bubble.

The Gulf sells oil and gas to Europe and the United States and in return obtains machinery for its industrial development and consumer products, such as cars, trucks, and IT products. The genius of Dubai was that it was to be the transshipment center for these exchanges, with the free economic zone of Jebel Ali as the hub of choice. Large firms selling in the Gulf, the idea went, would receive goods in huge warehouses in the city, repackage them, and send them on to places such as Saudi Arabia and Kuwait. The harbor at Jebel Ali is certainly one of the largest and most efficient in the world, and the industrial area around the harbor is by far the largest in the region. To this day, the transshipment vision is working.

Dubai's problem came when it tried to translate this transshipment center for goods into a destination center for people. Plans to develop the world's largest buildings, hotels, artificial islands, amusement parks, passenger airline, and other fast growing real estate ventures abounded. These were built with the vision of millions of tourists from China, Russia, and Europe spending their annual holidays in the emirate. It seems easy to say post-crash that tourists are unlikely to visit a place where the climate in the late spring to early fall is avoided by the locals at all costs. Overbearing humidity and temperatures of 95 to 115 degrees F are not conducive to tourism and suddenly seem less attractive to a world suffering from a quasi economic depression. It is thus not a great surprise that most of the amusement parks and related developments have been cancelled. While the Burj Dubai, the tallest building in the world, is now finished and will be occupied as well as the area surrounding it, a kilometer-high tower announced in October 2008 and "The World," an offshore group of islands in the shape of the continents, have become white elephants that are likely to be abandoned.

Hidden behind the glitz and public relations efforts is the fact that Dubai's real estate growth was mainly due to large investments by Iranians directly or through local banks in which they deposit their money. $10 to $15 billion dollars per year found its way between Iran and Dubai, with 400,000 Iranian citizens living in the emirate—four to five times the number of local citizens.[7] With them come over 8,000 Iranian-owned or controlled companies that purchase goods from all over the world and re-export them to Iran after adding a substantial mark-up, allowing Iranian earnings from oil to stay in Dubai. As Iran suffers from the decline in oil income and a badly managed economy, the amounts of money available to stay in Dubai have declined, making the local banks less able to lend to real estate projects.

Dubai finds itself faced with a total debt to entities controlled by the emirate or by its ruler, Shaykh Mohamed bin Rachid al Maktoum, of over $120 billion (Buamin 2009).[8] As a result, Dubai has struggled to fund some of its most sophisticated international transactions, such as the purchase of 20 percent of NASDAQ, the U.S. stock trading organization. It has had to rely on its rich neighbor Abu Dhabi to provide large liquidity to its banks, including a loan of $1.5 billion for the NASDAQ deal. Abu Dhabi also purchased $10 billion in Dubai bonds, with another $10 billion transaction expected before the end of 2009.

Abu Dhabi will likely continue to support Dubai for the time being, but the support will be slow and not as large as many creditors would like. Abu Dhabi's funds are sizable but are invested. For Abu Dhabi to sell some of its portfolio to support Dubai would imply converting paper losses on stocks and bonds to cash losses in a very difficult market, which could lead to further losses. Between the problems of Iranian cash flow and the lack of significant financial support for most unfinished projects, a great deal of Dubai's independence will be surrendered to the UAE federal authorities.

Undoubtedly, Dubai will survive and prosper, though Abu Dhabi will likely play a greater role in the government of the UAE—a role formerly reserved for Dubai. The struggling emirate may also not continue as the image of the Gulf's future. Many Gulf leaders began projects that looked like Dubai; these will likely be scaled down substantially. In addition, Saudi Arabia and Bahrain aim to replace Dubai as a transshipment center. Saudi Arabia is developing the harbors of the Red Sea and is linking its east and west coast with railroads. This should cut delivery time of goods and bypass Dubai. Bahrain is also modernizing its infrastructure. The new port in Manama will be linked by rail to Qatar and could be used as a competitor to Dubai. These plans mean that Dubai will have to adapt and find other niches to exercise influence in the region.

Economic slowdown

Gulf industrialization efforts, like other industries worldwide, are naturally being impacted by the recession. It has been reported that Saudi non-oil exports declined substantially in late 2008 and early 2009. If this is the case, it is the first decline in non-oil exports since the Kingdom's chemical industry commenced in 1982.

The price of liquid natural methane gas (LNG) sold by Qatar, Oman, and the UAE to the Far East, based on a formula linked to oil prices, has declined from almost $20 per million BTU[9] to below $8 per million BTU. The world recession and new sources of supply have caused a glut in LNG, and the fall in prices started in the United States due to a decline in demand. But the glut is actually creating LNG deals between Kuwait, which is short on gas, and Qatar, as well as between Qatar and Oman and Qatar and Pakistan. Such deals would have been counterproductive before the sharp price decline, as a well-known rule of thumb is that LNG should be sold to markets more than 2,200 miles away from the supply source. This is because its export is cheaper by overland pipeline or, in the case of more than 900 miles, by underwater pipeline (Mariot 2006). But now, any sale is an attractive one.

Low LNG prices will seriously impact Qatar's income. Qatar invested over $120 billion in its LNG infrastructure, borrowing most of the funds from banks or from industry partners like ExxonMobil. One can estimate that Qatar requires $3 per million BTU to pay the loans and another $3 per million BTU for depreciation. After paying for the return of its partners and operational costs, in today's market Qatar barely breaks even or could be losing money. However, in cash terms, that is, excluding depreciation, Qatar is doing better than in 2008. Still, the low return will impact Qatar's plans and ability to continue spending à la Dubai on real estate and other ambitious ventures, industrial or otherwise.

The declining cost of methane has also signaled one of the more unexpected impacts of the global recession: economic tension between Saudi Arabia and China. China announced in June and July of 2009 that it would investigate Saudi sales of methanol—whose cost of manufacture is based on the price of methane—at a price below cost. In other words, China accused the Saudis of dumping their methanol into Chinese markets. Dumping, defined as selling below cost of manufacturing and/or below prices available to local buyers, is prohibited by international agreements, especially under WTO rules.

These rules are precise. Any country can sell to its producer at cost plus a "fair profit" (World Trade Organization 2005). The purpose behind this rule is to encourage countries to maximize their natural advantage and increase world trade for the benefit of all. Saudi Arabia is endowed with the cheapest feedstock in the world. Saudi methane is sold to Saudi–based companies, whether Saudi or foreign, at $0.75 per million BTU, which can ultimately translate into a very low production cost per ton of methanol FOB Damman.[10] WTO experts will undoubtedly evaluate the actual cost, which includes a high fixed cost as well as a low cost of feedstock. It is unlikely, though, that total methanol cost would be much above $60/ton, with a world price close to a breakeven at $160 to $320/ton.[11] Including a "fair profit," Saudis could sell FOB Damman at $80 to $100 per ton and still make a substantial profit. This, of course, is only 10 to 20 percent of world prices, but considering that not long ago the cost of Saudi gas was high and that it is coming as part and parcel of oil production, the cost of methane in the Kingdom is virtually zero.

The Chinese authorities, undoubtedly prodded by their chemical companies who must buy LNG or gas from within China piped over thousands of miles, are denying the Saudis their natural advantage. As long as Chinese companies had a growing export market for their products, paying world market prices for methanol was acceptable. Once the exports declined, the Chinese firms felt the competition. Since the Saudis can sell their methanol at almost zero cost plus a fair profit plus low cost transport, the only alternative for the Chinese is to shut their own production lines—hence the squealing.

There is little doubt that such a dispute in a WTO court would be won by the Saudi producers. These disputes create tension and take many years to adjudicate. Methanol represents only $2 billion of trade between the two countries, but it is indicative of numerous fights to come. Because the Kingdom is poised to be the largest and cheapest producer of chemicals in the world within a few years, many Chinese plants, whether locally owned or in joint ventures with the German BASF (the largest chemical company in the world) or others, will shut down. As long as the recession continues, such commercial disputes and trade tensions will intensify, creating a major roadblock to the development of the Gulf beyond producing primary commodities such as oil and gas.

Overview of the book

Section 1/Chapters 1–3: Financing the growth

Steffen Hertog proposes a new structure of development in the Gulf that links large local state companies and development in complete opposition to the common thinking of many market oriented theorists or theorists of development based on export-led growth. Most theories of development have been based on import substitutions such as the type used by Latin American countries in the second half of the twentieth century. This approach proved a monumental failure, as it only increased capital flight, created unreasonable foreign exchange rates, and caused foreign exchange debts.

The more popular development approach then became that of export-led growth among the Far Eastern Tigers—Singapore, Taiwan, Thailand, and Korea. These countries were hugely successful, but their initial success was largely due to their ability to produce high-quality products at very low wages. Eventually high wages were introduced via new and efficient operation lines.

The Tigers were also able to export to a willing market. The United States—the world's largest economy and importer—accepted the products of the Far East through highly subsidized foreign exchange values. This allowed inflation in the United States to remain low and made these countries the bulwark of resistance to the communist world. This was done on the back of American business and labor, which lost entire industries to the Far East. However, this model of export-led growth would not work for the Gulf, as the region's citizens did not have the necessary expertise to produce advanced goods for low prices. Furthermore, it was unlikely that the United States would accept Gulf competition to its industries. Indeed, it is difficult enough for Gulf investors to invest in the United States without undercutting productions there.

Thus, as mentioned above, the Gulf countries went into industries where they have a natural advantage, such as chemicals, cement, and aluminum. Hertog's development paradigm maintains that this development has mainly taken place through highly structured state-owned companies. This may seem counterintuitive, but unlike the state organizations of the former Soviet Union and other communist states, Gulf state-owned companies are both efficient and by and large immune to corruption.

Employees of such companies as Saudi Aramco, SABIC, and Ma'aden Mining Company are over 85 percent national, including women. These companies are state owned or state controlled, but unlike state firms in many other countries, they are managed on the basis of merit, not personal or family connections, often referred to as *wasta*. It appears that the management—strongly prodded by the Ministries of Finance, Oil, and Labor—make substantial efforts to train their employees extensively. As such, the companies develop their own technology and manage most of their global sales with great success. They envision becoming leaders in their field. One might define Saudi Aramco's management as seeking to be a larger ExxonMobil, and SABIC's management as seeking to be a larger BASF.

Of course, these three state companies have access to the cheapest feedstock in the world. This low cost plus enormous access to capital, as explained above, gives SABIC, Saudi Aramco, and Ma'aden a huge profit margin that allows them to spend large sums on training employees and purchasing new production lines worldwide. Hertog sees that state-owned companies in the Gulf are the fundamental engine of development. This framework could be applied to a number of other countries with similar success, although the lack of corruption and the meritocratic management system may be difficult to implement elsewhere.

The writer, in Chapter 2, describes new development paradigms related to Hertog's. In particular, his paper also focuses on the profit-making role of the state, discussing how state companies are using local private capital to develop huge projects without overarching control by governmental bureaucracy. While these two papers look at the reasons for economic growth in the region, a third, by Alastair Hirst, addresses limitations on development. Hirst describes how corporate governance's aims are to achieve transparency and accountability, thus enhancing performance and shareholder value. Three local factors, he argues, inhibit corporate governance in the Gulf: deep conventional respect (at least in public) for the authorities; an ingrained culture of public politeness; and a distaste for public confrontation.

Section 2/Chapters 4–6: Competing models: the Gulf Arab states and Iran

Contributors also explore the relationship between the GCC and Iran. Paul Aarts and Joris van Duijne develop four possible scenarios outlining relations between the two in the year 2030: peaceful hegemonic competition, friendly neighbors, alienation, or continued fragile pragmatism. These scenarios should not be seen as true predictions of the future, Aarts writes, though they are based on probability and plausibility.

John Duke Anthony and Matteo Legrenzi examine GCC strategic relations vis-à-vis Iran by looking to history rather than to the future. Anthony delineates illustrative instances in which Iran, in the eyes of the GCC, failed to pass tests of trust, such as when Iran laid claim to the UAE's Greater and Lesser Tunb islands and to the island of Abu Musa. Legrenzi explores episodes in the GCC's history that show the organization to be a loose forum when it comes to diplomacy, rather than one that boasts supranational powers. For Legrenzi, this setup allows the organization to weather differences among its constituent states—such as their varying policies regarding Iran during the Iran–Iraq War—and shields it from making decisions that could lead to its breakup.

Section 3/Chapters 7, 8: Labor constraints and migration issues

At the symposium, the question of foreign labor provoked an interesting dialogue between the panelists and the audience as well as within the audience. Some audience members felt that the panelists were too critical of how foreign workers live in the Gulf states, and pointed out that by and large the life of expatriates is better in the Gulf than it is in their countries of origin. Indeed, many within the audience had lived in the Gulf as expatriates and had witnessed hundreds of others like them. Yet many criticized this approach, seeing the expatriates' lives as perhaps better from a financial standpoint, but often, especially among the poorer among them, fraught with enormous violations of basic human rights. This discussion was triggered particularly by an exposé of foreign workers' lives in Dubai by Sarah Leah Whitson of Human Rights Watch (unfortunately not available for this volume).

In Chapter 7, Gwenn Okruhlik addresses this lack of human rights given to foreign workers in the region, and discusses the way in which the Gulf's overwhelming dependence on foreign labor fosters social distance and political confrontation among locals and expatriates. She argues that segmentation and differentiation are becoming more rigid among these groups, and that economic and legal distinctions are heightened by physical and social space, such as the walled-off compounds in which foreign workers live. Mary Ann Tétreault approaches the issue of migration to the Gulf through a different lens, focusing on Western-style educational institutions in the region, particularly in Kuwait. She looks at the benefits and drawbacks of such institutions, and advocates for an in-depth assessment of them, noting that there is still time and space for intervention if needed.

Most interestingly, the symposium's keynote speaker, Shaykh Mohammed bin Isa al-Khalifa, Chairman of the Economic Development Board in Bahrain, gave full support to the critical views regarding foreign labor presented by the panelists and opposed some of the more positive views shared by the audience. He argued that employment will cease to be a problem in the Gulf when all laborers, foreign or local, are treated the same. He supports the same cost of labor for both locals and foreigners, with the desired outcome of the hiring of more locals and the discontinuation of discriminatory practices against foreigners such as sponsorship, work permits, and the confiscation of passports by employers.

Of course, this vision implies taxing the use of foreign labor to equalize costs between foreigners and locals. Needless to say, small and large merchants in the Gulf strongly oppose such policies, as they view them as a direct attack on their right to earn a substantial living. Bahrain implemented a new labor law that limits the need for sponsors and other discriminatory practices while taxing the use of foreign labor. Yet the law's impact is limited and has been discussed but not implemented in other Gulf countries.

Section 4/Chapters 9, 10: The role of women in industrialization

These chapters, also controversial due to their critical nature, evaluate the enormous problems regarding the rights of women in the traditional and religiously charged Gulf societies. Hatoon al-Fassi, a Saudi scholar, addresses the effects of modernity on Saudi women, describing the use of closed-circuit television (CCTV) in the Kingdom's universities. Through this technology, women can see a male teacher without being seen, thus following the society's laws of male–female segregation. CCTV, argues al-Fassi, has encourage women to join the education system but at the same time preserves their isolation and invisibility. Munira Fakhro, from Bahrain, also addresses the role of modern industrialization in women's everyday lives. She discusses the subtle increase in the number of Bahraini women joining the industrial sector and how such jobs expose women to longer working hours, making it difficult to balance work and family. These transformations in women's lives, notes Fakhro, have not been accompanied by legislation that would protect women's rights and advocate on their behalf.

Section 5/Chapters 11, 12: Gulf industrialization in perspective

A section in which the contributors define the issues at stake rounds out the volume. While this information was presented at the beginning of the symposium, we have positioned it as the concluding section of the volume for those non-specialists who need extra background. Hazem Beblawi outlines two basic concerns for the Gulf, namely that oil is a depletable natural resource and that the region depends too heavily on imported labor. Beblawi argues that the Gulf economies must diversify in order to solve the first concern, and that an acceptance of Yemen into the GCC would provide the states with a much-needed, local labor force. Ambassador Frances Cook discusses other fundamental issues facing the region, such as the danger of large numbers of Gulf youths in need of employment, and how a greater awareness of the importance of women to economic development and the industrialization process is required for Gulf society to continue to advance.

The 2008 Center for Contemporary Arab Studies symposium, "Industrialization in the Gulf: A Socioeconomic Revolution," was a great success in that the discussions resulting from the papers were fruitful and benefited both the panelists and the audience. It is the hope of the organizers and editors that this compendium of the papers presented will continue this discussion and will make a difference in understanding the importance of the changes taking place in the region today.

Notes

1 The seven sisters in the 1950s consisted of the main international oil companies of the time: Standard Oil of New Jersey (Exxon), Standard Oil of California, Mobil Oil, Gulf Oil, Texaco, Shell Oil, and British Petroleum.
2 SABIC partners in joint ventures with 10 companies, such as ExxonMobil, but it has complete control over 36 other firms. It has acquired the advanced plastics division of GE, the assets of Huntsman in Europe, and it also runs seven companies in Saudi Arabia.
3 These figures are not precise, as Gulf governments seem wary of providing real figures for political reasons. STRATFOR has made an attempt to show the ratios: http://web.stratfor.com/images/middleeast/Mideast_pop_800.jpg.
4 Stéphane Lacroix has explained that the Saudi religious establishment is managed by the *Sahwa* (the Islamic reawakening). The *Sahwa* came about as an alliance between the Muslim Brothers, forced out of Egypt in the 1950s and 1960s, and the old line *Wahhabi*. The Brothers were welcomed in Saudi Arabia and, being well educated, were employed as teachers. In 1979, King Fahad had to make a deal with this alliance of *Wahhabi* and Muslim Brothers to protect the legitimacy of the al-Saud family. The deal basically gave control of society—education, media, the role of women—to the *Sahwa* in exchange for an affirmation of state control by the al-Saud.
5 See McKinsey Global Institute 2008 and Kern 2007.
6 See Seznec 2008.
7 See Davidson 2008, who argues that there are only 80,000 locals in Dubai.
8 Mr. Buamin's presentation was attended by the writer and reported by *Gulf Today* on 2 March 2009. Interestingly, a few days prior, Shaykh Mohamed bin Rashid mentioned that the debts totaled $80 billion. When asked by a journalist about the discrepancy, Mr. Buamin stood by his figure.
9 Natural gas is normally priced in millions of British thermal units (BTUs).
10 The prices given are Free On Board (FOB), that is, exclusive of transportation costs.
11 Methanol in September 2009 was selling for $210/ton; it was selling for $360/ton in mid-2008. Cost of manufacturing methanol is still somewhere between $4 and $8 per million BTU. This implies a world price close to a breakeven at $160 to $320 per ton of methanol. These figures are estimated from the prices reported in *Chemical Week*,

the leading chemical industry magazine published in the United States. The prices are for methanol in the United States and methane imported by pipeline in the United States as reported by the International Energy Agency for March 2008 and 2009. I converted cents/gallon to dollars/tons using 42 gallons per barrel and 10 barrels per ton for methanol.

Bibliography

Buamin, H. (President of the Dubai Chamber of Commerce) (2009) Presentation, Dubai, 1 March.

Davidson, C.M. (2008) *Dubai: The Vulnerability of Success*, New York: Columbia University Press.

Kern, Steffen (2007) "Sovereign Wealth Funds: State Investments on the Rise," Deutsche Bank Research, 10 September.

Lou, J. (2009) "NYMEX Light Sweet Crude Oil Futures Prices." Online HTTP: www.eia. doe.gov/emeu/international/crude2.html (accessed 21 October 2009).

Mariot, C. (2006) Presentation at the LNG Financial Summit, Doha, 12 September. Reported in *Middle East Economic Survey* (2006) 49 (45): 7–8, 6 November.

McKinsey Global Institute (2008) *The Coming Oil Windfall in the Gulf*, McKinsey Global Institute, January.

Seznec, J.-F. (2008) "The Gulf Sovereign Wealth Funds: Myths and Reality," *Middle East Policy* 15 (2): 97–110.

STRATFOR "Foreign v. Native Population in the GCC." Online HTTP: http://web. stratfor.com/images/middleeast/Mideast_pop_800.jpg.

World Trade Organization (2005) "Report of the Working Party on the Accession of the Kingdom of Saudi Arabia to the World Trade Organization," WT/ACC/SAU/61, 1 November.

Section I

Financing the growth

1   Lean and mean

The new breed of state-owned enterprises in the Gulf Monarchies

Steffen Hertog

Introduction

Although economists increasingly agree that the state plays an important role as facilitator of economic development, there is still near-consensus that it should not play a direct role in the production of private goods and services. Another received wisdom is that oil-rich states suffer from particularly bloated and inefficient public sectors. State-owned enterprises (SOEs) outside of the infrastructure and utility sectors are generally seen as a bad, outmoded, and fiscally deleterious idea—especially in rentier states, which derive all or a substantial portion of their income from natural resources. Several of these states have had catastrophic experiences with state-led industrialization.

As such, it is surprising that a new generation of dynamic, profitable, and rapidly growing SOEs have emerged in the oil monarchies of the Gulf in recent years, and are increasingly operating on global markets. These SOEs operate successfully in both manufacturing and service sectors, and stand in striking contrast to the politicized and inefficient SOEs in more populous and more populist oil states such as Venezuela, Iran, or Russia. The new breed of Gulf SOEs necessitates a rethink of conventional assumptions about state-led development.

This paper first describes the commonalities that underlie the general success of Gulf SOEs. It then presents Saudi Arabia's SABIC as a case study, speculates about the motivations that have led to the creation and expansion of the Gulf SOE sector, analyzes the political circumstances in the Gulf Cooperation Council (GCC) that have made the political insulation of profit-oriented public companies possible, and concludes with some thoughts on the future of GCC SOEs.

Commonalities

The new SOEs in the GCC have several characteristics in common that distinguish them from old-school SOEs created during the age of import substitution industrialization.

Their management is structured in line with international corporate practice. They are not subject to civil service regulations, can engage in competitive hiring, and have profits as their main, though not only, operating goal. Supervised by boards

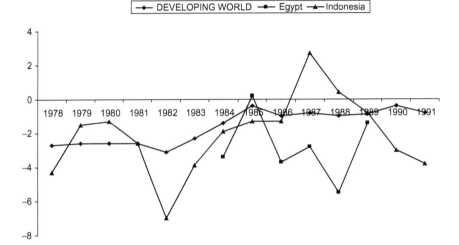

Figure 1.1   SOE overall balances before transfers (% GDP).
Source: Derived from World Bank Bureaucrats in Business Database and World Bank
Development Indicators and SAMA Data.

that usually include both senior bureaucrats and private sector representatives,
executive level posts carry the same titles and responsibilities as those of large
private companies.

Their leadership is judiciously selected by the ruling families with managerial
capabilities as the overriding selection criterion. Some rulers, it is reported, send
out informants to scour for high potentials in local business, bureaucracy, and
universities (Huyette 1985; Davidson 2008). While ruling family members often
act as company chairmen, the CEOs are almost invariably commoners. This
makes SOEs different from large swathes of the state apparatus, in which princes
or shaykhs often play a large role, such as in Qatar and Bahrain, where they dominate cabinets, as well as in Kuwait and the UAE, where they have a significant
cabinet presence. Many CEOs come from merchant families and other elite clans
close to the rulers, but they also include bright upstarts with less distinguished
backgrounds.

SOE managers thus often enjoy *special access to the ruling family*, allowing
them to bypass the sluggish national bureaucracy on matters of regulation and
infrastructure. Senior managers tend to develop long-term relationships of
trust with rulers, resulting in less personnel fluctuation than in other developing
countries.[1] Confidants of the rulers, such as Sultan Ahmad bin Sulayem in Dubai,
Abdulaziz Al-Zamil in Saudi Arabia, or Abdullah Al-Attiyah in Qatar, have been
entrusted with a variety of senior managerial posts over time.

Highly paid foreign experts often play an important role in management,
although less so in more populous Saudi Arabia than in the smaller shaykhdoms.
However, in all cases, SOEs employ much larger shares of nationals than the
local private sector does.

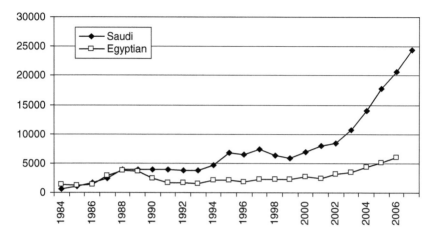

Figure 1.2 Saudi and Egyptian non-oil exports since the mid-1980s (million US$).
Source: Calculated from World Bank Development Indicators and SAMA Data.

Different from the developing country SOEs of the 1960s and 1970s, the new breed of SOEs is also *outward-oriented*, exporting its goods and services region-ally and, in many cases, globally. That Saudi Arabia has become the largest non-oil exporter in the Arab world is owed, to a large extent, to its state-owned heavy industry (Figure 1.2 compares its exports with that of the most populous Arab state, Egypt). Banks, service, and logistics companies from other GCC states are also increasingly exporting their services in the Middle East and North Africa (MENA) region and beyond.

Actors and sectors

The new brand of Gulf SOEs is not limited to infrastructure and heavy industry, but is active in a plethora of old and new growth sectors. Some of them predate the oil boom of the 2000s, but have been given new impetus by the new era of economic expansion and growing budgets.

- *Heavy industry* is the one manufacturing sector in which Gulf governments already had a sizeable presence before the current boom, which has strongly accelerated developments and boosted global ambitions. Saudi Basic Industries Corporation (SABIC), founded in 1976, is the regional leader. It has picked up large assets in U.S. and European markets since 2002, and recorded an unprecedented profit of $7.2 billion in 2007. Industries Qatar, established in 2003, has followed the SABIC model and recorded a profit of $1.37 billion in 2007. In 2006, Abu Dhabi established ADBIC, inspired by SABIC in more than name, which plans to invest $6.5 billion to build a plastics factory and expand an existing steel plant. Further heavy industry

SOEs include aluminum ventures Alba in Bahrain, Dubal in Dubai, and the EMAL joint venture of Dubal and Abu Dhabi's Mubadala. Several Gulf governments have also initiated new refinery projects at home and abroad, and through SOEs IPIC and Taqa, Abu Dhabi has been investing in international upstream energy assets.

- *Real estate* has traditionally been a sector in which Gulf governments have invested heavily but contracted out the implementation of projects to private players. In recent years a number of state-created or at least partly state-owned large corporations have entered the sector with their own projects. Dubai's Emaar has been the trendsetter, and has become increasingly active in tourism and realty projects in the wider Middle East and Asia. Its 2007 profits amounted to $1.73 billion. Its main local rival, Nakheel, also has ambitious international expansion plans. Qatar's Diar, created in March 2005 with a capital of $1 billion, seems clearly modeled on the Emaar paradigm, as is Ras Al-Khaima's RAK Properties.
- *Logistics and transport* is another sector in which Dubai has set the pace of regional development. Through Dubai World's various daughter companies, it is not only operating a local free zone, airport, and ports infrastructure, but is exporting logistics services worldwide. Whereas other GCC countries have not yet ventured into international non-hydrocarbon logistics markets, they have followed Dubai's lead into international aviation; its Emirates Airline, profitable since its inception in the 1980s, has been imitated by Abu Dhabi's Etihad as well as Qatar Airways. Ras Al-Khaimah has also announced its own airline. Dubai recently ventured into aviation technology with its 2006 Dubai Aerospace venture, closely followed by Abu Dhabi's Mubadala, which announced its own aerospace plans in February 2008.
- Fully or partially state-owned companies are also dominating the Gulf *telecoms* sector, and have been highly profitable. Although turning a profit in only partially liberalized home markets is not difficult, the UAE's Etisalat, Qatar's Qtel, and Bahrain's Batelco have also been successful in foreign markets in the Middle East region and beyond. For example, Etisalat's Saudi Arabian joint venture, Mobily, turned a profit of $370 million in 2007 after only two and a half years of operation, and Saudi Arabia's STC and Oman's Omantel have recently started to invest in Asian markets.
- Reversing a trend of gradual denationalization, Gulf governments have recently created several new companies in the *banking* sector. In January 2008 Dubai Holding launched the new Noor Islamic Bank with a capital of $1 billion. The Saudi government has set up a new bank, "Inma," that raised $2.8 billion in an IPO in April 2008. Kuwait reportedly also has plans to establish a new Islamic bank, "Jaber Bank," 76 percent of the shares of which are to be distributed to Kuwaiti citizens.

Furthermore, Gulf governments have initiated new ventures in tourism, media, and new technologies, such as renewable energy. Some of the SOEs whose managerial capacities have been proven are also venturing into new sectors; Industries

Qatar has recently announced a joint venture in real estate with another partially state-owned company, while Etisalat is moving into the real estate management business.

The various free zones, specialized "cities," and other investment enclaves in the GCC are often run by administrations very similar to the SOE model, organized along corporate lines and enjoying special regulatory status. The new generation of charities initiated by Gulf ruling families, most notably "Dubai Cares," is also run along corporate lines. There are, of course, overstaffed, sluggish, and corrupt SOEs in the GCC, as in most developing countries. These inefficient SOEs coexist, however, with a significant number of islands of efficiency that are unique in the rentier universe—and possibly in the developing world at large.

Clusters and industrial strategy

One advantage of SOEs is that their activities can be easily embedded in national sectoral strategies, and their activities can be coordinated so as to maximize synergies. Examples of targeted state support and SOE coordination include:

- The provision of state lands for SOEs in the real estate sector, including for Emaar and Nakheel in Dubai and Barwa in Qatar.
- The provision of cheap petrochemical feedstock for SABIC, Industries Qatar, and other state-owned petrochemicals companies by their respective national oil companies.
- Access to national infrastructure for logistics companies, such as airport facilities for the new national airlines, which helps both budding airport companies and national airlines.
- Close cooperation on governance matters, such as coordinating with SOEs in the introduction of e-governance services, smart cards, and other government transactions.
- Creating a critical demand for the consumption of locally produced goods and services. In 2007, for example, Qatar Airways announced that it would soon run its fleet on locally produced gas-to-liquids fuels, while Dubai government departments are renting space in local real estate projects struggling to find private tenants.
- DP World's listing on the new Dubai International Financial Exchange (DIFX), itself run along corporate lines, helped the latter toward its aim of listing a critical mass of blue chip stocks. The listing of a $2 billion *sukuk* Islamic bond by the Jebel Ali Free Zone Authority served the same purpose. The Qatar Financial Center hopes for similar synergies in the course of large-scale debt issues for national industrial projects.

Another important developmental use of SOEs is the training of national manpower, which the local private sector is not willing or capable of undertaking. This is increasing in urgency with growing local underemployment. Next to

Saudi national oil company Aramco, SABIC has been the most important trainer of qualified national labor.

A case study: SABIC

SABIC is the Gulf SOE with the longest successful track record, and in many ways it is the most impressive company in the MENA region. Its genesis, structure, strategy, and relationship to regime elites are in many ways representative of the leading GCC SOEs. Its history is therefore worth investigating in depth.

Patron–client politics at the creation

SABIC came into being in 1976 through a royal decree of then-king Khaled. The real driver of Saudi industrialization in the royal family, however, was Khaled's half brother and crown prince Fahd, who had positioned himself as a modernizing figure since the 1960s (*Activities of Prince Fahd* 1970; *Survival Prospects for the House of Saud* 1966; *Signs of a Modernizing Establishment* 1971). After the assassination of King Faisal in 1975, Fahd became the main player in the field of economic and administrative development. He reared a number of young technocratic clients for high office and started sidelining or replacing several of Faisal's older clients (former UK ambassadors to Saudi Arabia 2005; Gillibrand 2005). Fahd scoured local universities for promising technocrats and consulted with his ministers to identify talented managers (Huyette 1985: 78). Fahd became king after Khaled's death in 1982.

Fahd's industrializing ambitions resulted in two pivotal entities: the Royal Commission for the Industrial Cities of Jubail and Yanbu (RCJY), which he chaired, and SABIC, which was chaired by Western-educated Ghazi al-Gosaibi, a young client of his who was appointed to the new post of Minister of Industry and Electricity in a 1975 cabinet reshuffle. SABIC's first CEO was Abdulaziz Al-Zamil, a U.S.-trained engineer and, like Gosaibi, a scion of a prominent Saudi merchant family with roots in the Central Province (*MEED* 1976b: 25).

Under the stewardship of Fahd and his full brothers, SABIC became the main agent of heavy industrialization in Saudi Arabia, taking the responsibility for petrochemicals as well as steel and fertilizer projects away from the General Organization of Petroleum and Minerals (Petromin). Petromin had been established in 1962 under the Ministry of Petroleum and Minerals as a would-be future national oil and heavy industry company.[2] Zaki Yamani, a long-time protégé of Faisal, headed the Ministry from 1962 to 1986; Petromin's CEO, Abulhadi Taher, was himself a client of Yamani. Like many of Faisal's commoner clients, both were from the Kingdom's more developed Western province, which lost some of its privileged standing in the technocracy after Faisal's death.

Faisal's interest in economic development had been limited, and Petromin had a history of delayed and cancelled projects as well as a reputation for corruption, disorganization, and clientelist over-employment (former Saudi bureaucrats 2007;

Holden and Johns 1982: 391; *MEED* 1974: 930–93). Reduced to refining and mining operations after 1976, but still growing in scale until the mid-1980s, it was gradually dismantled after 1988, when Aramco took over, dissolved, or reha-bilitated its largest assets (APS 1993a).

Like Petromin, SABIC was founded as a 100 percent state-owned entity. But in contrast to Petromin, it was incorporated as a company. The state supported SABIC through soft loans from the Public Investment Fund, but SABIC's core mandate has always been to generate returns (Montagu 1994: 80; bin Salamah 2007; Former Saudi deputy minister 2007). Indeed, the ambition of the young technocrats at its core—prodded by Fahd—was to set a clear counterexample to Petromin. With an authorized capital of about $3 billion—easily affordable in a period of rapid fiscal expansion—it operated on a scale that was clearly beyond the means of the local private sector at the time (*MEED* 1976a: 22).

A systematic buildup

SABIC's initial management team was small, and corporate expansion proceeded only after several years of careful project studies by a team of around half a dozen Saudi managers and engineers (bin Salamah 2007). Ghazi Al-Gosaibi reportedly insisted on SABIC operating like a private company with fully autonomous management (SABIC Americas 2001: 34).

Several multinational petrochemical companies rated SABIC's profit outlook as dim (*MEES* 1976: 3). After extensive negotiations, Dow abandoned its planned Petrokemya joint venture with SABIC, which SABIC then converted into a 100 percent Saudi-owned project (SABIC Americas 2001: 64f). Given the Kingdom's underdeveloped administrative apparatus and lack of industrial history, the odds indeed seemed against Saudi Arabia as a successful rentier modernizer.

This did not prevent SABIC and the Ministry of Industry from planning a range of import substitution projects in chemicals, plastics, and building materials (*MEED* 1977: 40). In the meantime, Fahd gave the RCJY under its vice-chairman and Minister of Planning, Hisham Nazer, a close advisor of his (and rival of Yamani), the task of setting up two world-scale enclaves of industrial infrastructure to host SABIC and private industry. Reporting directly to Fahd, the RCJY could avoid entanglements with the rest of the national bureaucracy, rapidly issue international construction contracts, and circumvent the sluggish line agencies usually responsible for water, electricity, and roads (Gillibrand 2005).

Between 1979 and 1981, SABIC started construction on a number of large-scale petrochemical projects, the majority of which were joint ventures with multinationals. By the mid-1980s, most of the large plants at Jubail and Yanbu were coming on stream (APS 1993b), including Petrokemya. Twenty-five percent of SABIC shares were sold off to the Saudi public and to GCC investors in 1983, while a parallel plan to privatize Petromin never got off the ground, as the organi-zation proved impossible to value (Gillibrand 2005).

Transitions and self-defense

SABIC is perceived as an institutional "fortress" that has defended itself success-fully against bureaucratic encroachments or rent-seeking by minor royals (Colitti 2006). This has to do both with the direct royal interest in keeping SABIC func-tional and, relatedly, with the protection afforded the company by successive Ministers of Industry and by two powerful Ministers of Finance, Mohammad Abalkhail and Ibrahim al-Assaf. Both were close technocratic advisors to Fahd (Senior Ministry of Petroleum Representative 2007).

Different from the national bureaucracy, SABIC has had autonomous control over its competitively rated recruitment (Anonymous interviewees 2003–2008; Colitti 2006). Although it has been to some extent overstaffed to train locals (Montagu 1994: 31), admission requires significantly better qualifications than for most bureaucratic posts, and the company appears to maintain internal meri-tocracy. Its senior management still consists mainly of managers who joined the company in 1976. When Abdulaziz Al-Zamil was promoted to Minister of Industry and Electricity in 1984, he was succeeded as CEO by Ibrahim bin Salamah, previously responsible for the company's project planning. SABIC's current CEO, Mohammad Al-Mady, joined the company in 1976 as director of one of its joint ventures.[3]

SABIC and the business class

SABIC has had its share of conflicts with the local private sector over the avail-ability of local feedstock and over who gets to develop more profitable chemicals (Montagu 1994: 68; *Saudi Arabia Monitor* 1987: 3). The government has liter-ally had to force SABIC to sell some of its feedstock locally to enable industrial development (*Saudi Arabia Monitor* 1987: 5). At the same time, however, SABIC has offered local investors shares in several of its large-scale projects, including the 1984 Ibn Hayyan plastics venture and the 1993 Ibn Rushd Industrial Fibers project; both are undertakings without any foreign equity. SABIC feedstock has also allowed a large and wholly private Saudi plastics industry to emerge, with more than 800 companies active in the sector (*ICIS News* 2008). Although it is a rival to large private investors, SABIC has also blazed the trail for large-scale petrochemicals ventures in the GCC, which conservative local businesses would have been unlikely to engage in without a clear paradigm to follow.

SABIC's performance in comparison

Although SABIC's market entry coincided with a phase of depressed global petrochemicals prices, it has been consistently profitable since its large plants came on stream. It did not incur the losses that other international petrochemicals companies incurred in the early 1990s (*ICIS News* 1995), and its output has increased dramatically from 13 million tons in 1992 to 55 million tons in 2007 (*Al Bawaba* 2008). While petrochemicals projects in other oil exporters, such as

Iran, Venezuela, Mexico, Algeria, and Libya, have often run below capacity and at considerable deficit, SABIC is rated a more than sound investment.

Also, SABIC has constantly produced higher returns than its main international rival, Dow. When Dow incurred losses during the market slump in 2001 and 2002, SABIC produced returns of $500 and $760 million, respectively. Dow produced pre-tax profits of $4.3 billion on sales of $53.5 billion in the more benign market climate of 2007, while SABIC produced profits of $7.2 billion on sales of $33.7 billion. BASF, the main international rival of SABIC and Dow, produced pre-tax returns that year of $6.9 billion on sales of $58 billion (BASF 2007; Dow Chemical 2007; SABIC 2007). SABIC is therefore about twice as profitable as its international rivals, or roughly three times as profitable if the latter's tax liabilities are factored in. Given SABIC's local feedstock advantage, this is entirely explicable, yet it stands in stark contrast to other cases of rentier state heavy industry outside of the Gulf.

SABIC as global SOE

Eighty-five percent of SABIC's 17,000 employees are Saudi nationals, and its workforce relative to its sales volume is considerably smaller than that of its rivals (SABIC 2009).[4] Although this likely has to do with SABIC's stronger focus on capital-intensive basic chemicals, it is difficult to argue that the company's payroll is excessively bloated. SABIC has also built up considerable in-house expertise and pursues domestic projects without foreign partners, either on its own or with the local private sector.[5] While other rentier states are compelled to open their obsolete heavy industry sectors to foreign investors, SABIC, like Aramco, has increased its technological autonomy over the years.

Reversing its role vis-à-vis international industry, SABIC has pursued a global expansion strategy since 2002, acquiring aging European assets such as the Dutch DSM Petrochemicals (2.2 billion Euros in 2002) and the UK's Huntsman Petrochemicals ($700 million in 2006). In 2007, SABIC moved downstream with its $11.6 billion acquisition of GE Plastics. Although SABIC's statute demands the sale of 75 percent of its shares to the public, it is still 70 percent state-owned and will likely remain so for the time being (*MEED* 1977: 40).

SABIC as a model case

Although some parts of the SABIC story are specific to its Saudi political context and its specific role as an early player in heavy industry, other parts are strongly reminiscent of the successful SOEs in other Gulf states. Factors such as the patronage of senior ruling family members over select technocrats, special dispensations to circumvent existing bureaucracy, targeted state support coupled with a clear mandate to generate returns, and meritocratic recruitment and substantial managerial autonomy are all characteristic of the other cases mentioned above. Trusted lieutenants like Zamil and Gosaibi find their equivalents in figures like Mohammad Al-Abbar and Sultan Ahmed bin Sulayem in Dubai,

Khater Al-Masaad in Ras Al-Khaimah, Khaldoun Al-Mubarak in Abu Dhabi, and Abdullah Al-Attiyah in Qatar.

Why does it happen?

There are a number of motivations for the creation of the SABICs and Emaars of the GCC. SOEs represent an attempt to put oil surpluses to productive local use while not simply redistributing them to the private sector. While pro-business, the GCC regimes are also very conscious of keeping some degree of strategic control over the diversification process. SOE-led development also allows for breaking new ground in sectors in which local business is reluctant to invest due to lack of experience or perceived risk.

Through the numerous partial IPOs of new SOEs, governments have also managed to redistribute some of the oil wealth without creating direct budgetary entitlements among national populations, as they did through indiscriminate public employment during the last boom.

The IPO of minority SOE holdings is often restricted to nationals, and shares are often sold below fair price. This leads to a windfall income for nationals in the short run and, as rulers hope, could contribute to a "popular capitalism" that in the long run would create a steady stream of dividends (read: rents) to the national population that does not directly burden the public purse, creating a more refined, less politically burdensome mode of rent recycling through widespread share ownership. IPO subscription rules are often engineered to allow hundreds of thousands or even millions of nationals to acquire small numbers of shares.

Etisalat, DP World, Saudi Telecoms, Saudi Arabia's mining and fertilizer company Maaden, and Qatar Petroleum have sold off minority shares or shares in subsidies. Further sell-offs are envisaged for Batelco, Alba, and potentially Emirates. In an age of large oil surpluses, there is no fiscal necessity for such sell-offs; instead, the habitual under-pricing seems to indicate a distributional motive. A number of public banks have been set up with an IPO as immediate aim.

As counterpart to the distributional function of SOE IPOs, regimes might themselves look to SOEs for new sources of non-oil state income through SOE dividends. Although unlikely to supplant oil income as the main source of state budgets, dividend payments can help to marginally boost the state fisc and further postpone the delicate politics of domestic taxation with which GCC regimes will have to engage in the long run.

Why does it work?

The Gulf states stand alone among oil-rich states in having created a wide spectrum of efficient state-owned corporations. Competition between the GCC governments, often initiated by Dubai, is part of the explanation. More important perhaps, most GCC governments have enjoyed considerable autonomy from popular demands in how to use the new surpluses. Kuwait, the one Gulf monarchy with meaningful participatory politics, has not managed to set up efficient SOEs due to the constant bickering over the use of new riches and the strong populist spending demands from parliament.

This relative autonomy, combined with a non-populist ruling ideology, distinguishes the Gulf states from cases such as Iran or Venezuela. In the latter, regimes have engaged in populist spending sprees that have precluded the creation of managerially autonomous, profit-oriented structures. Although GCC regimes do pursue policies of patronage in significant parts of their bureaucracies, they have been able to insulate choice bits of their public sector from the logic of distribution.

Outlook and conclusion

It remains to be seen whether the new paradigm will spread beyond the GCC. Much will depend on the coming years, as many of the more recent projects— both experimental ventures into new sectors and "copycat" undertakings inspired by Dubai's SOEs—have yet to prove their viability. Total failures are unlikely, however, as the export orientation of most new SOEs exposes them to international competition, and, different from more populist oil states, SOE managements will stand and fall by the profitability of their companies.

The recent financial crisis has dented the profits of most of the SOEs and some, like Dubai's real estate companies, have incurred substantial losses. Yet, their SOE status has made it easier for them to refinance thanks to either sovereign backing or direct state loans. It increases their independence from short-term shareholder pressures, favoring long-term strategy. The crisis might have curbed individual SOE ambitions, but does not undermine the SOE model.

It also seems unlikely that the new SOEs will crowd out the local private sector. If anything, they set precedents for new types of investments that local businesses tend to imitate, be it air transport in the case of Emirates, luxury real estate in the case of Emaar, or large-scale petrochemicals in the case of SABIC.

The GCC's experience with state-owned corporations calls into question the conventional wisdom that public sectors in the developing world tend to be inefficient. They have given a new lease on life to the "developmental state" in the Gulf, which is able to maintain a leading role in the economy while avoiding over-bureaucratization. The new generation of SOEs is another sign that Gulf governments have learned from the errors of the last boom. They might even be able to create a new paradigm of enclave development that negates important assumptions of both the "resource curse" theory and research on public sectors more generally.

Notes

1 Cf. Waterbury 1993.
2 For details, see Hertog 2008.
3 Cf. Saudi Arabian Basic Industries Americas 2001 for further biographies. Both Zamil and bin Salamah joined the private sector after the end of their public careers. The current chairman of SABIC, Prince Saud bin Thunayyan, is also chairman of RCJY.

4 BASF employed about 95,000 people in 2006; Dow had 46,000 workers in 2007.
5 For details cf. Jean-François Seznec in this volume, "Financing Industrialization in the Arab-Persian Gulf."

Bibliography

Activities of Prince Fahd (1970) London: Kew Public Record Office, FCO 8/1508.
Anonymous former Saudi bureaucrats (2007) Personal interviews, Riyadh, February.
Anonymous former Saudi deputy minister (2007) Personal interview, Riyadh, February.
Anonymous former UK ambassadors to Saudi Arabia (2005) Personal interviews, London, November.
Anonymous senior Ministry of Petroleum representative (2007) Personal interview, Riyadh, February.
APS (1993a) "Oil Market Trends," *APS Review*, 30 August.
APS (1993b) "Downstream Trends," *APS Review*, 6 September.
BASF (2007) Annual Report.
Al Bawaba (2008), 14 April.
Colitti, M. (former head of EniChem) (2006) Phone interview, December.
Davidson, C. (2008) *Dubai: The Vulnerability of Success*, London: Hurst.
Dow Chemical (2007) Annual Report.
Gillibrand, M. (former advisor to various Saudi ministries) (2005) Personal interview, London, November.
Hertog, S. (2008) "Petromin: The Slow Death of Statist Oil Development in Saudi Arabia," *Business History*, 50 (5): 645–67.
Holden, D. and Johns, R. (1982) *The House of Saud*, London: Pan Books.
Huyette, S. S. (1985) *Political Adaptation in Saudi Arabia: A Study of the Council of Ministers*, Boulder/London: Westview.
ICIS News (1995) 2 January.
ICIS News (2008) 31 March.
Middle East Economic Digest (MEED) (1974) 16 August.
Middle East Economic Digest (MEED) (1976a) 10 September.
Middle East Economic Digest (MEED) (1976b) 29 October.
Middle East Economic Digest (MEED) (1977) 29 April.
Middle East Economic Survey (MEES) (1976), 13 September.
Montagu, C. (1994) *The Private Sector of Saudi Arabia*, London: Committee for Middle Eastern Trade.
bin Salamah, I. (2007) Personal interview, Riyadh, February.
Saudi Arabia Monitor (1987) 2 March.
SABIC Americas (2001) *The SABIC Story*, Houston: SABIC Americas, Inc.
Saudi Arabian Basic Industries Corporation SABIC (2007) Annual Report.
Saudi Arabian Basic Industries Corporation SABIC (2009) "People at SABIC." Online HTTP: www.sabic.com/corporate/en/career/peopleatsabic/default.aspx.
Signs of a Modernizing Establishment - Evolution Within a Traditional Regime (1971) College Park, MD: National Archive and Record Administration, Box 2585, folder POL 15 SAUD, 1 January.
Survival Prospects for the House of Saud (Airgram, 6 June) (1966) College Park, MD: National Archive and Record Administration, Box 2645, folder POL 15-1 SAUD, 21 May.

Waterbury, J. (1993) *Exposed to Innumerable Delusions: Public Enterprise and State Power in Egypt, India, Mexico, and Turkey*, Cambridge: Cambridge University Press.

World Bank Bureaucrats in Business Database. Online HTTP: http://go.worldbank.org/9CVTM1EKL0.

World Bank Development Indicators and SAMA Data. Online HTTP: http://go.worldbank.org/6HAYAHG8H0.

2 Financing industrialization in the Arab-Persian Gulf

Jean-François Seznec

The states of the Gulf Cooperation Council (GCC) have been growing at breakneck speed. From an industrial base of near zero 30 years ago, the Gulf has become a major world production center for petrochemicals, fertilizers, aluminum, cement, prefab metal building, fiber-optic cables, air conditioners, and all manner of products related to construction. Yet the achievements made until now in 2008 are small compared to what is on the books for production in the near future.

Of course, the present course has been greatly encouraged and fueled by the large inflow of cash into the region from the increase in oil prices since 1999, but as has been seen in Iran, Iraq, Nigeria, and Venezuela, money alone cannot buy growth. Successful development requires vision from the elites of each of the Gulf countries, political stability, and financial structures able to match the demand for investments and the supply of capital.

This paper argues that the financial structures developed in the Gulf, in particular those of Saudi Arabia, have provided a turbo effect to the supply of capital. These structures, when combined with a very aggressive civil service promoting rapid industrial development, have funded the unprecedented economic growth that can be seen by all visitors to the Gulf.

Overview of industrial development in the Gulf

Chemicals

Today the GCC countries produce over 60 millions tons per year (hereafter ts/y) of chemicals and fertilizers. The main products are chemicals derived from methane (Cs), ethane (C2s), propane (C3s), butane (C4s), and aromatics such as benzene and toluene, which are mostly derived from oil distillation.

Most chemicals are presently made from natural gas. However, a shortage of gas is looming. The escalating demand for electricity and the desalination of water and chemicals are pushing Gulf companies to build major plants producing the same chemical chains as natural gas, but based on naphtha and liquid petroleum gas (LPG) produced from crude oil. In particular, Saudi Aramco, in a $10 billion PetroRabigh joint venture with Sumitomo, is expected to start production this year of chemicals based on naphtha and LPG downstream from regular refined products from crude oil.

Saudi Aramco is also negotiating with Dow Chemical to start a huge oil-based chemical production center in Ras Tannura. SABIC, the main chemical company in the Gulf, already has 63 separate companies, 17 of which are based in Saudi Arabia. SABIC acquired GE Advanced Plastics for $14 billion in 2007 and is now producing high tech plastics worldwide. The other major Gulf producers, such as Borouge in the UAE, a joint venture between Borealis, OMV (a leading oil and gas corporation in Austria), and Abu Dhabi National Oil Company (ADNOC), and Equate in Kuwait, a joint venture between Kuwait Petroleum Corporation (KPC) and Dow Chemical, are expected to double production within a year and have plans to triple it within three to four years. Altogether the Gulf is expected to produce 120 million ts/y of chemicals and fertilizers by 2015, which will make the region the largest producer of petrochemicals, chemicals, and fertilizers in the world.

Most of the newer productions in the Gulf are not merely basic petrochemicals. Most of the new plants are expected to produce very advanced chemicals, downstream from the basic ones already produced. Technology is key in this development, and Gulf governments—particularly that of Saudi Arabia—spend much effort and money to obtain know-how and technology either through the purchase or development of research centers and university-based research.

Aluminum

The Gulf is increasingly a large producer of aluminum. The two largest plants in the world are Alba in Bahrain, with a capacity of 850,000 ts/y, and Dubal in Dubai, with a similar capacity. The main cost of making aluminum is electricity. Since the region has plentiful energy, it has a natural advantage in electricity generation. Even though Bahrain and Dubai have only very limited oil resources, they have some natural gas, which has allowed them to provide very cheap electricity to their state-controlled aluminum manufacturing plants. Unfortunately, though, both Bahrain and Dubai have severe constraints on the amount of natural gas available in the future, and have had to shelve plans to increase their production capacities to 1.2 million ts/y.

The aluminum sector, however, is in full development. Sohar Aluminum Company (SAC) in Oman began production on a plant with 350,000 ts/y capacity in early 2008. SAC is in joint venture (JV) with RioTinto-Alcan. Abu Dhabi is planning a 1.4 million ts/y plant in JV, also with RioTinto-Alcan. Importantly, Saudi Arabia's state-owned Ma'aden, already a shareholder in Alba, is developing its own bauxite mines in Northern Arabia, and will transform the bauxite into alumina, which is then made into aluminum via energy and caustic soda. The required electricity will be provided by generators powered by crude oil. Since bauxite is available locally and caustic soda can be a byproduct of any chlor alkali plant,[1] Saudi Arabia is in a position to have the cheapest aluminum production in the world. Ma'aden expects to produce up to 650,000 ts/y in JV with RioTinto-Alcan.

When these plans come to pass, the Gulf will produce 25 percent of the world's aluminum and will compete directly with U.S. and Russian producers on all the world markets.

Services

Banking is growing rapidly to service the industrial and commercial boom of the region. The most remarkable growth taking place is in Islamic finance, with Islamic institutions being established with a very large capital base. Many have emerged from Bahrain, which has managed to establish the proper regulatory base for their development and thus has built the most credibility in the region. Even Saudi Arabia, which discouraged Islamic banking for many years, has now gotten the message that the public in the region wants it offered, and there are now three Islamic banks in the country. The most recently established one, Al Inmar Bank, was floated on the stock market in Riyadh to huge demand in April 2008. More than 8.8 million Saudis (about half of Saudi citizens) subscribed to the shares offered during the IPO.

Shipping has become extremely efficient. Dubai Ports World is the second largest port manager in the world. Dubai has become an enormous transshipment center, with goods from around the globe arriving in Jebel Ali and redirected to the rest of the Gulf and Iran in particular.

Logistics and distribution centers are opening all over Arabia. Western firms with extensive experience in managing large projects and distributing highly diversified and sometimes highly flammable or sensitive goods have been established in the region with great success. State of the art quality control, packaging, labeling, shipping, and accounting (ARE) now as available in the Gulf as anywhere in Europe or the United States.

The airports in the region are very efficient, and the local airlines are becoming world class. Emirates in Dubai, for one, is growing rapidly and offers connections to the entire world. It has bought $34 billion worth of airbuses and is increasing the present airport's capacity to receive 120 million passengers per year—about six times its present level. This expansion is nearly finished with the new terminal having opened in October 2008. Dubai is obviously aiming to become the center of the new Silk Road. All the other Gulf states are developing airlines as well whether they be Gulf Air, Etihad, or Qatar Airways. Their fleets, unlike the U.S. fleets, are very modern and their services are first-rate. The region has also become home to three local discount airlines, which service the Gulf and a few select Indian cities. These low-cost airlines are greatly benefiting from the economic growth that requires frequent transport of local citizens as well as foreign workers.

Real estate, of course, is another major activity in the region. Not only does it provide apartments, houses, offices, and shopping centers to the growing public, it also creates industrial development in its own right. The cement industry is growing rapidly, and steel beams and rebars are now mostly made locally. There are numerous marble plants in Saudi Arabia, and red brick factories using local clay and cheap energy have also grown in many areas. Very large plaster factories produce sheet rock, and there are even a couple of floated glass plants for the new glass buildings sprouting all over the Gulf. Shopping centers are opening daily, and are both huge and among the best in the world. Except for the normally forbidden products under Islam, these centers and supermarkets offer much more choice than their counterparts in the West.

Financing in the Gulf: the stock markets

There are a few trillions of dollars of projects on the books. Perhaps not all will see the daylight, especially in the economic slowdown of the end of 2008 and 2009, but many are being developed and built at this writing. All the projects require extensive financing and can only commence when the financing package has been signed and sealed. Most of the large projects are beyond the scope of a single financial institution. In fact, some of the projects are so large that even rich states and state-owned companies cannot fund them alone. Hence, very intricate financing packages must be structured. These innovative financing packages do not reflect traditional bureaucratic tendencies, and thus demonstrate the essence of growth in the region. Below, I present three examples of the newly structured mega-facilities that have allowed projects to commence relatively quickly and in a format most unusual for traditional states and lenders.

PetroRabigh[2]

PetroRabigh is a joint venture between Saudi Aramco and Sumitomo. The project was first mulled over in 2003 and was scheduled to cost about $3.5 billion. At the time, Saudi Aramco had modernized an oil refinery built by John Lastsis of Greece that had never run properly or profitably. At about the same time, it became clear that Saudi Arabia's need for natural gas under its industrialization plans was higher than its capacity could bear. Further, there were fears that the WTO negotiations could abort under European Union pressure and force Saudi Arabia, especially SABIC, to abandon its access to low-cost feedstocks. Saudi Aramco's board and the government decided to push Saudi Aramco into petrochemicals, using its own products downstream from its refineries, thereby escaping the issues of transfer pricing, which the EU was trying to tag on to SABIC.

The project proceeded with the Saudis linking with Sumitomo of Japan. By the end of negotiations, however, the project had expanded a great deal. Saudi Aramco and Sumitomo felt that they could go downstream from ethylene, propylene, benzene and the like, and develop more advanced and very large production lines for ethylene dichlordie, ethylene glycol, ethalnolamines, and polypropylene. While the negotiations proceeded but took much time, the cost of engineering, procurement, and construction (EPC) increased rapidly worldwide. By 2007, the total cost of the project had climbed to $10 billion.

Saudi Aramco could have raised the capital needed from the government, but the Japanese would then have been left with a very small share of ownership or would have had to pay a much larger sum than the $0.5 billion they had originally planned. Further, Saudi Aramco was likely not keen on begging the government for a hefty sum, as the money would probably carry some control clauses to which the company would not have been accustomed. Also, in line with the traditional approach of the Ministry of Finance, it is likely that the Ministers and the King wanted to bring as many Saudis into the industrialization of the Kingdom without losing control of the company.

Thus, a sort of mixed-ownership company[3] called PetroRabigh was founded. Capital was set at $4.03 billion, close to the original cost of the project. Both Sumitomo and Saudi Aramco put up $1.41 billion, a large sum but basically easily available in the treasuries of both companies without special requests to their ministers and directors. This gave both firms an "equal" say at 37.5 percent. The balance was floated on the stock exchange in Riyadh, and it gave the small shareholders who joined the IPO 25 percent interest. Of course, in reality Saudi Aramco has complete control. It will automatically represent the small Saudi shareholders, and Sumitomo is barred from buying more shares on the market. Should relations deteriorate, Sumitomo can only sell its shares and leave the company.

The balance of the funding comes from various debt instruments. Trade credits from the Japan Bank for International Cooperation (JBIC) provided $2.5 billion in 15-year loans to be used for the purchase of equipment and construction loans to Japanese companies involved in the project. The Saudi state-owned Public Investment Fund (PIF), an organization closely linked to the Ministry of Finance, made a loan of $1 billion at an undisclosed interest rate for a period of 15 years.

Normally the Saudi government has used SABIC to capitalize some of the major industries of the Kingdom. For example, PIF owns 75 percent of SABIC and 100 percent of Saudia, the airline of Saudi Arabia. In the case of PetroRabigh, PIF made a loan instead of taking a share of ownership. This means that the Ministry of Finance will have much less influence on PetroRabigh than it does on other state-financed firms. On the other hand, it may mean that the government decided to leave most of the capital funding to the private sector through the Riyadh stock market. This decision may be based on a policy to include as many individual shareholders as possible in order to have widespread support of the industrialization policy of the Kingdom.

Banks got together in a syndicate and arranged for $1.74 billion in funding. The lead banks were HSBC and its Saudi affiliate, Saudi British Bank (SABB). Mostly Saudi banks were involved, such as SABB and Riyadh Bank, as the syndicated loan included only local banks, except for HSBC. This syndicated credit is for 14 years. Finally, a $674 million Islamic portion of the syndicated loan is shared by the Islamic departments of the participating banks as well as Al Rahji Bank and Bank Albilad, the two main Islamic banks in the kingdom.

It is worth noting that all lenders, whether state-owned, Islamic, or commercial banks, signed an intercreditor agreement. Intercreditor agreements are notoriously difficult to agree on for most large projects. This agreement required a special addendum for the Islamic portion of the loans, and as such is groundbreaking for the cooperation between very different institutions and signals a likelihood of accelerated financing packages for future projects.

The share offering—219 million shares offered at SR 21 ($5.60) per share— was extremely successful, and was oversubscribed by a ratio of 4 to 1. Almost five and a half million people signed up for the offering, about 30 percent of all Saudi citizens. The public's approval of the offering is understandable, as from an investor's point of view, the shares are very safe. Leverage is limited at 1.45,[4] which means that the senior lenders feel well protected by a large equity cushion. It is also apparent to small shareholders and bankers alike that on paper the new enterprise is a standard publicly traded company, but in reality, the state is in control. Saudi Aramco has 37.5 percent of the shares, the government is lending a further $1 billion, and most of the rest of the funding is provided by local financial institutions, themselves under tight supervision from the Saudi Monetary Agency. Thus, both lenders and shareholders know that ultimately, albeit not legally, this funding is an obligation of the Saudi state.

Yansab

In December 2005, SABIC also raised funds on the stock market in a quest to obtain $5 billion to fund its largest project to date—a huge ethylene and propylene complex in Yanbu called Yansab. Considering the rapid growth of SABIC and its subsequent need for capital, it made sense for it to tap the public at large for funds to maximize their ability to continue acquiring companies and developing new projects. However, it is most important for SABIC's management to keep complete control of the projects. As a result, it floated shares to the public and a set of private investors on a private placement basis, but it kept 50 percent of the company. SABIC's share of the capital was $765 million, the public received $525 million worth of shares, and the balance was privately placed. The total equity amounted to $1.5 billion. Just as was the case for PetroRabigh, SABIC obtained trade credits, this time from European government agencies, mainly the SACE Group of Italy, for about $700 million. It obtained a loan of $1.067 billion from the Saudi state's PIF, and it also raised commercial loans; $850 million came from Islamic banks, and $1 billion came from a consortium of international banks. The offering was oversold 2.6 times, and almost 8 million buyers subscribed.

Yansab was the first "corporation with state funds" in the Kingdom. SABIC, a state-owned company, made a bet that the public would want to join them in their growth without having to surrender control. This bet was obviously successful and laid the path for PetroRabigh and other huge projects.

Saudi Kayan

In 2007 SABIC organized an IPO for Saudi Kayan, its affiliate and one of its most ambitious projects. Saudi Kayan will produce a total of 5.6 million ts/y of chemicals, some basic like ethylene, propylene, and benzene, and some more advanced, like ethanolamines and polycarbonates. It required $2.7 billion of investments.

In May 2007, SABIC offered $1.8 billion worth of shares to 3.6 million public subscribers at 45 percent interest. The IPO was four times oversubscribed. The structure of lending was very similar to that of Yansab, with $1 billion from the PIF and commercial banks making a large syndicate for the balance. Again the public and the banks saw the state and SABIC as having control of the project and thereby ensuring the safety of the investments. (It is also important to mention that the public considers SABIC an extremely well managed and globally competitive company.) The public has come to view the extensive state involvement in SABIC's ownership as a "government guarantee" that implies that the state will not let the company down under any circumstances, thereby making any investment controlled by SABIC very attractive.

The success of these three issues has been overwhelming and is the harbinger of many new industrial investments to come. The largest ones expected in the near future are the $9 billion aluminum joint venture between Ma'aden (the Saudi state's mining concern) and RioTinto-Alcan. The $24 billion mega chemical project between Saudi Aramco and Dow Chemicals in Ras Tannura is also expected to have a similar financial structure and to also be vastly oversold.

Main features of Gulf financing

Banking facilities

The very large volume of liquidity in the Gulf mainly ends up in the area's local banks or branches of foreign banks. There are about $205 billion in deposits in Saudi banks, $173 billion in the UAE, and $50 billion in Qatar (Central Bank of Qatar Monthly Bulletin 2008; Central Bank of the UAE Quarterly Bulletin 2007; SAMA Monthly Bulletin 2008). The banks in turn are eager to find proper investments to place the funds with which they have been entrusted. It has not been difficult for them to realize that the region holds a major advantage in feedstock prices, and thus they are willing to lend to any energy-based venture and its related service and industrial industries.

Therefore, bank involvement in Gulf industrialization is massive. The large loans provided either directly or in syndication between various banks are based on the banks' evaluation that the credit risk is excellent. Banks today will lend for up to 15 years, when only a few years ago they only lent sparingly and for short terms. This change in policy came about for a number of reasons:

- The analysis that the companies will be very profitable due to the low cost of feedstock.
- The Far East is growing so fast that its demand for chemical and metal products cannot be met locally, and it is increasingly dependent on Gulf productions.

- The unspoken view of banks that the risk inherent in the industrial project is a state risk rather than a private company risk, that is, in case of trouble, one can count on the state to bail out the banks.

- However, since the state does not guarantee the loans per se, the banks can lend to companies as if they were private firms and therefore not be subject to international banking regulations on limits to a single borrower.

- The large liquidity available in the market allows banks to make very large loans, substantially increasing profitability.

The largest deals in Saudi Arabia are led by HSBC, GIB of Bahrain, and National Commercial Bank (NCB) of Jeddah. Most local banks and affiliates of foreign banks also participate extensively in the deals. Other important banks in the syndication of loans have been CaLyon of France and Deutche Bank of Germany; both have very active offices in Riyadh, Bahrain, and Dubai. Because the business is extremely competitive, most large banks have established project finance departments in the region supplemented by large departments in London.

As mentioned above, Dubai has become an important center for project finance along with Bahrain. Dubai benefits from the very large deposit base of the UAE, which is close to that of Saudi Arabia though its population is one-sixth that of the Kingdom. Of course, a great deal of the deposits in the Emirates come from outside the UAE, mainly Iran and Pakistan. These funds are in turn invested by the banks and finance the UAE's real estate boom, especially in Dubai, and find their way to industrial projects in the entire region.

Islamic banking

The growth of Islamic finance in the region has been just as dramatic as the growth in industry. The number of *shari`a* compliant institutions and their volume of business is growing by the day. There are now 26 Islamic banks in Bahrain, as well as 19 Islamic insurance companies, and they hold $26.9 billion in deposits as of June 2009 (Central Bank of Bahrain 2008). Among these is Al Baraka, one of the largest Islamic banks in the world. In its annual report Al Baraka showed total assets of $11 billion and $697 million in paid up capital (Al Baraka Annual Reports 2009). The balance will come from private investors led by Al Baraka's founder, Saudi tycoon Saleh Kamel.

Three very large Islamic banks in Saudi Arabia are also in operation. AlRajhi Banking and Investment was established in 1990 as the successor to the largest money-changing firm in the Kingdom. Al Bilad was established in 2007, and a new bank, Al Inma Bank, was licensed and floated shares on the Riyadh stock exchange in April 2008. This last bank raised about $2.8 billion in an issue that was 174 percent oversold to 8.8 million shareholders. The success of this issue for an unproven bank is likely based on the amount of liquidity available in the Kingdom, but also on the fact that the bank is *de facto* controlled by the Ministry of Finance and its very able and honest civil servants. Indeed, the founding shareholders of Al Inma are the pension funds and the Social Security funds of the Kingdom (alinma.com and Tadawul Stock Exchange 2009). It is interesting to note that the Ministry of Finance has now not only fully accepted the concept of Islamic banking, which for many years it had rejected, but is taking the lead in developing it.

A good deal of the growth in Islamic finance is due to the Central Bank of Bahrain's insistence that all Islamic financial institutions follow standard accounting practice. It established the Auditing and Accounting Organization of Islamic Finance Institutions (AAOIFI), which calls itself "the main standard-setting organization." Its website in 2008 declared: "We have now issued up to 70 standards on accounting, auditing, and governance, in addition to codes of ethics and *shari`a* standards" (AAOIFI 2008).

One of the most popular products presently issued and/or bought by Islamic finance companies are *sukkuk*. *Sukkuk* are long-term bonds that carry a coupon rate providing an established return to investors on long-term investments. Bahrain's Central Bank was the first to issue such instruments, and they have become hugely popular, as in the financing of PetroRabigh and Yansab mentioned above. Over $18 billion of *sukkuk* have been issued in the past seven years in the Gulf, a number expected to increase rapidly as new projects come to the markets for financing.

Consequences of the Gulf financial structures

The combination of professional banks, large liquidity, and new types of financial institutions, as well as active stock markets draining the savings of private citizens, is making for a debtor's market. The economic growth of the Gulf has become quite awesome, and the private sector, especially in Saudi Arabia, is becoming very active in heavy industrial investments. Most of the states of the Gulf have started new plants or are in the building or planning stage of major industrial developments. In Kuwait, Equate will increase capacity to 1.6 million ts/y. In Abu Dhabi, Borouge is planning to augment capacity to 1.8 million ts/y. In Qatar, the industrial growth has been so rapid and the plans so numerous that the government has had to place a moratorium on allocation of natural gas to new projects until they can ascertain whether the country with the third largest gas reserves in the world can actually provide feedstock to all the projects. The growth in the Gulf states can therefore be described as very rapid. Even more rapid is the growth in Saudi Arabia, where the private sector is seeking industrial ventures while state companies are using local private capital to develop huge projects, such as PetroRabigh, Yansab, and the soon to come $26 billion Dow Arabia. Importantly, these projects occur without overarching control by the state bureaucracy.

These new financial structures allow Saudi Aramco and SABIC to mobilize the huge amounts of liquidity available in the market and build themselves into world-class chemical corporations. When Ma'aden's 3 million ts/y diammonium phosphate (DAP) plant comes on stream by 2011 together with its 650,000 ts/y aluminum plant, it will also be a world-class producer.

Among the fears generated in the Gulf by a strike on Iran, one could list:

• Potential retaliation by Iran in the Straits of Hormuz, which would cut sharply into oil income. Even though the Straits are not easy to block, and the U.S. Navy is probably well prepared to keep them open, the fear would lead to a pull back on investment.

• All the states of the Gulf have large Shi'i populations. While most of these Shi'a in the Gulf are Arabs and are mostly anti-Iranian, there could be a disgruntled element, which, if armed and supported by Iran, could create major disruptions to the daily life of people and the economy at large, again bringing a substantial pull back on investments. The stock markets would crash, making the small shareholders lose hundreds of billions of dollars.

Iran could open up to the world

Almost as difficult, but more manageable, would be the opposite of military action against Iran. If Iran changed from being a closed hierocracy to an open and transparent economy, much of foreign investments would be directed to Iran. Iran could start to compete with the newly developed industries of the Gulf, whether via petrochemicals or aluminum. Further, a large amount of the capital now poured by Iranian clergy and businessmen into Dubai and redirected in projects across the region would stay in Iran and bring to it a turbo effect on development somewhat similar to what is seen today in the GCC.

Large increases in EPC costs

The natural advantage of low-cost energy in the Gulf can be eroded by the large increases in EPC costs in the region. EPC costs have more than doubled in the past four years, as seen in the huge increases in the PetroRabigh plant in Saudi Arabia. New refinery projects in the Gulf have also shown signs of inflation, with no refineries estimated to cost below $4 billion, when $1 billion would have been the norm a few years ago. However, these increases are relative, as costs are also increasing in the quickly developing markets of China and India. For the Gulf to lose its natural advantage on feedstock, its costs would have to rise much faster than those of China and India.[5] Since the cost of steel products, advanced machinery, and high-quality engineering is the same worldwide, the main difference lies in labor costs in plant construction, which is likely to be a relatively small amount of the total plant costs. Therefore, at this point, in spite of increasing EPC costs, the Gulf is maintaining its production cost advantage.

Conclusion

The impressive economic growth in the Gulf is tantamount to a modern-day industrial revolution. It is certainly triggered by the financial structures and instruments offered by the market to potential investors. Yet, these structures as well as all the incentives geared to increase industry in the region are based on political decisions by the various leaderships of the GCC. It seems that King Abdullah, his advisors, and key ministers are pushing hard to bring Saudi Arabia into the twenty-first century by encouraging small investors to participate in the development of the Kingdom—a policy initiated under King Faysal by Mohamed AbalKhail, the then Minister of Finance.

King Abdullah is also encouraging the participation of women in the economy and trying hard to improve the quality and relevance of the educational system, which puts him at odds with the conservative Salafi groups in the Kingdom. One can imagine that the speed of growth is encouraged by the monarch, the civil servants who manage the economy, and the merchants who benefit from it in order to marginalize the Salafi elements in society who had been allowed to impose harsh rules under King Fahad. Similar approaches are noticeable in the other states of the GCC, with perhaps the exception of Kuwait, which is embroiled in constant controversy between an Islamist-controlled parliament and the Emir and his family.

Notes

1 Caustic soda is a product of the electrolysis of brine, which is plentiful in the Gulf as a mainly unused by-product of water desalination.
2 The prospectus on PetroRabigh, as well as those of most large stock IPOs, is available in English at Capital Market Authority's website: www.cma.org.sa/cma_en/subpage. aspx?secserno=160&mirrorid=390&serno=160.
3 Many French industrial concerns, such as Renault, were for many years structured in the same manner. The government had substantial ownership, and a large number of shares were publicly traded on the Paris Bourse. However, ultimate control remained with the state, securing small shareholders. These companies are called "société anonyme à capitaux d'état" (corporations with state funds).
4 This corresponds to $5.84 billion of debt for $4.032 billion of equity.
5 This is not an attempt to dismiss the problem of EPC inflation, but it should be noted that for the Saudis and other Gulf states to start losing their advantage on feedstock (somewhere between 1 to 10 and 1 to 20), their depreciation and interest costs would have to be about 2.5 times higher than their equivalents in the Far East. This is a very rough, "back of the envelope" estimate based on the rule of thumb that 50 percent of the cost of petrochemicals is the cost of the feedstock.

Bibliography

Accounting and Auditing Organization for Islamic Financial Institutions (AAOIFI) (2008) Online HTTP: http://aaoifi.com.
Al Baraka Annual Reports (2009) Online HTTP: www.albaraka.com/default.asp?action=article&id=55 (accessed May 24, 2010).
Capital Market Authority. Online HTTP: www.cma.org.sa/cma_en/subpage.aspx?secserno=160&mirrorid=390&serno=160 (accessed May 24, 2010).
Central Bank of Bahrain (2008) "Islamic Finance." Online HTTP: www.cbb.gov.bh/cmsrule/index.jsp?action=article&ID=19 (accessed May 24, 2010).

Central Bank of Qatar Monthly Bulletin (2008). Online HTTP: www.qcb.gov.qa/ENGLISH/PUBLICATIONS/REPORTSANDSTATEMENTS/Pages/BankMonthlyStatement.aspx (accessed May 24, 2010).

Central Bank of the UAE Quarterly Bulletin (2007). Online HTTP: www.centralbank.ae/statistical_bulletin.php (accessed May 19, 2010).

Al Inma Bank. Online HTTP: www.alinma.com (accessed May 19, 2010).

Saudi Arabian Monetary Agency (SAMA) (2008) Monthly Bulletin.

Tadawul Stock Exchange. Online HTTP: www.tadawul.com.sa (accessed May 19, 2010).

3 *Hawkamah* in the Gulf

Local reception of modern corporate governance standards for publicly traded companies in the Arab Gulf States

Alastair Hirst[1]

Resort to the capital markets for funding for industrial projects in the Gulf region varies from country to country. In several Gulf states the major source of capital is the government itself, as is seen, for example, with SABIC in Saudi Arabia or GHC in Abu Dhabi in the UAE. In such states resort to capital markets, if it happens at all, takes place at a later stage and is often not primarily a capital-raising exercise at all, but rather a privatization measure with the object of giving local nationals a stake in the future of their own economy or of satisfying an international treaty obligation of the state to liberalize the market in question. In other states, notably Bahrain and the Sultanate of Oman, where the resources available to the government for funding capital projects are relatively more limited, major projects are more likely to require the mobilization of private capital at an early stage.

Whatever the source of their funding, companies in the industrial sectors of the securities market listings in the Gulf are, like the companies publicly traded in the other sectors, subject to the securities market rules and increasingly to standards on corporate governance, for which the term *hawkamah* in Arabic has been coined.[2] These standards are intended to achieve transparency and accountability in the way publicly traded companies are directed and controlled, as well as to enhance performance and shareholder value.

Corporate governance standards often bring a distinctly ethical dimension to the functioning of the ordinary company law rules. For instance, under ordinary company law rules, board members choose the chairman and the chief executive officer from amongst themselves as they see fit, but corporate governance standards operate so as to prevent the board members from choosing the same person for both positions, as this would place too much corporate power in the hands of a single person and thereby increase the chance of that power being abused. Similarly, under ordinary company law rules, the shareholders in their general meeting appoint the company's auditors each year as they see fit, but under corporate governance standards, they are not allowed to appoint the same firm of auditors for more than a stated limited number of successive years, typically three or four, in order to avoid the danger of the auditors becoming too friendly with the management whose work they are supposed to be scrutinizing in the shareholders' interest.

Formal statements of corporate governance standards intended for international adoption are found in the OECD Principles of Corporate Governance and their accompanying commentary, as well as in the Institute of International Finance (IIF) Code. These standards are of course not set in stone, and will evolve as market mechanisms and practices themselves evolve. They do, however, represent international benchmarks by which relations between a publicly traded company and actual or potential investors in it are measured, and due observance of these standards is seen as important for the healthy functioning of the capital market.

In this paper I will take a brief look at how these international standards accord with prevailing views in the Gulf on matters such as the relationship between the individual and the authorities in the public sphere, the nature of collective decision-taking, and the dissemination of significant information within the community—in this case, the community of investors. First, however, some background.

Legislative background: company law and securities market law

As indicated in the examples of corporate governance standards given above, the first, and still the most basic, part of the legislative platform for activity in stocks and bonds in the Gulf countries is the body of rules constituting the local commercial companies legislation. When these countries first made their entry as players on the international economic stage, commercial companies law was an essential component of the basic package of modern business laws enacted in each in order to fill what was in effect a legislative vacuum. This took place in Kuwait in the early 1960s, then in Bahrain, and finally in the Lower Gulf in the early 1970s.[3] Broadly, the corporate models adopted by the Gulf states derive from French company law as it stood in the first half of the last century and as it was transmitted mainly through Egypt into the wider Arab world. The largest of these corporate models is the *société anonyme*, and the local companies nowadays publicly traded on Gulf securities markets are all incorporated along the lines of this essentially civil law model, which, for convenience, I will refer to as the "public joint stock company," or "PJSC," following the commercial English vernacular used in the Gulf for the Arabic *sharika musahama 'amma*.

The company law provisions relating to PJSCs include a number of rules that are basic to securities market activity. For instance, the rules on the incorporation process deal at a basic level with what happens in IPOs and other public offers, and the rules on ownership rights deal at a basic level with the transfer and trading of shares.[4]

As regards the working of the securities markets themselves, the applicable legislation—where there is any—is typically styled as a "Capital Market Law," and tends to be of an essentially English/U.S. common law character or origin. This law is often the product of studies commissioned by securities market experts from common law countries, such as the United States, the United Kingdom, Australia, Singapore, etc. The two legal systems—civil law and common law—can have significant differences, both in terms of underlying legal concepts, and also in terms of legal techniques, such as drafting conventions, rules of interpretation, and so on. Commercial companies legislation of civilian origin and securities market legislation of common law origin do not always bed down comfortably together, and this can give rise to technical complications in the regulatory authorities' task of rule-making and enforcement.

The institution of the "regulator"

The regulator, as a formally constituted authority, is a relatively new figure on the Gulf business landscape. Securities market laws normally include provision for a regulatory body to exercise a rule-making and watchdog function over the market-making mechanism of the exchange itself. Generally speaking, the exchanges were initially self-regulating—the Kuwait Stock Exchange largely still is—but the need for an independent regulatory body was soon perceived. In Oman, for instance, the independent regulatory body was set up as one of the consequences of the market crisis that took place in 1998 and 1999. In other Gulf states the independent regulator is usually of more recent date. In Qatar, for example, the regulatory body was set up in late 2005, but has still not started to operate in practice.

While the regulator may be constituted as a separate body independent of the exchange itself, it is difficult to see the Gulf regulators as independent from the political authorities. In all these countries, the government has a major say in appointing the senior officers of the regulatory body. In many, the chairman of the regulatory body is the competent minister himself. This naturally attracts criticism internationally, since a regulator is supposed to be free from political control or influence.

In fact, the whole concept of a regulator—in the sense in which market economists and lawyers use the term nowadays—is founded on a western, English/U.S. common law country paradigm. The regulator's function is to patrol the middle ground between the political authorities and the market. He is expected to be vigilant in two separate directions. On the one hand, he has to repel government attempts to exert political influence on the working of the market, and, on the other hand, he also has to repress attempts by the market players themselves to abuse the market mechanisms or bend the market rules. Conventional respect for authority in the Gulf states makes it difficult to discern the existence of any such middle ground in any publicly acknowledged way. Generally speaking, one is either with the authorities or against them. Since a regulator is commonly seen issuing rules and pursuing miscreants, he is inevitably perceived as being simply another part of the apparatus of the public administration.

Exercise of company law powers and rights

In the Gulf states there is not only conventional public respect for the authorities, but there is also a deeply ingrained culture of public politeness[5] and a distaste for public confrontation, or *fitna*, within the community.[6] These established attitudes inhibit the robust adoption of international standards of corporate governance along the lines set out in the OECD Principles or the IIF Code.

This can be considered more closely in relation to the way company law powers are exercised, first, in terms of the exercise of shareholders' rights, and second, in terms of the exercise of management powers by the board of directors.

Exercise of shareholders' rights

The listings of companies publicly traded in the Gulf contain unusually high proportions of state-controlled companies and family-controlled companies.

In Saudi Arabia, for instance, public sector bodies hold some 40 percent of the shares in publicly traded companies. In Qatar, the majority of publicly traded companies have significant, if not controlling, participation by the government or by political decision-takers. Substantial statal shareholdings are particularly common in public utility companies. Contrary to the case in Western countries, most Gulf private investors tend to see this as an attractive feature. The expression "the dead hand of government" is not one that strikes a chord with them. On the contrary, they assume their money is safer if they have the government as a co-investor with them. They assume their personal interests are synonymous with those of the government. The current market success of 70 percent government-owned SABIC in Saudi Arabia, for example, confirms for private investors the wisdom of this assumption. It means they are reluctant to use their voting rights to oppose measures which the government shareholders support.

As regards family companies, many of these have converted into PJSCs in order to secure a capital base wider than the founding families' own resources are capable of providing.[7] These family companies are typically local merchant houses which were founded 40 or 50 years ago to conduct import and commercial agency business. They have subsequently grown and diversified—often into manufacturing and light industry projects—as the local economy itself has developed, and the original merchant's children and grandchildren have progressively moved into positions of responsibility in the business. Their assuming of such positions is facilitated, and sometimes dictated, by traditional family and social expectations. There can easily be residual feelings amongst local investors that a particular business, even though it has converted into a PJSC and its shares are publicly traded, still represents in some inchoate way the traditional *diyar*[8] of the family or group who started the business, and therefore that new shareholders who come in should exhibit the due deference of a guest or visitor.

For reasons like these, shareholder activism is rare. There is a general cultural reluctance to invoke company law rules in order to set up a public confrontation which would be decided by a general meeting vote or subsequently in the courts,[9] and would therefore inevitably lead to a public loss of face for the losing party. One result of this is that significant areas of company law remain largely untested. For example, in Oman, the Gulf country with the most developed regime of corporate governance,[10] the regulator (the Capital Market Authority) has the power to suspend, upon reasoned request by shareholders owning at least 5 percent of the capital, resolutions of the general meeting which favor or disadvantage a particular category of shareholders, or which benefit members of the board of directors but not the company as a whole. However, over the 10-year period this law has been in force, there is no record of this article ever having been invoked, far less having elicited any formal intervention by the regulator on the basis of it.

Another factor may be, again, traditional attitudes to authority, particularly the respect accorded to the collective wisdom of the notables of the place—the *ahl al-hall war-rabt*[11]—who discuss issues amongst themselves, usually face to face, and decide matters by consensus. This process is sometimes referred to as the "*majlis*[12] culture," and is assumed to produce decisions reflecting the interest of the community as a whole. It is unusual for such a decision to be publicly challenged by an individual member of the community standing outside this circle of notables. In company law, the same word—*majlis*—is used to denote the board of directors, and inevitably the directors of PJSCs acquire in the minds of the ordinary shareholders something of the status and respect that attaches to the *ahl al-hall war-rabt* in the wider community.

An important concomitant to shareholder activism is well-informed investigative financial journalism. The Gulf states are sometimes criticized for lack of investigative journalism and facilities providing training for it. The fact, however, is that in the public media in the Gulf, words do have to be chosen thoughtfully. An important and legitimate function of such media is to present a decorous and orderly picture of local public life and to show the country's institutions as prospering and developing. Securities market misconduct would not necessarily escape media mention, but would not, as a rule, be presented in terms which would imperil the growth of the tender plant of local investor confidence or which would pillory a particular named individual, as that would mean obloquy by association for other innocent and loyal citizens who happened to be members of his clan or tribe.

The method of voting in elections for board membership is an important indicator of the degree of local adoption of modern standards of corporate governance. In the conventional PJSC model each share generally carries one vote, and in electing board members, each shareholder is therefore able to cast the full weight of the votes he holds for each candidate on the ballot sheet, one by one. In effect, each candidature is seen as a separate vote for the meeting. In this way, a large shareholder or a group controlling a significant number of shares acting in concert can ensure that every candidate elected is a person acceptable to them. A board can thus easily be packed with yes-men and cronies. In Oman one of the main reasons for the Muscat Securities Market crisis in 1998 and 1999 was perceived to be the ease with which individual large shareholders could impose their will on other shareholders and their fellow board members, thereby directing the company's resources and activities in a manner not necessarily in the best interest of all the shareholders. One result of this is that Oman is the only Gulf country to have mandatory application of what is called the "cumulative voting" rule for board elections.[13] Under this method of election, each shareholder has to divide up the total number of votes he holds amongst all the names on the ballot sheet. Individual candidatures are no longer determined by separate votes. This means the way is open to tactical voting, therefore to wider representation on the board, and therefore—in principle—to better-quality decision-taking. This, of course, depends on the shareholders being prepared to make the effort necessary for organizing tactical voting. In Oman, it is not unusual for board member-ship candidates to exercise, for lobbying purposes, their right of access to the company's shareholder roll with its information on names, addresses, and size of shareholdings, but in other Gulf states such access is less common, if indeed legally or practically permitted at all.

Exercise of board authority

Many of the corporate governance standards are directed to improve the quality of decision-taking at board level, yet there is a widespread perception in the Gulf region that any large shareholder should be entitled to automatic repre-sentation on the board.[14] A shareholding in the company is still a common pre-condition for board membership. This means that wealthy individual investors who lack the necessary qualifications and experience required for the manage-ment of a large business organization can occupy many seats on the boards of PJSCs. In cases where the company employs foreign nationals who do possess appropriate qualifications and experience, they often cannot become board members because the law does not permit the company's shares to be owned by foreign nationals. Added to this, in many Gulf countries the number of local nationals who do possess the requisite qualifications and experience is relatively limited, and there are simply not enough of them to go round.[15] This dearth of board-level ability is difficult to alleviate as very few of the Gulf countries openly address the issue of board member education. A constraint here is the widespread social perception that a directorship in a PJSC is something too grand for an incumbent to need to go back to school to learn the basic skills required for the position. In addition, the local commercial companies legislation will usually impose an absolute numerical cap on the number of joint stock company directorships any single individual can hold: typically this cap is set at four or five directorships, with the result that competent and experienced people in the pool of potential local national candidates for board membership may find their availability underutilized. These are all factors that tend to impair the quality of board decision-taking.[16]

Very few Gulf countries seek to promote candid, informed, and, if necessary, adversarial deliberation at board level in PJSCs, by say, making mandatory the corporate governance standards requiring a minimum level of participation by non-executive board members or by prohibiting the same individual from occu-pying the positions of chairman and chief executive.

Equally, very few of these countries have binding requirements as to internal audit and the key role of non-executive directors in that process.[17]

Dissemination of price-sensitive information

The corporate governance requirement of transparency extends to the making available of price-sensitive information. The object is to make this information equally and simultaneously available across the whole investment community—a "level playing field" for every market participant. Commercial company laws usually contain some high-level pious wording prohibiting a board member from securing a personal benefit from company information not available to the investing public generally, but there are obvious practical difficulties in enforcement. Securities market laws usually have provisions requiring regular reporting of results, and also for prompt disclosure and publication of information on events which have a material effect on the publicly traded company's activities and financial position. In some countries the regulatory body can, on its own initiative, arrange for press publication of price-sensitive company information at the company's expense if the company is dilatory in doing so.

These are rules of law that ignore the traditional information channels of the Gulf states. Arab society is extremely gregarious, and there is a natural talent for networking (Allen 2006: 111). There are the rituals of visiting and hosting, as well as the conventions of conversation and exchange of news, particularly within the long-established social units of tribe, clan, or family—the "ineradicable internal geometry" of Arab society (Allen 2006: 137). Ties of loyalty within these units can be extremely strong, and it is asking a lot for these ties to be subordinated, by a mere stroke of a rule-maker's pen, to a modern Western insistence that the generality of the investing public—whether friend or foe, local national or foreigner, co-religionist or otherwise—should have free, equal, and simultaneous access to price-sensitive information.

Conclusion

A recent survey by a corporate governance institution based in Dubai measured the corporate governance regimes of each of the Arab Gulf Cooperation Council States against the IIF Code. The findings were that Oman's corporate governance framework met more than three-quarters of the IIF Code requirements; Bahrain met slightly more than half; Kuwait and Saudi Arabia met about one-half; the UAE met less than half; and Qatar met a little over one-third (Hawkamah Institute for Corporate Governance 2006).

When coupled with the one-man-one-vote and one-share-one-vote principles of the existing commercial companies legislation, these international corporate governance standards portend significant change in the tenor of relations between publicly traded companies and the investing public in the Gulf, as well as relations among the various internal organs of the companies themselves. Assimilation of these standards into the local commercial communities in the Gulf is taking place progressively at varying speeds from country to country, but for the reasons I have outlined above, the process will not always be comfortable nor quickly completed.

There are three factors that could have the potential to expedite this process. The first are the moves towards cross-listing among the various Gulf exchanges. Plainly cross-listing can only work properly if corporate governance standards are applied uniformly across all the countries concerned. Plainly also those who stand to gain most from cross-listing are the smaller countries such as Bahrain and Oman. Both already exhibit the greatest degree of commitment to international standards, driven primarily by their own economies' need to attract foreign capital. For them, the question will be how quickly the large markets, particularly the Saudi market, can be induced to emulate them in terms of corporate governance requirements. They will have been encouraged to see the Saudi regulator, the Capital Market Authority, recently beginning to flex its muscles and bring some discipline into the market.[18]

The second factor is increased interest in Gulf stocks by non-Gulf investors, as opposed to direct investment by them in specific projects. Significant nationality-based constraints do still obtain. In a number of states non-GCC foreigners can only participate in the local market through investment funds. Not all the Gulf markets will feel the need, economically, for a substantial increase in the volume of foreign indirect investment, or the readiness for that politically. However, if the level of participation by investors from countries with well-established systems of corporate governance does increase, plainly also the pressure for improved standards in the Gulf countries will also increase.

The third factor which may expedite assimilation of such standards is the appearance, in two of the Gulf countries, of "offshore" financial centers with exchanges for the trading of stocks and bonds. These centers have been set up with the object of developing an international—as opposed to a local—capital market role. One is the Qatar Financial Center and the other is the Dubai International Financial Exchange in the Dubai International Financial Center (DIFC). These centers have been set up in special zones with their own laws and rule-making powers. In many ways they are like mini-states, albeit under the same head of state as their host country. The DIFC, for instance, has its own special zone legislation on companies and capital market operations. These reflect current international standards, particularly in regulatory and corporate governance matters. They also reflect a distinctly English common law approach, and resort to common law features not present in the civilian system, such as trusts. These zones even have their own courts: the DIFC has judges brought from England and rules of court procedure of a very English stamp.[19] Part of the rationale of these new zones is the belief that the merits of international best practice standards will be there for all to see and will accordingly percolate into the rest of the country outside the zones—in effect, institutional renewal by a sort of surreptitious reverse take-over. Hitherto however, in the capital markets in these zones, the volume of activity has remained modest, but if this changes, and the regulatory regimes and the corporate governance standards they enforce, are perceived as effective and beneficial, the effects on the onshore institutions and regulatory regimes will be interesting to observe. However, as with cross-listing and foreign participation in the markets, these are still early days.

Notes

1 Alastair Hirst, Barrister, FCIArb, Consultant with Denton Wilde Sapte, Abu Dhabi, Visiting Lecturer in Oman Business Law at Sultan Qaboos University, Muscat. The views expressed in this paper are my own, and are not to be attributed to either of these institutions. These views have been formed over more than 30 years of practicing commercial and corporate law in all the Arab Gulf states, but particularly in the Lower Gulf, where I have been resident longest, and where the most interesting part of my work is currently in the administrative law and legislative drafting fields, which aims to ease the concepts and terminology of structural economic change into the form and linguistic register of modern legislative Arabic.
2 This neologism is a nonclassical configuration of the basic three consonant radicals H-K-M in Arabic, which carry the sense of "rule." Another instance of the use of this unusual consonantal configuration for a term in the modern business field is the Arabic for "globalization," 'awLaMa, derived from 'aLiM meaning "world."
3 The United Arab Emirates were some way behind the others in introducing commercial companies legislation for various local reasons, including the federal/local division of legislative and executive competences and the large number of sui generis Ruler's Charter companies, which had in the meantime been created across the different Emirates.
4 Particular features of the traditional PJSC that are inimical to modern capital market operations include: the rule that profits can only be distributed after the shareholders have approved the accounts for the period in question, which creates complications in relation to interim dividends; or the rule that all existing shareholders are entitled to participate pro rata their existing shareholdings in any increase of capital, which creates complications in relation to private placements of increased capital in order to accommodate a substantial new investor.
5 See, for instance, Jones 2007: 161.
6 See Allen 2006: 103 and elsewhere.
7 The proportion of family companies amongst publicly traded companies generally would be higher but for the fact that in a number of countries the company law rules make such conversion difficult. For example, in the UAE, until very recently any public offer of shares had to be for at least 55 percent of the capital, which meant that the founders—the original owners of the business being converted—faced an obvious risk of loss of control.
8 Meaning "territory," often used to denote the geographical ambit of a tribe's habitation or movements.
9 The exception here is Kuwait, whose courts have been the scene of several battles over control of PJSCs.
10 Even though the Muscat Securities Market is the smallest securities market in the region in terms of capitalization.
11 Literally, "those with power to bind and loose"—the decision-takers.
12 Literally, "meeting-place" and, by extension, "council." See Allen 2006: 97; also Jones 2007: 190 on the Majlis Reform movement in Dubai in the late 1930s.
13 In some other countries, for example, Saudi Arabia, cumulative voting for board member elections is recommended, but not mandatory.
14 Some countries even have, or had, a rule that any shareholder is entitled to one seat on the board for every 10 percent of the capital he owned.
15 This is aggravated when the country's commercial companies legislation requires that a majority of the board members in any PJSC be local nationals; see, for instance, UAE Commercial Companies Law, article 100.
16 These quality issues are particularly relevant to family businesses that have gone public. The assumption of leading positions in the company by family members is not always supported by the requisite qualifications and experience. Family members,

especially senior ones, can sometimes find it difficult to submit to public company procedures for collective decision-taking, whether amongst shareholders or amongst board members, and for disclosure of company information to the market. Another complication can be family disputes, often triggered by the death of a senior family member and consequential inheritance issues. The usual way to deal with this dimension is through the creation of the "family office" entity, in which these family issues are resolved privately so that a common family position can be presented to the other shareholders through the family office. In some Gulf countries the creation of this sort of entity can be quite complicated, and often local company law is inadequate or even completely silent on the subject of holding companies. For a skeptical insider's view on family businesses going public, see the comments of Kanoo 2008.

17 In fact, in most Gulf countries it is the commercial banks that spearhead the development of corporate governance, particularly in relation to internal audit. This is driven by the banking regulator seeking to implement the standards of Basel II.

18 Early in 2007 the Capital Market Authority suspended trading in two ailing agricultural stocks that had long been popular with market professionals, and in April last year it initiated investigations into 80 companies for what it referred to as "cheating."

19 This common law enclave set in the midst of a very different surrounding legal culture is strangely reminiscent of the old British capitulatory jurisdiction in the Gulf, with extraterritorial British courts sitting in the various emirates and shaykhdoms (and originally also on the south coast of Iran) exercising a jurisdiction that only came to an end in 1971 on the completion of its progressive absorption into the new national court systems of the Gulf states with their civil law allegiance in commercial matters.

Bibliography

Allen, M. (2006) *Arabs*, London: Continuum.

Hawkamah Institute for Corporate Governance (2006) "Hawkamah-IIF Surveys – Corporate Governance from an Investor's Perspective," Dubai: Hawkamah Institute for Corporate Governance.

Jones, J. (2007) *Negotiating Change*, London: I.B. Tauris.

Kanoo, M. (2008) Quoted in "[Mishal] Kanoo Says Vanity Driving IPO Surge," *Emirates Business*, 247, 4 June.

Section II

Competing models

The Gulf Arab states and Iran

4 The political economy of Saudi–Iranian relations

Present and future

Paul Aarts and Joris van Duijne

Introduction

During the late 1970s, Louis Turner and James Bedore published a number of articles and books on Middle Eastern political economy that proved standard reading for over a decade. Some of their work predicted future developments in the region, particularly future relations between Iran and Saudi Arabia. Thirty years later, though time has left much of their analysis obsolete, a rereading of these works certainly provides useful insights into the past, present, and future of the regional political economy. After assessing Turner and Bedore's predictions and discussing past and current political and economic factors at play in the relationship between Saudi Arabia and Iran, we move to a predictive analysis of our own: Saudi–Iranian relations of the year 2030.

In "Saudi and Iranian Petrochemicals and Oil Refining: trade warfare in the 1980s?" Turner and Bedore are mainly concerned with tensions that could arise from Saudi and Iranian exports and possible protectionism of the "pioneers" in North America and Western Europe. While they do predict a limited cooperation between Western companies and such new producers [for instance, a specialization in higher-value products in the core regions, leaving the basics to nontraditional producers (Turner and Bedore 1977: 581–582)],[1] they are generally pessimistic. The current virtual absence of a Western lobby and the huge participation of Western companies in Middle Eastern petrochemicals and refining were clearly unexpected at the time.[2]

Other aspects of Turner and Bedore's predictions turned out to be inaccurate as well. In 1977, they argue that Iran, not Saudi Arabia, is the most promising site for industrialization, particularly because of its larger population that is both a source of labor and a domestic market for goods (Turner and Bedore 1977: 574). Clearly, this has changed, in large part due to the Islamic revolution, which involved eight years of devastating war and long-standing sanctions.

The authors also predict limited possibilities for the Middle East due to competition from another newcomer to the scene: the Soviet Union, who at the time had quite similar ambitions (Turner and Bedore 1977: 581). The current economic rise of Saudi Arabia is thus at least partially explained through the political upheaval of the early 1990s. If we want to fully grasp the future political economy, we have to take such global changes and paradigm shifts into account.

How can this be done? How can one predict longer-term social and global political affairs that surpass current paradigms and states of being? To get an idea of the possibilities, we have written four scenarios of the future of Saudi–Iranian relations: Peaceful Hegemonic Competition, Friendly Neighbors, Alienation, and Continued Fragile Pragmatism. Scenario thinking and writing is a method, first developed in business, to look beyond the present into the uncertain future to adapt policies to changing structures and events in a strategic way. According to Peter Schwartz, a scenario is "a tool for ordering one's perceptions about alternative future environments in which one's decisions might be played out"[3] (Schwartz 1996: 4).

Concretely, scenarios are a set of stories, built around carefully chosen driving forces. Each story resembles a possible future environment on a larger or smaller scale. To build a scenario, one must apply systematic and strategic thinking to dynamic, complicated, and seemingly unpredictable realities by exploring the interrelated imponderables between the different factors that influence those realities. Scenarios should not be seen as true predictions or indisputable schemes of the future, and may seem unrealistic sometimes, but they are based on plausibility and probability. Scenario writing is a way to map the future in all its complexities and inconveniencies (Aarts and Van Rijsingen 2007: 23–58).

Using political and economic variables, we can create different scenarios, none of which predict actual future outcomes of Saudi–Iranian relations. They do, however, shed light on possibilities that under current circumstances seem remote or indeed impossible.

If we want to shed light on these political-economic relations in 2030, we clearly must take global and regional politics into account. We will argue that, though many regional issues determine short-term political processes and relations, it is the global context in which such politics are embedded that is essential for our long-term view. Economic cooperation between Saudi Arabia and Iran, especially in the core industrial sectors, constitutes the other variable.

The second half of the 1990s saw a true leap in the study of economic integration and cooperation in the Middle East, both at universities and at international institutions such as the World Bank and different UN institutions.[4] Central to this emphasis was the notion that "peace is good for business." History also teaches us that "business is good for peace" (Klaus Schwab, cited in Aarts and Tempel 1995: 39). The exploration of the possibilities of economic cooperation in the region has, however, mainly resulted in pessimism. At the end of the millennium, intra-regional exports in the Arab world stood at 8 percent of total exports, while in the European Union, the figure was 57 percent.[5] These figures seem unlikely to change, as large-scale economic and political reforms would be required.

Though regional trade has never caused the kind of political cooperation that was envisioned by many at the end of the twentieth century (with the possible exception of the already closely related states of the GCC), Steffen Hertog notes that there is reason for hope: GCC petrodollars, Saudi Arabian in particular, are slowly but steadily moving away from traditional bonds and bank deposits in the West toward Foreign Direct Investments (FDI) in a wider selection of regions, with about a third of Arab outward FDI being intra-Arab (Hertog 2007). Thus, writes Hertog (2007: 59), "FDI has been at the core of regional economic integration since 2000. It has accelerated much more massively than trade and is cross-cutting subregions in a way that commerce has never managed."

While the emphasis above is on Arab economic affairs, the same could logically apply to Arab–Iranian economic affairs. During the time of Saudi–Iranian rapprochement after the Iraqi invasion of Kuwait in 1990, economics and industry were among the most important issues discussed. Indeed, in 1997 a $15 million joint industrial committee was established, and later Saudi foreign minister Saud al-Faisal and Iranian president Khatami agreed on bilateral investments in mining, transport, and the petrochemical industry, as well as possibly tourism. Furthermore, billionaire and entrepreneur prince Waleed bin Talal announced his eagerness to invest in Iran—if invited to do so—and there were talks between Saudi Arabian Basic Industries Corporation (SABIC) and Iran's National Petroleum Company (NPC) about petrochemical cooperation (Okruhlik 2003: 116–119).

This occurred over a decade ago, however, and talks and agreements do not necessarily entail actions. What is more, there are still issues of politics, security, and identity that hinder such cooperation between Iran and the Arab part of the Gulf, and some doubts still exist regarding the Iranian investment climate. Still, it is worthwhile to assess whether, in the long run, investments in core industries can cross-cut subregions.

Saudi–Iranian political relations: ongoing pragmatism?

In explaining Saudi–Iranian political affairs throughout the years, one has to consider three important factors. The first is the regional, strategic factor: in the oil-rich Persian Gulf, three powers—Iran, Saudi Arabia, and Iraq—have long been rivals for dominance. Much of the region's balancing game can be applied to this triangle. When the Ba`th took power in Iraq for the second time in 1968, Iran and Saudi Arabia were quick to join forces. Quite similarly, the Islamic revolution drove Saudi Arabia and Iraq toward each other, and later the Iraqi invasion of Kuwait brought Saudi Arabia and Iran together again (Fürtig 2002: xiii). Though for the time being Iraq as a formidable power seems remote, it is certainly not unthinkable that the logic of such a triangle will return some day.

The second factor relates to ideology, though one has to be careful in choosing the most relevant type. For example, many stress a Sunni-Shi`a divide or a rift due to claimed leadership of the Islamic Umma, which are important in an instrumental manner, but fail to explain the shifts in alliances noted above as well as long periods of peaceful coexistence between Sunnis and Shi`as. Rather, as David Long aptly points out, the divide in previous decades was between conservatism (or status quo, i.e. the Al Saud and the Pahlavis) and radicalism (or anti-status quo, i.e. first Nasserist pan-Arabism, then Ba`thist nationalism, and later Khomeinism) (Fürtig 2002: 4).[6]

Concerning the first decade of the Islamic republic, this notion of Islamic leadership as the variable in divided relations between Iran and Saudi Arabia is appealing and indeed advocated in almost all literature, albeit with varying importance. There is indeed an element of truth to it, but two points should be made. First, it is impossible to decisively establish the exact level of instrumentalism in any political ideology, but there is bound to be some. For example, Tehran's eagerness to appease secularly governed but equally anti-status quo Arab states like Syria and Libya is telling, as it disregards Islam in these relations (Ehteshami 1995: 130). Second, and relatedly, playing an Islamic virtue card can be an important domestic imperative, not only in Iran where it was needed to rally support for a regime trying to consolidate its power (Ehteshami 1995: 130), but equally in Saudi Arabia, where the Islamic Revolution coincided with internal opposition that expressed itself in the seizure of the Grand Mosque.[7] As a result, King Fahd felt the need to polish up his Islamic credentials (Okruhlik 2003: 115–116).[8] Still, as we will argue below, the current disregard of the Islamic "card" in bilateral relations, even in the light of intensifying sectarian strife in Iraq, contributes to explaining the ongoing pragmatism between Tehran and Riyadh. As such, and especially since there is a clear difference in their pro and anti status quo positions, such ideological explanations of earlier rivalry cannot be completely disregarded.

The third factor of concern is the international environment. Much of the Middle East has been colonized in some form by Western powers except for Iran and Saudi Arabia; the Cold War manifested itself vividly in Yemen, Iraq, and Afghanistan, among many other countries, and outside involvement in all three Gulf wars has had a major impact on Gulf affairs. We will not go into too much detail here,[9] but suffice it to say that most bilateral relations in the Gulf region— and probably the wider Middle East and North Africa—could not be explained without taking global power politics into account.

Before the Islamic revolution, Saudi Arabia and Iran were both firmly in the Western camp. Indeed, the two were essential in the American "Twin-Pillar" policy. There was already an element of rivalry between them concerning supremacy in the Gulf and leadership of OPEC, but the common interests of the two monarchies kept such rivalry low. The nonthreatening nature of the Pahlavi secular ambitions vis-à-vis the Saudi claims of Islamic leadership also kept things in balance.

It is interesting to note that initially the Al Saud, in their common nonconfrontational manner, congratulated Ayatollah Khomeini on his victory and applauded the establishment of an Islamic Republic. This, however, quickly changed when it became clear how diametrically opposed Khomeini was to what he called the "American Islam" of the Gulf monarchies. Soon, Iran challenged the Al Saud's ability to govern Mecca and Medina, and Riyadh in turn labeled the Iranian regime "unIslamic" and supported the invasion of Iranian territory by Saddam Hussein. As a result, Iran and Saudi Arabia were bitter opponents during the remainder of the 1980s (Fürtig 2002: 23–27).

It is common knowledge that relations between the two improved during the 1990s, though there is some disagreement on the exact timing and reason for

these improvements. Many suggest the rapprochement came with the election of
Mohammad Khatami in 1997, but this is problematic for several reasons. First, as
noted before, the Iraqi invasion of Kuwait played an important role. Second, there
were clear signs that many in the Iranian establishment, including commander of
the armed forces Hashemi Rafsanjani, opted for a policy of rapprochement even
before the death of Khomeini in 1989 (Fürtig 2002: 95–96). Finally, the importance of the "succession" by Crown Prince Abdullah after King Fahd's stroke
in 1995 is often underestimated (Okruhlik 2003: 114).[10] Thus, many factors
between 1988 and the end of the millennium contributed to the improvement of
ties between Iran.

Two important facts, however, have left these improvements tentative and
cautious. First, while Saudi Arabia is firmly under the U.S. security umbrella,
Iran is an important adversary of the Americans in the Gulf. The second factor
is that during the 1990s, mounting economic problems in both Saudi Arabia
and Iran (though more pressing in the latter) and the reduced leverage ability
of OPEC resulted in fierce competition between Iran and the Arab Gulf states
both in the oil market (and often within OPEC) and over foreign investments
(Fürtig 2002: 237–238; al-Suwaidi 1996: 344). This dark cloud, however, had
a small silver lining: it was these same economic difficulties that started a drive
for economic diversification and a stable regional environment to attract needed
foreign investments. Thus many in the Gulf had a firm interest in the pragmatism
that was developing (Okruhlik 2003: 120; al-Suwaidi 1996: 345–356).

Some have argued that the first obstacle to regional cooperation has also been
eroding. Gwenn Okruhlik argues that the rapprochement between Saudi Arabia
and Iran can be partially explained by growing Saudi disillusionment with the
United States and its policies in Israel, Afghanistan, and Iraq. This convergence
of interests between Tehran and Riyadh is most obvious in the case of Israel: both
Iran and Saudi Arabia are opposed to Israeli aggression and are concerned about
Israeli–Turkish military cooperation. The 9/11 and United States threats against
Iran, she argues, only further enhance Saudi distancing from the West and thus the
improvement of Saudi–Iranian ties (Okruhlik 2003: 120–122).[11] The recent grow-
ing discussion in both academia and the media about the growing influence of
China in the Gulf may also signal a converging ally for Saudi Arabia and Iran.[12]

We have argued elsewhere that Saudi Arabia has a long history of balancing
between different external powers and that its "special relationship" with the
United States has largely remained intact and will stay intact for the foreseeable
future (Aarts and Van Duijne 2009).[13] Moreover, while Iran during the 1990s
engaged in many foreign relations [though not with Israel and only limitedly
and unsuccessfully with the United States (Menashri 2006: 120)], the election
of president Mahmoud Ahmadinejad has largely reversed this process. As such,
the differences between Saudi Arabia and Iran in terms of global alliances have
remained intact.

While it is tempting to suggest that Saudi–Iranian relations will be plunged
into bitter rivalry again, current affairs show that this has only very limitedly
been the case. Sunni-Shi`i tensions in Iraq as well as Iranian nuclear ambitions

seem preeminent in this hypothetical deterioration. Facts on the ground, however, show that while Iran is certainly unhappy with Saudi diplomacy in the case of the Lebanon war in 2006, in which the Saudis strongly condemned Hezbollah, as well as Saudi mediation in the Palestinian infighting between Hamas and Fatah, thereby "clipping the wings" (Gwertzman 2007)[14] of the Iranians, Tehran has remained remarkably silent in both cases. In fact, Saudi–Iranian cooperation has been crucial in helping to ease tensions, particularly in Lebanon (Aarts 2007: 545–546). In much the same way, Saudi Arabia has been weary of Iranian nuclear ambitions[15] and its policies in Iraq, but has carefully remained on speaking terms with Iran. Essentially, Saudi Arabia wants to contain Iran and its ambitions, but simultaneously does not want to clash with it (Aarts 2007: 549–550).[16]

In addition, the Saudi elite largely views Iranian ambitions as power politics and not as a quest for sectarian domination.[17] And while Ahmadinejad has positioned himself internationally as the spokesman of the deprived, be it Muslim or non-Muslim, focusing on anti-imperialism and justice for the Global South (Ehteshami and Zweiri 2007: 106–108), he has done so without attacking the Al Saud or other Gulf monarchies. Quite the contrary, his blame of the United States for its Iraq policy is clearly detached from regional actors.[18] As such, the iconography of Muslim leadership that troubled relations previously has largely vanished and, as Valbjorn and Bank convincingly argue:

> What initially appears as a Sunni-Shi`i split may in fact be a pattern of alliance making with motives far less sectarian in nature. The split not only coincides with the divide between pro- and anti-U.S. orientations, but it also nicely complies with a classic balance of power logic, according to which other regional states will ally in order to balance a rising regional power, Shi`i or not.
> (Valbjorn and Bank 2007: 7)

Thus, while the deep-felt animosity of the 1980s has largely vanished, Saudi Arabia and Iran remain embedded in different camps and thus mistrust and suspicion will continue to play an important role in bilateral relations. But, as both the regional environment and their ideological positionings have changed significantly since the 1980s, there is room for common ground and tentative, pragmatic cooperation. This is especially true since Arab Gulf leaders have taken a somewhat more independent position from the United States in recent years. Under current circumstances and in the near future, we suggest that this cooperation will largely remain cautious and limited. However, to predict bilateral relations in the longer run as we will soon do, much will depend not only on the regional situation and on outside involvement in the Middle East (and reactions to this within it), but also on levels of convergence of economic interests.

Industrialization and the new era of regionalism?

During the second half of the 1960s and in the 1970s, the Middle East and North Africa (MENA) region, and the Gulf in particular, was characterized as a success story. International institutions, not least of which the World Bank, saw some countries, such as Iran, Israel, and Turkey, as potentials for new industrialization and vehicles for leading the way for others, especially Saudi Arabia and Egypt. Growth rates in the region were higher than in Latin America, Africa, and most of Asia, and the area outranked those in terms of income distribution as well. The six Arab Gulf states, for instance, saw a rise in GDP from $11 billion in 1971 to $211 billion in 1981. High oil revenues largely, of course, contributed to these growth rates. Moreover, they shifted the regional balance of economic power from the Levant (and Egypt) to the Persian Gulf (Ehteshami 2007: 132–135).

However, while oil was the primary reason for this economic prosperity, it also proved its Achilles heel. Not only did prices sharply decline in the mid-1980s, but oil income also made the economies stagnate. When the revenues shrank, restrictive practices, inflexible labor bureaucracies, and other inefficiencies took their toll. This "Dutch Disease" affected the entire Gulf, and in the late 1990s, oil still accounted for 96 percent of Iranian and even 99 percent of Saudi Arabian exports. This poor economic performance in sectors other than oil is also identifiable through the inflow of FDI: total GCC inflows in 2001 were $38.7 billion, as opposed to $451 billion for Hong Kong alone (Ehteshami 2007: 135–139).

While this situation resonated throughout the entire Gulf region and largely in the wider Middle East during the 1990s, the new millennium saw a divergence of economic performances. Between 2004 and 2006, Saudi inward FDI as a percentage of gross fixed capital rose from 4.5 to 32.1 percent, while in Iran, it rose from 0.7 to 1.9. (The average in the developing world in 2006 was 13.8 (UNCTAD 2009).) Clearly, the Arab side of the Gulf has in recent years been able to attract large sums of foreign capital, while its Persian counterpart has not. Why is this of critical importance?

As noted above, both Iran and Saudi Arabia had a potential for large-scale development 30 years ago in the downstream oil and gas sectors, namely petrochemicals and refining. Indeed, they are today the two most important petrochemical players in the Middle East (Qatar is a good third): Saudi Basic Industries Corporation (SABIC) is the Middle East's number one company with a capacity of roughly 23 million tons per year, followed by Iran's NPC with 17 million tons per year (Zawya 2007). On a global scale, they are also important players, despite the prediction of Western protectionist measures in the late 1970s, and this role is expected to increase further in the coming years:

> Even if only half of the planned capacity *additions* in Iran and Saudi Arabia come to pass by the end of the decade, the region will still be nearly the size of Western Europe in terms of ethylene production. The growth of the region has been underpinned by stunningly low production site cash costs, which in turn are driven by low feedstock costs.[19] (Italics by the author.)
>
> (Rooney 2005)

Ethylene is the single most important building block in the petrochemical industry. The estimated increases in its capacity between 2005 and 2011 are 7.2

and 8.4 million tons per year for Iran and Saudi Arabia, respectively. However, while these figures are impressive, they still comply with what Turner and Bedore estimated: a move away from the developed world of the basics. The true leap forward for the Gulf region would be to further downstream developments into high-value products, such as polymers, polyester products, chlorine, and semi-finished plastic goods. This downstream development requires large sums of capital as well as technical know-how. One country (and largely one company) has been particularly successful in generating both: Saudi Arabia, with the help of its second "national flagship" SABIC (HSBC Global Research 2007; Rooney 2005; *Tehran Times* 2006).[20]

Two important financial factors help Saudi Arabia and SABIC in their developments. First, large petrodollar surpluses in the Gulf remain in the region. As a result, 15 of the top 20 banks in the Arab world are located in the GCC, and there is a large increase in intraregional investments. Regional markets for equity are also growing. The second factor is the growth in FDI mentioned earlier. Large participation of numerous foreign companies, such as Shell, ExxonMobil, Dow, Total Petrochemicals, Sinopec, Sumitomo, and ChevronPhillips has been established in Saudi Arabia (Rooney 2005).[21]

This long-term foreign participation also helps the Saudis acquire the necessary technological know-how. Besides this rather passive strategy, SABIC is also actively striving to increase its knowledge base by undertaking large takeovers of DSM and GE Plastics in Europe, which offer a broadening of their product slate and a global reach (Aarts *et al.* 2008).

The Iranian case, on the other hand, shows a different image. While many still emphasize the Iranian potential, it largely remains potential vis-à-vis more sophisticated product slates, since Iran lacks the two assets above that its neighbor is endowed with. Foreign participation is, as noted, low, and figures in this regard tend to be exaggerated to (rather unsuccessfully) boost international confidence (Amuzegar 2005: 58; 2007). Moreover, economic difficulties limit available capital surpluses, despite current oil prices, and much is lost in mismanagement and bureaucracies (Amuzegar 2005: 46–63; 2007; 2008). Indeed, the state bureaucracy has seen an unusually high level of expenditure throughout the years, partly to stave off a crisis of unemployment, and partly to provide subsidies in foodstuffs and domestic energy. These subsidies have been increasing regime legitimacy, but they are huge budgetary burdens (Howard 2007: 130–137). The Ahmadinejad government is particularly blamed for squandering the oil windfalls (Amuzegar 2008). As for technology, much the same applies, since further downstream development for any company, country, or region requires other partners with specific skills and know-how.

Cross-cutting subregions?[22]

In 1995, Charles Tripp rightly argued that the GCC was overwhelmingly a political success, but with a very limited economic backdrop. However, he also argued, and with hindsight much less convincingly, that the possibilities were limited in part due to the fact that the economies were too similar and thus not complementary (Tripp 1995: 293–294). Much has changed since then, not in terms of trade, but rather in terms of finance and investments. Certainly, the current oil boom and capital surpluses have a role in this, but it is also important to stress that a decrease in protectionism, industrial development, and foreign confidence to invest within the region have largely contributed to this integration.

When it comes to investments and large-scale joint ventures or acquisitions, clearly the noncomplementarity is less of an issue, a point also convincingly made by Steffen Hertog. In this sense, it is evident that—in theory—the same could apply to economic relations between Iran and Saudi Arabia. Saudi Arabia has access to the technological expertize of which Iran is in dire need, and it has enormous amounts of petrodollars to invest abroad. In return, Iran could be a welcome market for Saudi petrochemical output due to its large population, and would constitute a further step for Saudi expansion eastward. Lastly, and certainly not least, business is good for peace.

There is also the issue of gas. The Saudi Arabian petrochemical industry has an ever increasing need for natural gas, and Iran holds the second largest reserves in the world. Whether this means a future courting of Iran by Riyadh, however, is a source of disagreement. Much of this depends on the Saudi gas explorations, especially in the Rub al-Khali (the Empty Quarter). Until now, results of these drillings have remained disappointing, and thus it is questionable whether Saudi gas resources will be able to keep up with its petrochemical demands (HSBC 2007: 9–10).[23] Iran, on the other hand, holds 15.5 percent of the world's proven reserves. The downside, however, is that its production rate is particularly low [3.7 percent of total world production at the end of 2006, compared to Saudi Arabia, which, having only 3 percent of proven reserves, at the same time produced 2.6 percent (BP 2007: 22–24)]. As such, Iran even had trouble meeting its domestic gas needs in the winter of 2007/2008. However, ambitious plans exist to upgrade production more than threefold from 130 billion cubic metres (bcm) in 2007 to 475 bcm in 2020, leaving room for exports.[24] It must be noted, however, that such increases require structural industrial changes and a conducive foreign and domestic investment atmosphere (Ghorban 2008).

All in all, it would thus seem that there is indeed an opportunity for improving Saudi–Iranian economic relations, especially in the core industrial sector that the two countries share. But at present, such links are still extremely limited, if not absent. Why is this? Two important reasons come to the fore.

First, there is an obvious political component. Saudis are not thrilled about the current Iranian leadership and distrust continues to strain bilateral economic relations. Also, under the current circumstances, Saudi Arabia would prefer to import gas from other sources than Iran, such as Qatar, if the need arises.[25] On the other hand, Iran is not keen on Saudi and GCC FDI, as long as Chinese FDI is available that has no political strings attached.[26] The result is that the minor economic steps taken are largely politically motivated: Iran reaches out to the GCC to disrupt U.S. policy in the Middle East, and some "Gulfis" reach back to keep cross-Gulf relations within the realm of normality. Hence, if we want to address bilateral affairs in 2030, this political context is of special importance.

The second explanation for the absence of bilateral economic ties solely focuses on Iran and can be summed up as economic governance.[27] The Iranian government has no control over parts of its economy; notable examples include the huge economic powers of many *Bonyads* (foundations) and the trouble the government experienced in establishing the new Imam Khomeini Airport just outside Tehran. The economic context in Iran is thus highly volatile and specific interest groups actively defend their turf. All this severely limits the possibility of large-scale FDI projects. Several GCC companies are known to want to invest in Iran, but this lack of economic pragmatism has resulted in limited success and thus overall pessimism about the possibilities of making money. While Iran boasts about foreign, especially Asian, participation, Gulf investors realize that this is very different in nature—especially in duration—from participation in their home countries: foreign investments in the GCC countries tend to be massive in volume and fixed for decades. In Iran, however, contracts involve less capital, are fixed for a limited period and generally hold escape-clauses for the foreign partners. As such, Iran also needs a better overall investment climate for non-Gulf FDI to inspire Saudi and other GCC investors.

Most observers are pessimistic about changes in Iranian economic governance, but be reminded again that we are thinking of 2030 and "outside the box" of the current state of affairs. We will not make any predictions as to whether Iranians will be able to create a better business environment. Rather, we will try to paint two separate futures, one in which they can and another one in which they cannot. This will be our X-axis. The political component is the Y-axis, and thus four scenarios emerge.

Saudi–Iranian ties in 2030

We will largely let the following scenarios speak for themselves, but a few introductory remarks are necessary. First, it is important to note the interrelation between the axes we have chosen: political relations influence business, and vice versa. However, the two are also independent to some extent, which justifies their separation; the above has shown that Iranian economic governance, largely an internal affair, will partially determine future economic cooperation between Saudi Arabia and Iran. It thus also has an independent impact on the future outcome of bilateral ties.

The second point concerns our choice of the global nature of the political axis. Many scenarios focus on regional affairs and particularly regional stability.[28] Initially, we did the same, but it soon became clear that this distorted the situation. We soon understood that when the subject is, for instance, the development of a country or region or the future importance of an outside actor in the Middle East, then stability makes all the difference. However, since we are concerned with bilateral relations of two important states *within* the Middle East, stability is not necessarily a driving force. Quite the contrary, it has been argued,

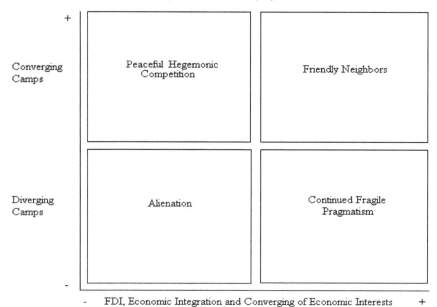

Figure 4.1   The four scenarios.

for example, that the invasion of Kuwait by Iraq improved Saudi–Iranian ties in the early 1990s. Our scenarios equally show that further escalation in Iraq can both result in the improvement or deterioration of these relations.[29] Thus, we needed another driving political force. Regional issues (such as an increase versus a decrease of a Sunni-Shi`i split) could be suggested as independent variables. However, as argued above, these often conveniently coincide with global alliances. Thus the following scenarios take regional developments into account, but in a more short-term and instrumental manner. We argue that the overriding factor that will influence Saudi–Iranian relations in 2030 is whether they belong to the same or a different *global* camp at that time.

Peaceful hegemonic competition

2010 saw a further deterioration of the situation in Iraq. The elected government was weakened even further, and militias effectively ruled much of the territory. Death tolls increased, and the United States gradual withdrawal that started in early 2010 backfired, resulting in the massacre of hundreds of American troops in central Baghdad in May 2011. Two regional players, Saudi Arabia and Iran, however, did not let sentiments escalate, and steered a pragmatic course in this tragedy. This did not go unnoticed, and UN Secretary Ban Ki-Moon applauded their wise and moderating efforts on many occasions.

A milestone event occurred in October 2012, when the Iranian Supreme Leader Ayatollah Khamenei repeated the Iranian government's May 2003 offer in an interview with the Islamic Republic News, saying that "after 30 years of distrust and animosity, it is high time to settle our differences. More than ever, the great American people, as well as the entire Muslim Ummah, now need peace and stability, not conflict, war and deprivation." Much to the surprize of many observers in the West, the Obama administration eagerly accepted this offer and within weeks, Secretary of State Hilary Clinton was on a plane to Tehran. Clearly, the 2006 Baker-Hamilton report had not gone unnoticed in Democratic circles.

It still took some time and the resolution of many issues, but full diplomatic ties between the United States and Iran were restored in 2013. Soon, the situation in Iraq showed serious signs of improvement, largely due to Iran's active attempts to end sectarian infighting in Iraq through its affiliates in the country and in close consultation with the Saudi government.

As all sanctions against Iran have been lifted, and because the Gulf region as a whole became a much more stable business environment, analysts predicted that economic development in Iran could effectively leap forward. Between 2012 and the end of the decade, many Western, East Asian, and Gulf companies and investors actively sought to get a piece of the pie. But, in the mid-2020s, after Ayatollah Ali Mesbah (son of deceased Ayatollah Mohammad Taqi Mesbah Yazdi) took over as Supreme Leader, it became increasingly clear that Iran still clung to its economic independence. Many protectionist measures were kept firmly in place and the government was unable to gain control of the *Bonyads* and other interest groups, leaving the business climate in Iran far from ideal. With Chinese investments (Iranian leaders still saw them as least threatening), however, the Iranian industry boomed, particularly in the downstream oil sectors where it soon started to match its Arab Gulf neighbors.

In 2030, Iran and Saudi Arabia have warm and friendly relations in diplomatic terms. However, in economic terms, the two are competitors par excellence: they have developed practically identical industries, and a fierce competition is taking place between SABIC and NPC over the American, European, and Asian markets. The U.S. strategic umbrella, however, keeps these frictions firmly in check, a situation that is, among older observers, reminiscent of the period prior to the Islamic revolution in the late 1970s.

Friendly neighbors

What started as minor disagreements between former close allies the United States and Saudi Arabia has slowly but gradually grown into a diplomatic rift. While criticism of Saudi policy after September 11, 2001, or Washington's opposition to the Israeli–Syrian talks in 2007 (a clear obstruction to the Arab League peace initiative, as King Abdullah called it years later) were pragmatically ignored, the continued United States obstruction of Saudi attempts to mend the rift between Fatah and Hamas increased the belief among Saudi policymakers that its ally had no intentions of peace in the Arab–Israeli conflict. Conversely, between 2008 and the beginning of 2010, American criticism of the Saudi role in Iraq became ever more audible, especially when more and more reports emerged about the involvement of Saudi nationals in the Sunni insurgency, though Riyadh kept denying any direct involvement. In 2012, relations further deteriorated when Washington, supposedly under Israeli pressure, took an oppositionist attitude vis-à-vis the GCC states' openly stated nuclear-energy ambitions.

Within this fragile environment, a newcomer entered the Middle Eastern political scene, though it had enjoyed an economic presence for quite some time: China. The East Asian nation decided that the days of peaceful coexistence and diplomatic silence should end, and it launched a public peace plan to settle the Arab–Israeli conflict on December 1, 2014. That same day, Moscow and Tehran issued statements fully supporting the initiative, though Russia has since remained a cautious bystander. Within a week, Riyadh's King Sultan joined forces and thus the end of the alliance that some said would last indefinitely was now a fact. In the following 10 years, the contours of the "New Cold War" slowly emerged in the Middle East. Today, two camps are firmly entrenched: the United States, Israel, Turkey, and Syria (which made a U-turn in 2017) are in linear opposition to China, Iran, and Saudi Arabia. Sadly, the largest hotbed of the New Cold War today remains Iraq. While the country had been rather stable (though still with a large United States presence) roughly between 2010 and 2016, violence again escalated because of a joint Iranian–Saudi effort to destabilize the American-supported government.

Meanwhile, the second decade of the twenty-first century saw a leap in Chinese investments in Iran, where Mehdi Hashemi Rafsanjani (son of Ali Akbar Hashemi Rafsanjani) became president in 2013. Sinopec's multi-billion dollar—and even more important, long-term—deals with the Iranian NPC in 2012 and 2014 as well as Iranian hard-fought reforms of its economy have not only resulted in very prosperous economic developments, but also in a huge increase in cross-Gulf investments and cooperation. SABIC and Aroco (formerly Aramco) have together started to aid the Iranians with their gas exploration and infrastructure. FDI has skyrocketed, and Iran became a full member of the GCC in 2019. All in all, though the Middle East has again been plunged into a global conflict with no end in sight, Saudi–Iranian bilateral relations are today better than ever.

Alienation

2010 saw a further deterioration of the situation in Iraq. The elected government was weakened even further and militias effectively ruled much of the territory. Death tolls increased, and the United States gradual withdrawal that started in early 2010 backfired, resulting in the massacre of hundreds of American troops in central Baghdad in May 2011. What is more, sectarian infighting in Iraq increasingly resulted in the support of radical insurgents by both Iran and Saudi Arabia. The Saudi domestic scene also witnessed an increase in sectarian conflict with the bombing of a Shi`i gathering in Dammam in 2014 and the riots that followed in the streets of every major city and town in the Eastern Province.

Lebanon proved to be another major battleground when the Saudi government, backed by the United States, decided to aid radical Sunni militias in a desperate attempt to diminish the ever-growing influence of Hezbollah. Iran, on the other hand, felt emboldened after finally acquiring nuclear weapon capability in 2015. Thus, at the end of the second decade, many analysts concluded that a Sunni-Shi`i divide was responsible for the tense situation throughout the Middle East. Others, however, aptly pointed out that this divide coincided largely with a global division between American and Chinese–Russian spheres of influence in the region. Be that as it may, the result of Iranian–Saudi bilateral ties has been a continuation, if not an increase, of mutual distrust and largely a return to the ideological campaigning of the early 1980s.

The continued civil war in Iraq, increased tensions between the two major powers in the Gulf, and the increase in domestic unrest in many countries in the region had another devastating result. While the beginning of the twenty-first century witnessed an increase in intra-Arab FDI, the Gulf petrodollar is now firmly back in American banks, and while oil income for the Gulf is now higher than ever, the binding factor of mutual economic interests in the Middle East has largely disappeared. Though the economic diversification strategy has remained intact in both Saudi Arabia and Iran, and both are still doing reasonably well—in the case of Iran, particularly through enormous, politically motivated investments from China—no cross-Gulf interaction occurs in this regard, or hardly in any regard.

Continued fragile pragmatism

Saudi Arabia and Iran dealt with many issues during the first 30 years of the twenty-first century, such as opposite visions on the future of Iraq, Iranian obstruction of the Arab League peace initiative, and a divergence of interests vis-à-vis both Hezbollah and the influence of Syria in Lebanon. These differences continued and deepened when China entered the political equation. The Chinese peace initiative of December 1, 2014 further drove Riyadh and Iran in opposite directions: both Russia and Iran fully supported the plan, while King Sultan saw it as "undermining Arab independence and a blatant denial of the interests and well-being of the people of the Arab world, as well as their ability to deal with the issue by itself."

Since this new Chinese diplomatic drive, Saudi Arabia has clearly taken sides and improved its relations with Egypt and Turkey, though relations with Israel have remained cautious and secretive. This is understandable, because the domestic repercussions of the mid-2010 talks between the Kingdom's foreign minister Prince Turki bin Faisal and Israel's prime minister Benyamin Netanyahu were still fresh in Saudi memory. Thus, during the past 30 years, political relations between Riyadh and Tehran have remained cautious and full of mutual distrust.

However, much has changed since the turn of the century. In the early twenty-first century, much talk about increasing cross-Gulf investments occurred, though analysts correctly pointed out that these were mainly politically motivated. Two significant changes then altered this situation rather drastically: first, the newly elected pragmatic-conservative government of Ali Larijani in 2012 soon implemented drastic reforms of the Iranian economy; the downstream oil sector was privatized, and foreign investment laws were radically changed.

The second important change came in the spring of 2013, when the three large joint ventures that had been drilling for oil and gas in the Rub al-Khali years longer than expected presented their disappointing conclusions. Some oil was found, but no natural gas.

These two changes paved the way for an unprecedented spur of economic cooperation between the two politically opposed neighbors. SABIC established a multi-plant joint venture with NPC, both in Jubail and in the Iranian Pars Special Economic Zone, and Aramco offered its assistance with the exploration of the abundant Iranian natural gas resources as well as the improvement of infrastructure. In return, the Saudis were granted a long-term gas supply contract.

Today, while Saudi Arabia and Iran are exposed to many political differences, it is safe to say that indeed, business is good for peace: neither is willing to jeopardize these important economic interests, and thus they ensure that disagreements stay within the limits of normal diplomatic engagement. The political success of these economic interests has been especially visible in Iraq: between 2008 and 2012, both Iran and Saudi Arabia were, it is currently known, two important destabilizing actors in that country, but since then, and despite the unchanged political differences between them, both have recognized the economic importance of regional stability. Thus, Iraq has slowly been recovering from 10 years of conflict. How much pressure this balance can take, however, remains an open question.

Conclusion

We have argued that the future configuration of bilateral relations between the Kingdom of Saudi Arabia and the Islamic Republic of Iran will largely depend on two main factors: the convergence of economic interests and cross-Gulf investments and alliances in global political configurations.

While some of the four sketches of Saudi–Iranian ties in 2030 seem far-fetched and remote, the suggested steps and events that led to these future configurations are in themselves not unthinkable. Thus, scenario writing circumvents the social scientist's tendency to predict the future with a strong emphasis on the current state of affairs. We too would suggest that these bilateral relations in 2030 will remain cautious and full of distrust, and as such, the difference between poor and reasonably good relations will largely depend on economics. However, due to pessimism regarding the ability of the Iranian government to make necessary changes, economic relations will continue to have a strong political rationale. But, in an uncertain world, the unthinkable at least becomes thinkable.

While the political axis can have groundbreaking effects in these scenarios, the economic one largely works out the "details" within these political configurations. For instance, while true improvements of bilateral relations are currently prohibited by the diametrically opposed relations of Saudi Arabia and Iran with the United States, the importance of economic diversification and foreign investments has resulted in a mutual interest in continued pragmatism, despite tensions over Iraq or Iranian nuclear ambitions. In the future, economics will clearly still make a difference between (under current political circumstances) alienation and a continuation of this pragmatism or (under different political circumstances) between competition and cooperation.

The above has also shown that the convergence or divergence of global alliances is of central importance. It must be noted that it is much less relevant *which* global camp it will be. While in one scenario both Iran and Saudi Arabia align with the United States, and in another with China, it is important to stress that these configurations are interchangeable.

The future is full of uncertainty. Much will depend on economic developments and policy choices, not only in Iran and Saudi Arabia, but also in China, the United States, Europe, Russia, and other Middle Eastern states. The four scenarios are thus not the only possible futures, and there is indeed thinkable middle ground between them. Essentially, they present an analytical exercise that allows us to think outside of current paradigms. They can also, as in business, be a tool for decision-makers to grasp possible future outcomes of a given course of action.

Notes

1 See also Aarts *et al.* 1987: 150–168.
2 See Aarts *et al.* 2008: 135–156.
3 Compare Ayoob 2006: 148–161. Ayoob delivers a set of "predictions" less adventurous than the "thinking the unthinkable" we do in this article, which is central to scenario writing.
4 Examples include Çarkoğlu *et al.* 1998; World Bank 1995; Aarts and Tempel 1995: 39–49; Aarts 1999: 911–925; Laura Guazzone (ed.) 1997; and Michael Hudson (ed.) 1999.
5 Interestingly, intra-regional trade has shown to take mainly the form of intra-industry trade; see Miniesy *et al.* 2004: 46. For a recent, more general observation, see Noland and Pack 2008: 60–69.
6 See also Gargash 1996: 139.
7 On November 20, 1979, the first day of the Muslim fifteenth century, a group of young Islamists seized the Grand Mosque of Mecca and took several hundred pilgrims as their hostages. See Hegghammer and Lacroix 2007: 103–122. For a journalistic account of the events, see Trofimov 2007.
8 Fahd changed his name from "Your Majesty King Fahd" to "Custodian of the Two Holy Mosques of Mecca and Medina, King Fahd" in these days, and he often linked events in Iran to international communism in an attempt to discredit Iranian Islam. The regime also moved closer to the *Wahhabi* establishment and increased its financing of militant jihadism abroad—mainly in Afghanistan—to gain credibility among the Islamists and keep the jihadis among them busy outside of the kingdom.
9 See for instance Roberson 2002: 55–70; Hinnebusch 2003; Louise Fawcett (ed.) 2005; Halliday 2005.

10 Actually, Abdallah took over the reins of the kingdom in 1995, but it took another 10 years before he officially became the new king of Saudi Arabia. As a Crown Prince, he for instance invited then President Rafsanjani to visit the Kingdom.

11 Equally, some have argued the United States was distancing itself from Saudi Arabia. See for instance Hammond 2007 or da Lage 2005, who argues that "[the United States is] openly wary of the Saudi regime and doesn't seem any longer to consider its survival a strategic priority." For another example, see Bronson 2005: 372–398.

12 See for instance the Gracia Group 2002 and also Aarts and Van Rijsingen 2007: 23–58. Both recognize that the short-term strategic implications are rather limited, but do not rule out serious mid- or long-term consequences of growing Chinese energy needs. Niblock 2006: 170 concludes that "[I]n the long term, Saudi Arabia's interests may well be best served by shifting its international cooperation towards the countries of South Asia and the Far East."

13 See also Nonneman 2005: 315–351.

14 The relaunch in April 2007 of the Abdullah peace plan should be seen in the same perspective; to date it has not been very successful.

15 Kaye and Wehrey interestingly note, however, that many regional actors do not perceive a direct nuclear attack from Iran to be the greatest threat. They point out it will be the reactions to or the spillover from a nuclear Iran that poses the greatest threat. Even more interesting is what they noted as the smaller states' worry that the Saudis might undertake a "hegemonic overreaction," "[i]n which Riyadh would exploit the threat from Tehran to win Washington's recognition of Saudi pre-eminence in the Sunni Arab world" (Kaye and Wehrey 2007: 112).

16 See also Hiro 2007.

17 "Iran's attempt to exploit the current instability in Iraq to consolidate and assert its political leverage at the expense of the other parties sends wrong signals. It is not just a direct intervention in the affairs of an Arab country whose political stability and security are directly linked to the Gulf environment as a whole, but it is seen as an attempt to destabilize the regional balance of power and sends clear signals that Tehran's foreign policy is still motivated by narrow interests" (Sager 2005). See also Gause 2007.

18 These views are evidenced by statements such as "Without the presence of the foreign troops, the region will live in peace and brotherhood," in "Iranian President Ends Iraq Tour" (*Al Jazeera* 2008). See also Amer 2008.

19 See also Aarts *et al.* 2008.

20 The term "national flagship" refers to Saudi Aramco; see Jaffe and Elass 2007. The emphasis the Saudis recently have put on industrial development and the prestige SABIC has offered them certainly justify a similar label.

21 See also Woertz 2007: 77–106, Luciani 2007: 149–197, and Saudi Energy Forum 2006 for additional information on key players and joint ventures.

22 For this section, it has proven extremely difficult to find convincing evidence. As such, we owe a great deal of gratitude to several seasoned analysts, especially Giacomo Luciani, Steffen Hertog, John Calabrese and Anoush Ehteshami.

23 HSBC Global Research 2007: 9–10. This was confirmed by Jean-François Seznec during the symposium "Industrialization in the Gulf: A Socioeconomic Revolution," organized by the Center for Contemporary Arab Studies at Georgetown University, March 27–28, 2008.

24 Some estimates of possible production are even higher, up to 600 bcm/y.

25 It seems, however, that Qatar's export potential (for neighboring Saudi Arabia) has inbuilt limits due to its large-scale long-term commitments in LNG deals.

26 For more on Iranian "dreams" about Chinese investments, see Calabrese 2006 and Aarts and Van Rijsingen 2007: 31–34; 38–40.

27 See "Doing Business Indicators" in www.doingbusiness.org/economyrankings/?regionid=4 and note the wide divergence between Saudi Arabia's and Iran's ranking (viewed May 1, 2008). See also Sullivan and Nadgrodkiewicz 2008.

28 For a clear example, see World Economic Forum 2007. See also Aarts and Van Rijsingen 2007.
29 Though Iraq is the most probable cause for such changes or continuities in alliance-making, it is not necessarily *the* regional immediate cause. Other conflicts, such as in Lebanon or Israel–Palestine, could equally serve as that trigger. An improvement of the situation in Iraq in the immediate future, on the other hand, would most probably have a less dramatic effect on the political axis, though it would certainly have an impact in terms of regional balancing. Still, the exact configuration of such balancing is dependent to a large extent on global alliances. The most eminent effect of an improvement of the situation in Iraq therefore lies on the economic axis: business is not only good for peace, but vice versa.

Bibliography

Aarts, P. (2007) "Saudi Arabia Walks the Tightrope," *The International Spectator*, 42 (4): 545–550.

Aarts, P. (1999) "The Middle East: A Region without Regionalism or the End of Exceptionalism?" *Third World Quarterly*, 20 (5): 911–925, October.

Aarts, P. and Tempel, M. (1995) "Economic Integration in the Middle East," *JIME Review*, 31: 39–49.

Aarts, P. and Van Duijne, J. (2009) "The Saudi Security Environment: Plus Ça Change...," in D. Pioppi and L. Guazzone (eds.) *The Dynamics of Change in the Arab World: Globalisation and the Re-structuring of State Power*, Ithaca, New York: Ithaca Press.

Aarts, P. and Van Rijsingen, M. (2007) "Beijing's Rising Star in the Gulf Region: The Near and the Distant Future," in E. Woertz (ed.) *Gulf Geo-Economics*, Dubai: Gulf Research Center.

Aarts, P., Eisenloeffel, G. and Renner, M. (1987) "OPEC's Industrialisation and European Restructuring," in C. Stevens and J.V. Themaat (eds.) *Europe and the International Division of Labour: New Patterns of Trade and Investment with Developing Countries, EEC and the Third World: Survey 6*, London: Hodder and Stoughton.

Aarts, P., Meertens, R. and Van Duijne, J. (2008) "Kingdom with Borders: The Political Economy of Saudi-European Relations," in M. al-Rasheed (ed.) *Kingdom without Borders: Saudi Political, Religious and Media Frontiers*, London: Hurst & Co.

Amer, P. (2008) "U.S. Fails to Isolate Iran from Arabs," *Al Jazeera*, 14 January. Online HTTP: www.aljazeera.net (accessed March 10, 2008).

Amuzegar, J. (2005) "Iran's Third Development Plan: an Appraisal," *Middle East Policy*, 12 (3): 46–63.

Amuzegar, J. (2007) "An Overview of Petrochemical Industry," *Iran Daily*, April 8.

Amuzegar, J. (2008) "Iran Deals with the Oil Windfalls," *Middle East Economic Survey*, 51 (9): 25–28.

Ayoob, M. (2006) "The Middle East in 2025: Implications for U.S. Policy," *Middle East Policy*, 13 (2): 148–161.

BP (2007) *BP Statistical Review of World Energy 2007*, June.

Bronson, R. (2005) "Understanding U.S.-Saudi Relations," in P. Aarts and G. Nonneman (eds.) *Saudi Arabia in the Balance: Political Economy, Society, Foreign Affairs*, London: Hurst & Co.

Calabrese, J. (2006) "China and Iran: Mismatched Partners," *Occasional Papers*, The Jamestown Foundation, August.

Çarkoğlu, A., Eder, M. and Kirişci, K. (1998) *The Political Economy of Regional Cooperation in the Middle East*, London: Routledge.

DoingBusiness.com, "Doing Business Indicators." Online HTTP: www.doingbusiness. org/economyrankings/?regionid=4 (accessed May 1, 2008).

Ehteshami, A. (1995) *After Khomeini: The Iranian Second Republic*, London / New York: Routledge.

Ehteshami, A. (2007) *Globalization and Geopolitics in the Middle East: Old Games, New Rules*, London/New York: Routledge.

Ehteshami, A. and Zweiri, M. (2007) *Iran and the Rise of its Neoconservatives: The Politics of Tehran's Silent Revolution*, London/New York: I.B. Tauris.

Fawcett, L. (ed.) (2005) *International Relations of the Middle East*, Oxford: Oxford University Press.

Fürtig, H. (2002) *Iran's Rivalry with Saudi Arabia between the Gulf Wars*, Reading: Ithaca Press.

Gargash, A. (1996) "Iran, the GCC States and the UAE: Prospects and Challenges in the Coming Decade," in J.S. al-Suwaidi (ed.) *Iran and the Gulf: A Search for Stability*, Abu Dhabi: The Emirates Center for Strategic Studies and Research.

Gause, F.G. III (2007) "Saudi Arabia: Iraq, Iran, the Regional Power Balance, and the Sectarian Question," *Strategic Insights*, 6 (2) (accessed March 10, 2008).

Ghorban, N. (2008) "Iran's Future Gas Development and Exports in View of the January 2008 Gas Crisis," *Middle East Economic Survey*, 51 (8): 24–28.

The Gracia Group (2002) "The Sino-Saudi Energy Rapprochement: Implications for U.S. National Security," The Gracia Group, January 8.

Guazzone, L. (ed.) (1997) *The Middle East in Global Change: The Politics and Economics of Interdependence versus Fragmentation*, Houndmills: Macmillan.

Gwertzman, B. (2007) Interview with F. Gregory Gause III, "Saudis Aim to Roll Back Iranian Influence," Council on Foreign Relations. Online HTTP: www.cfr.org/ publication/12895/ (accessed April 10, 2008).

Halliday, F. (2005) *The Middle East in International Relations: Power, Politics and Ideology*, Cambridge: Cambridge University Press.

Hammond, A. (2007) "Saudi Diplomatic Drive Runs into U.S. Opposition," Reuters, February 21.

Hegghammer, T. and Lacroix, S. (2007) "Rejectionist Islamism in Saudi Arabia: The Story of Juhayman al-'Utaybi Revisited," *International Journal of Middle East Studies*, 39 (1): 103–122.

Hertog, S. (2007) "The GCC and Arab Economic Integration: A New Paradigm," *Middle East Policy*, 14 (1): 52–68.

Hinnebusch, R. (2003) *The International Politics of the Middle East*, Manchester/ New York: Manchester University Press.

Hiro, D. (2007) "Iran--Saudi Arabia: A New Beginning?," *The Nation* (Bangkok), March 13.

Howard, R. (2007) *Iran Oil: The New Middle East Challenge to America*, London/ New York: I.B. Tauris.

Hudson, Michael (ed.) (1999) *Middle East Dilemma: The Politics and Economics of Arab Integration*, New York: Columbia University Press.

HSBC Global Research (2007) *Company Report Saudi Basic Industries Co.*, 12 April.

"Iranian President Ends Iraq Tour" (2008) *Al Jazeera*, 4 March. Online www.aljazeera.net (accessed March 10, 2008).

Jaffe, A.M. and Elass, J. (2007) *Saudi Aramco: National Flagship with Global Responsibilities*, The James A. Baker Institute for Public Policy, Rice University.

Kaye, D.D. and Wehrey, F. (2007) "A Nuclear Iran: The Reactions of Neighbors," *Survival*, 49 (2): 111–128.

da Lage, O. (2005) "Saudi Arabia and the Smaller Gulf States: The Vassals take their Revenge," The Gulf Monarchies in Transition (colloquium), CERI, January.

Luciani, G. (2007) "The GCC Refining and Petrochemical Sectors," in E. Woertz (ed.) *Gulf Yearbook 2006–2007*, Dubai: Gulf Research Center.

Menashri, D. (2006) "Iran, Israel and the Middle East Conflict," *Israel Affairs*, 12 (1): 107–122.

Miniesy, R., Nugent, J. and Yousef, T. (2004) "Intra-Regional Trade Integration in the Middle East: Past Performance and Future Potential," in H. Hakimian and J.B. Nugent (eds.) *Trade Policy and Economic Integration in the Middle East and North Africa: Economic Boundaries in Flux*, London: Routledge.

Niblock, T. (2006) *Saudi Arabia: Power, Legitimacy and Survival*, London/New York: Routledge.

Noland, M. and Pack, H. (2008) "Arab Economies at a Tipping Point," *Middle East Policy*, 15 (1): 60–69.

Nonneman, G. (2005) "Determinants and Patterns of Saudi Foreign Policy: 'Omnibalancing' and 'Relative Autonomy' in Multiple Environments," in P. Aarts and G. Nonneman (eds.) *Saudi Arabia in the Balance: Political Economy, Society, Foreign Affairs*, London: Hurst & Co.

Okruhlik, G. (2003) "Saudi Arabian-Iranian Relations: External Rapprochement and Internal Consolidation," *Middle East Policy*, 10 (2): 113–125.

"Petrochemical Industry and Prospects for Development (Part 2)" (2006) *Tehran Times*, February 23.

Roberson, B.A. (2002) "The Impact of the International System on the Middle East," in H. Raymond and A. Ehteshami (eds.) *The Foreign Policies of Middle East States*, London/Boulder: Lynne Rienner, 55–70.

Rooney, P. (2005) "Factors That Influence the Petrochemical Industry in the Middle East," *Middle East Economic Survey*, 48 (23). Online HTTP: www.mees.com (accessed February 3, 2008).

Sager, A. (2005) *Saudi Arabia, Iran and the Search for Security*, Gulf Research Center, June. Online HTTP: www.grc.ae (accessed February 4, 2008).

Saudi Energy Forum (2006) "Event Sponsors." Online HTTP: www.saudienergyforum. com/index.php?page=sponsor (accessed February 4, 2008).

Schwartz, P. (1996) *The Art of the Long View: Planning for the Future in an Uncertain World*, New York: Doubleday.

Sullivan, J. and Nadgrodkiewicz, A. (2008) "Middle East and North Africa Reform: Rooted in Economic and Political Ground," Center for International Private Enterprise, No. 0804, February.

al-Suwaidi, J.S. (1996) "The Gulf Security Dilemma: The Arab Gulf States, The United States and Iran," in J.S. al-Suwaidi (ed.) *Iran and the Gulf*, Abu Dhabi: The Emirates Center for Strategic Studies and Research.

Tripp, C. (1995) "Regional Organizations in the Middle East," in L. Fawcett and A. Hurrell (eds.) *Regionalism in World Politics: Regional Organizations and International Order*, Oxford: Oxford University Press.

Trofimov, Y. (2007) *The Siege of Mecca: The Forgotten Uprising*, London: Penguin/ Allen Lane.

Turner, L. and Bedore, J. (1977) "Saudi and Iranian Petrochemicals and Oil Refining: Trade Warfare in the 1980s," *International Affairs*, 53 (4): 572–586.

United Nations Conference on Trade and Development (UNCTAD) *FDI Country Fact Sheets*. Online HTTP: www.unctad.org/Templates/Page.asp?intItemID=3198&lang=1 (accessed November 7, 2007).

Valbjorn, M. and Bank, A. (2007) "Signs of a New Arab Cold War: The 2006 Lebanon War and the Sunni-Shi`i Divide," *Middle East Report*, 242: 6–11.

World Bank (1995) *Claiming the Future: Choosing Prosperity in the Middle East and North Africa*, Washington, D.C.: The World Bank.

Woertz, E. (2007) "A New Age of Petrodollar Recycling?" in E. Woertz (ed.) *Gulf Geo-Economics*, Dubai: Gulf Research Center.

World Economic Forum (2007) *The Kingdom of Saudi Arabia and the World: Scenarios to 2025 – Executive Summary*, Geneva: World Economic Forum. Online HTTP: www. weforum.org/pdf/scenarios/gcc_ksa_executive_summary.pdf (accessed January 14, 2008).

Zawya (2007) "Exploit Oil to Diversify from Oil." Online HTTP: www.zawya.com/ industryinsight/petrochemicals.cfm (accessed March 15, 2008).

5 Strategic dynamics of Iran–GCC relations

John Duke Anthony

This paper focuses on the origins and dynamics of the GCC's strategic concerns in its relationships with Iran. It posits three overarching strategic constants. First, Tehran, unlike the six GCC members, governs a country that is Iranian, not Arab. Second, the mother tongue of millions of Iranians is Farsi, not Arabic. Third, the one regional organization to which all of the GCC countries have longest belonged and which constitutes their single largest association with fellow Arabs, the League of Arab States, is one in which, by definition, Iran is not a member.

This paper contends that three additional constants in Iran's strategic and geopolitical calculations are at odds with the aspirations of the GCC countries' governments, leaders, and majority of their citizens. One is the radical and revolutionary nature of Iran's system of governance and political dynamics. These are seen as the antithesis of the governmental status quo-orientation of the GCC countries' respective administrative structures.

Another constant is the GCC's objection to Iran's numerous policy pronouncements and actions toward what GCC leaders regard as primarily Arab issues. More specifically, the objection is to Iran's interference in the domestic affairs of Arab League members Iraq, Lebanon, and Palestine. Closer to home, the objection is to Iran's occupation of Abu Musa Island and the Greater and Lesser Tunb Islands. Before the GCC formed in May of 1981, these islands belonged to the Emirate of Sharjah and the Emirate of Ra's al-Khaymah, respectively. The GCC claims these islands should still belong to the Emirates.

A third constant is overall GCC resentment of Iran's opposition to the member-countries' support for a continuing Western defense presence in the region. Iran's continuing criticisms of GCC strategic decisions in this regard, the GCC leaders argue, ignore regional realities and preferences, namely that the GCC countries have no practical choice but to align their deterrence and defense needs with the assistance extended them by credible Great Powers. Buttressing their decision has been that these powers' foreign policy objectives coincide closely to the GCC peoples' legitimate interests in self-defense and the inherent right of their countries and governments to self-preservation.

Within the ever-present interplay of these constants, the paper's purpose is to describe and analyze a range of phenomena pertaining to the background and context of GCC–Iran relations that may not be readily apparent either to generalists or to many specialists. This paper also takes note of a range of Iranian viewpoints on the country's interests and objectives toward the GCC countries. Even so, it makes no pretense to being balanced. Rather, the goal is to enhance awareness of the relationships between the two peoples and their respective governments on issues of strategic importance primarily from the vantage point of the GCC.

The paper's approach to explaining what has driven the exceptional caution of the GCC country leaders' dealings with Iran from before and since the GCC's creation is as follows. It is to highlight specific instances in which Iran could have dispelled the grounds for the GCC countries' suspicions and mistrust but did not. Providing such an evidentiary trail should shed light on the pan-GCC contention that Iranian behavior has frequently fallen short of inspiring the requisite trust and confidence that GCC leaders seek in a neighbor from whom they want nothing more or less than the most cordial and reciprocally rewarding ties.

That many in Tehran take exception to the GCC's grounds for doubt and suspicion of Iranian motives in such matters should not be surprising. However, the response by GCC representatives has been to cite logic and the verifiable record. Iranian actions, policies, and positions on matters of importance to the GCC members, they maintain, provide ample justification for their reservations and ongoing concerns.

The implications of such a response are clear. GCC leaders see no reason why Iranians should question the GCC's approach to protecting and furthering their legitimate interests. Least of all, they contend, should Tehran find their actions irresponsible. The record, they argue, hardly differs from what they believe Iran would do were it to face the same range of foreign policy priorities and challenges as the ones that confront the GCC.

An additional objective of the paper is to illuminate GCC leaders' efforts, wherever possible, to avoid antagonizing Iran while finessing and/or countering Tehran's criticisms of their ties to international allies and working partners.[1] In pointing out instances in which GCC and Iranian strategic objectives have diverged more than converged, it is difficult for this writer to conclude other than that the GCC's approach to Gulf defense has been driven from the start by notions of elementary prudence. Essentially, the GCC countries have sought to enhance their abilities, aided by others, to protect themselves against possible intimidation or attack by Iran, Iraq, or any other country.

Seeds of distrust: background, context, perspective

Any examination of GCC–Iranian strategic relations needs to acknowledge that Iran, from the beginning, was not alone in opposing the GCC's criteria for membership. The criteria implicitly—no good purpose would have been served had it been made explicit—excluded from consideration four countries that thought they should be included: Iran, Iraq, Jordan, and Yemen. Among the four, Iran has been by far the most outspoken in its criticism of the GCC's exclusivist criteria for admission. Little wonder why: the organization, by design, is composed of Gulf Arab countries. Ethnic-based national differences alone, however, were and are not the sole attribute distinguishing the member-countries from Iran. Other common GCC attributes include a broadly common identity, culture, language, and history; a nearly identical set of developmental challenges; and similar systems of governance.

Seed one: Britain abrogates its special treaties

The seeds of the consensus determining the GCC's standards for admission were numerous, cumulative, and multifaceted. The earliest seed was planted in late 1967 and would be nurtured thereafter for the next four years. The context was Great Britain's political decision to relinquish its long unchallenged role as the paramount power in the Gulf. Great Britain declared that by the end of 1971 it would abrogate each of the longstanding treaties between itself and nine Arab Gulf states by which it administered their defense and foreign relations.

From a geopolitical perspective, the decision marked the end of an era in which the region's international economic, political, and military might had been dominated by Great Britain for more than 125 years. In this, there was something unique. Unlike the transitions from imperial rule to national sovereignty else-where in the Arab world, none of the representatives of the nine Arab signatories to the protected-state treaties had pressed the British to make such a decision.

Accordingly, the Gulf emirates affected by the decision initially responded with shock and trepidation. Nonetheless, once they realized the decision was irreversible, they quickly agreed to meet with British officials to explore the feasibility of forging as large, unified, and robust a successor state as possible.[2] To their good fortune, their efforts were supported by Kuwait, Oman, and Saudi Arabia, and, to a lesser extent, by Bahrain as well as Iran.

What emerged by the late summer and fall of 1971 as a result of numerous meetings, however, was not one country but three, namely Bahrain, Qatar, and the United Arab Emirates. The latter united the six east Arabian principalities of Abu Dhabi, Ajman, Dubai, Fujairah, Sharjah, and Umm al-Qaywayn into a loose confederation. A seventh member-state, the Emirate of Ra's al-Khaymah, joined in March 1972. As they began to chart an existence free from British rule, each of these polities was apprehensive of what the future might hold. Of particular concern was how Iran and Iraq would react to what they were setting out to achieve.

All nine of the east Arabian rulers had grounds for being suspicious of Baghdad's and Tehran's respective national agendas and ambitions toward them. Not without reason, they regarded Iran and Iraq as eager to fill the perceived power vacuum occasioned by the British decision. They believed that, left unchecked, both countries would likely pose challenges to the region's stability and security. Accordingly, neither the British nor the Arab participants were inclined to allow Baghdad or Tehran to be privy, let alone party, to the sensitive aspects of their discussions and negotiations.

Seed two: America ascendant

In marked contrast to the termination of imperial rule elsewhere, the ending of Great Britain's position as the paramount strategic external power in these polities' defense systems was not accompanied by violence. Instead, Britain's abrogation of its protected-state treaties not only occurred peacefully, but was followed almost seamlessly by the beginning of another epoch. In it, the United States would constitute the most powerful foreign military presence in the Gulf.

Without question, the elevation of Great Britain's most important ally to the semi-official status of preeminent global force in the Gulf was synonymous, certainly in this particular region, with an entirely new international adventure for the United States. However, the phenomenon of a Great Power administering the region's defense was not. Indeed, in the eyes of the Gulf's inhabitants, the protective measures that Washington proceeded to undertake in pursuit of its own and its allies' interests and key foreign policy objectives could not have been more familiar, and echoed a continuous theme in Gulf history stretching back to the Portuguese presence dating from the early sixteenth century.

For 400 years there had thus not been one day when the protection and international affairs of most of the maritime reaches of the western side of the Gulf, or practically the entire length of eastern Arabia, had not been administered by a Western Great Power. With Saudi Arabia the sole exception in this one geo-strategic feature, for during most of this period it had not yet formed the state and territory that it came to comprise from 1932 onward, the six contiguous countries that would later forge the Gulf Cooperation Council in 1981 were then and would remain unique. Nothing remotely like it had occurred before or since in the international experience of the rest of the Arab world's sub-regions, that is, the Fertile Crescent, the Levant, the Nile Valley, and Arab North Africa.

In the modern era predating the onset of the Iranian Revolution in 1979, the significance and strategic implications of this reality have long remained a major point of contention in Tehran. From an Iranian nationalistic perspective, it is galling that for four consecutive centuries the country at the center of the defense structures perpetuating international order and stability in the area has not been the country with by far the longest coast and largest population in the Gulf. Rather, it has been a non-Arab, non-Iranian, and non-Islamic foreign power.

Underscoring this ongoing strategic and historic reality is how the military might of one or more Western powers over much of the past half millennium has proven not only vital to maintaining Gulf peace and stability, but has also been central to the continued existence of a majority of the Gulf countries' traditional systems of governance. No less significant is that the presence of such concentrated superior foreign military force has improved the abilities of government leaders inside and outside the Gulf to better anticipate and prepare for scenarios that could affect their destinies.[3]

Seed three: Iran, Iraq, and the Gulf's intraregional balance of power

Although this paper is concerned primarily with Iran and the GCC countries, it is necessary to point out that, for the past half century, a challenge to Gulf security and stability has been Iraq. In 1958, Iraq's monarchy was overthrown and replaced by a radical revolutionary government. A succession of Iraqi post-monarchy leaders put the Gulf's seven remaining hereditary regimes on notice. For the next four and a half decades, one Iraqi government after another was dedicated to promoting the ideals of Arab nationalism, unity, secularism, and varying degrees of socialism.

This first of two demises of a Gulf dynastic regime over the course of the past 50 years was not without consequence. Indeed, leaders in Iran and all along the eastern edges of Arabia were thereafter keenly aware of Baghdad's interest in enhancing Iraq's role in Gulf affairs. An opportunity to do so was not long in coming. When Kuwait gained its independence from Great Britain in July 1961, Iraq sought to annex it by force. It was thwarted when Britain rapidly mobilized and deployed its armed forces back to Kuwait.

Even so, from 1968 onwards, an overarching reality for the Gulf countries could not have been clearer: within three years Great Britain would no longer perform its protective role in assuring the security and stability of the Gulf countries. Iraq continued its nationalist and expansionist aspirations in the face of this new regional balance of power, its leaders perceiving an opportunity to couple Iraq's pan-Arab ambitions with Gulf Arab polities soon to be free of British rule.

But a seeming paradox was at hand. Whereas Iraq had previously indicated an interest in challenging Great Power primacy in the Gulf's international affairs, the number of occasions when it had actually organized and dispatched forces in an effort to do so was significantly fewer than Iran's. Indeed, in modern history, Tehran's expansionist ambitions at Arab expense were, in marked contrast, more frequent and have existed over a much longer period of time.

Seed four: GCC apprehensions of Iran

In the eyes of the countries that would form the GCC, two Iranian reactions to Great Britain's decision to abrogate its remaining Gulf treaty relations were telling. The first reaction had to do with Iran's designs on Bahrain.

At the time, Bahrain's international status was viewed throughout eastern Arabia as one of first among equals. In 1948, Britain withdrew from what had been the seat of its Political Residency for the Gulf at Bushire on the southwestern Iranian coast and moved it to Bahrain, where it would remain until December 1, 1971. Bahrain henceforth served as the headquarters from which British interests and policy objectives were administered for the Gulf's nine remaining protected states.

Iran had once ruled Bahrain indirectly before its representatives were ousted in the late eighteenth century. Ever since, Iran had maintained irredentist claims to Bahrain and even set aside two seats for Bahrain in its parliament. It did so with much fanfare in preparation for the day when the Arab island state's citizens would be liberated from British rule.

When that point arrived, the Shah of Iran assumed Bahrainis would not likely opt for separate national sovereignty and political independence. Rather, he presumed they would acquiesce to rule by Iran. To that end, he wagered further that Bahrainis would proceed to elect delegates to represent their interests in Iranian institutions.

Thus, once Britain's decision to abrogate its treaty obligations to Bahrain and the other eight emirates became known, the Shah insisted Bahrain be dealt with differently than the other emirates, reminding anyone in doubt that a majority of Bahrain's citizens, like Iran's, were Shi`i Muslims. Tehran was not alone in such views. In a meeting with this author at the time, former U.S. Admiral Arleigh Burke, who as Chief of Naval Operations had only shortly before held the highest office in the United States Navy, also recommended that Bahrain revert to as close an association with Iran as possible.

Iran's claims to Bahrain were dealt a body blow when the results of a British-engineered informal sampling of public opinion in the archipelago by an official of the United Nations were made public in May 1970. The UN representative had met at length with numerous Bahraini cultural and social groups' leaders and members to inquire about which among several possible post-British rule options, inclusive of the possibility of Bahrain rejoining Iran, the respondents most wished to pursue. To the dismay of the Shah and the Iranian government, the Bahrainis whose views had been solicited declared overwhelmingly in favor of obtaining their national sovereignty, political independence, and territorial integrity as an Arab country.

Scarcely had the Shah realized he had no choice but to accept this fait accompli, which in being backed by Great Britain and the United States he knew would likely be irreversible, than the beam of his expansionist-focused searchlight shone elsewhere. The Shah laid claim to three Arab-ruled islands located inside the Gulf only a short distance north of what was even then arguably the world's most strategically vital maritime route: the Hormuz Strait. Two of the islands—the Greater and the Lesser Tunb—were administered by the Emirate of Ra's al-Khaymah. The larger and more inhabited island of Abu Musa was administered by the Emirate of Sharjah. At the time, the two emirates were part of the seven so-called Trucial States that would become the United Arab Emirates.

As mid-point in 1971 came and went and the end date of the British treaties' validity drew nearer, it became increasingly obvious that the Shah was determined not to be thwarted a second time in his bid to expand Iran's territorial reach and control. To that end, he waited for the precise moment when neither the British nor any other power would likely be able or willing to stand in his way.

The Shah's timing was impeccable. On December 1, 1971, the very day before the British treaties expired, he ordered the Iranian navy to seize the three islands. What happened then sowed the seeds of a continuous thorn in GCC–Iranian relations. With the flimsiest of evidence justifying his claim that the islands rightly belonged to Iran, the Shah wrested control of territories whose peoples were almost entirely Arab and over which the two emirates' flags had flown for more than a century. That the Iranian ship that seized one of the islands belonging to Ra's al-Khaymah was wider and longer than the island itself was predictably psychologically damaging to the Arabs.

As such, the act and the way it occurred imparted a lasting negative image of Iran, depicting a non-Arab country mercilessly imposing its will on defenseless Arabs. In retrospect, the heavy-handedness of Tehran's grab of Arab territory was but an omen of what would later be further Iranian adventurist actions against Iraqi and GCC interests.

Subsequent Iranian acts of antagonism against one or more Arab Gulf states' interests would also hardly be cost-free. Indeed, each one served only to vitiate further what little trust and confidence existed among the Arabs on the receiving end. Over the ensuing years, Iran would unilaterally engage in successive measures to increase its military domination of Abu Musa Island. In so doing, it directly violated the memorandum of agreement that an intimidated Ruler of Sharjah felt compelled to enter into in 1971, which specified that responsibility for the island's administration as well as receipt of revenues from its offshore oil production would be divided equally between the signatories.

Iran has consistently rejected the UAE's repeated calls for the dispute to be submitted to the International Court of Justice or international arbitration for settlement. Tehran has stated instead that the matter ought to be dealt with bilaterally between Iran and the UAE. In the fall of 2008, a UAE official, who insisted on nonattribution as he was not authorized to speak on the issue, informed this author that the UAE has interpreted Iran's position as "sending an unmistakable message that we are not important, that it does not need to take us seriously" (Anonymous UAE official 2008).

The example of these three islands is as good as any in illustrating the GCC countries' reservations regarding Iran's intentions at their expense. But the sense of distrust of Iran during the period prior to the GCC's formation was not unlimited, and did not in every instance prove an insurmountable barrier to the two entities agreeing to cooperate with one another in issue-specific matters. Instead, both sides acknowledged it was only prudent to try to find ways of accommodating each other's legitimate interests. As such, in more than one instance a mutually agreeable *modus operandi* was reached that enabled Iran and one or more Gulf Arab countries to cooperate in strategic matters pertaining to the region's stability and security.

Seed five: the Nixon Doctrine's Twin-Pillar Strategy

One such effort to enhance the nature and degree of strategic cooperation between the Gulf's Arab countries and Iran would become a fifth seed in which both Arab trust and mistrust vis-à-vis Iran were established. The effort, known as the Twin-Pillar Strategy (TPS) between Iran and Saudi Arabia, was devised soon after the abrogation of Britain's Gulf treaties.

The catalyst for the TPS was the early 1970s American decision to withdraw from Vietnam. In its wake, Washington sought to lessen the need to mobilize and deploy large numbers of American forces abroad in the then foreseeable future. The result was the Nixon Doctrine or the Guam Doctrine, the latter nomenclature deriving from the American-controlled island of Guam where the president first enunciated the strategy's scope and focus.

The cornerstone of the Nixon Doctrine as it pertained to Arab–Iranian relations in the Gulf was a strategic understanding between the United States and Riyadh, on one hand, and Washington and Tehran, on the other. The goal was to link Iran and Saudi Arabia in special separate bilateral relationships with the United States over and beyond what already existed between them. Only thus, the parties agreed, would they likely be able to enhance the prospects for maintaining national security and regional stability in Arabia and the Gulf.

But no sooner did conceptualization of the Nixon Doctrine become known than it proved problematic. The prospects for its success were limited in part due to its timing. More specifically, the early formulations of the TPS predated the outbreak of the October 1973 Arab–Israeli war and the ensuing Arab oil embargo against the United States, Great Britain, and the Netherlands. Indeed, the oil embargo pointed to the likely constraints on the TPS' efficacy, certainly in matters of mutual trust and suspicion as they pertained to Israel. The limits became apparent when Saudi Arabia and numerous other Arab countries opted to adhere to the embargo but, significantly, Iran did not, choosing instead to materially benefit from the situation at Arab expense, as it had done after the 1967 Arab–Israeli War.

Iran's refusal to participate in the embargo proved costly. It tarnished the country's image among many of its domestic political factions, and it angered Arab nationalists throughout the Gulf region. Furthermore, it sent a red flag to the Palestinians, Syrians, and most other Arabs.

Saudi Arabia and other Arabs found the rationale behind Iran's actions lacking in credibility. In a 2008 conversation with this author, a GCC leader reflected back on Iran's 1973 decision. In describing its effect upon a broad swath of Arab opinion, he said,

> We had seen the Shah do this before. When he did so again in this instance it was clearer than ever before that in matters pertaining to Israel and Palestine regarding issues of elemental justice and human rights, he was not only not with us, he was aligned with Israel, which was then, as now, unjustly occupying our fellow Arabs in Egypt, the Palestinian territories, and Syria.
>
> (Anonymous GCC leader 2008)

Confronted with the domestic and international damage to his image, the Shah moved quickly to try to restore favor with those whom he had offended. To that end, he opened Iran's coffers. For the next several years, he took care to ensure that Iran was one of the most generous providers of financial assistance to Egypt. The aid was rationalized as a means to help compensate Cairo for the economic losses incurred by the war's closure of the Suez Canal.[4]

The consequences of Iran's actions and inactions in response to the October 1973 Arab–Israeli War were therefore mixed. While the Shah's decisions did nothing to inspire confidence among Gulf Arab leaders regarding an issue of fundamental importance to their sense of justice, at the same time Tehran and Riyadh were careful not to challenge the overall efficacy of the Nixon Doctrine. To the contrary, the Cold War premises of the doctrine remained in place. Neither of the countries' leaders nor the leaders in Kuwait and the other soon-to-be-independent Gulf polities were inclined to cast doubt or renege on their underlying agreement to enhance their respective capacities for deterrence and defense.

Seed six: the March 1975 Algiers Accord

Adherence to the Nixon Doctrine was only one example of how the Arab side of the Gulf, notwithstanding its reservations about Iran, was able to forge a degree of policy unity with Iran in which both parties benefited. Another event gave them an additional reason to cooperate. The catalyst was the aftereffect of significantly elevated international oil prices that did not revert to their prewar levels following the end of the oil embargo in March 1974. Indeed, the earlier reluctance of the Arab Gulf states to grant Iran a regionally paramount defense role would rapidly and unexpectedly be eclipsed, albeit temporarily, by a development that neither Gulf Arabs nor Iranians had adequately anticipated.

The development was reflected in mounting Western anger at the continuing high price of oil being charged by Arabs and Iranians. Western leaders and Americans in particular cited the high oil prices as a major reason for a plethora of challenges faced by the world's industrialized economies. With no apparent end to the challenges in sight, a growing number of prominent American strategic and foreign policy analysts began to ponder an option that had previously not been under consideration. They began to weigh the pros and cons of the United States, either alone or in concert with other Western countries, seizing the Gulf's oil fields, if necessary, by force.

The highly charged tensions that accompanied the implications of such publicly voiced threats by American officials were not without effect. In the face of such intimidation, all eight Gulf governments reacted as one. They agreed to set aside their differences so as to meet and discuss how best to confront the challenges before them. Failure to do so, they acknowledged, risked the obvious: the possibility of powerful foreign interests trying to set them against each other in a quest for strategic advantage and economic gain at their expense. Worse, leaders on both sides of the Gulf envisioned that one or more Western Great Powers might have in mind returning to the Gulf with vastly larger, more advanced, and better equipped armed forces than ever before.

The reasons for pan-Gulf paranoia at the time were not imagined. Every Middle Eastern leader was painfully aware of two precedent-setting cases. In each, superior foreign forces inflicted their might on Arabs and Iranians with a view to overthrowing their leaders and undoing their governments' policies. Twenty years earlier, France, Great Britain, and Israel, united in their opposition to Egyptian leader Gamal Abd al-Nasser, hurled their respective armed forces against Egypt with the intention of toppling him and thereby dealing a body blow to the then-champion of the cause of Arab nationalism.

Three years earlier, the United States and Great Britain successfully engineered the overthrow of the democratically elected Iranian government led by Prime Minister Mohammad Mossadegh. The act restored British control over, and introduced a substantial American stake in, Iran's oil industry. With an eye to preventing the United States and its allies from using force in this instance, all eight Gulf countries' leaders agreed to convene in Algiers. They did so with a view to settling the most prominent differences between them, which at the time were those between Iran and Iraq.

The summit concluded with the Algiers Accord. In it, the representatives of Baghdad, Tehran, and all the other Gulf countries declared a set of principles by which they professed they would henceforth be bound. The accord's specific language underscored the signatories' intent "to reach a final and permanent solution of all the problems existing between the two countries [Iran and Iraq] in accordance with the principles of territorial integrity, border inviolability, and noninterference in internal affairs" (Algiers Accord 1975).

Against all expectations to the contrary, the Algiers Accord would last almost four years until broken by Iran in February 1979. Barely a day after Iranian Ayatollah Rouhollah Khomeini returned from exile abroad, Tehran called for the overthrow of the Iraqi government, violating a cardinal principle of the accord. Subsequently, in the 6 March 1991 "Damascus Declaration," the six GCC countries, together with the foreign ministers of Egypt and Syria, recommitted themselves to the principle of noninterference in one another's domestic affairs. The Damascus Declaration as of this writing is, of course, moribund. Even so, the significance of its life after death in terms of its direct bearing on GCC relations with Iran is this: the GCC countries have held fast to their insistence that adherence to this principle is the *sine qua non* of their relations with each other and with non-GCC members within the Gulf, namely Iran and Iraq.[5]

Yet as impressive as the extended adherence to the Algiers Accord by its signatories came to be, it only postponed a further manifestation of suspicion and distrust between the Gulf region's Arabs and Iranians. In this light, the accord merely temporarily brushed aside the signatories' differences. The most important of these differences was over the presummit Western and Iranian debate over why or why not the Gulf Arab countries should cede to Iran the premier position of military prominence and geopolitical advantage in pan-Gulf matters.

Confronted with this situation, Washington officialdom was faced with a quandary. With its preferred candidate to play the role of paramount regional power rejected by all seven of the Gulf's Arab countries, it had little choice but to explore other possibilities. To its good fortune, Saudi Arabia seized the opportunity to play an enhanced role in the strategic formulation and execution of the Gulf's defense policies. Doing so, its analysts reasoned, helped to further regional security and stability while allowing the Kingdom to pursue its own interests and foreign policy objectives.

Riyadh's inclination to take on this role followed year-long strategic surveys of the country's defense needs. The surveys were conducted in association with Great Britain, the United States, and other countries following the October 1973 Arab–Israeli War. The thrust of the strategic assessors' conclusions was that, within the time span of the next twenty years, the places from which Saudi Arabia would most likely be vulnerable to threat or attack would be Iraq and/or Yemen, but not Iran. This was not surprising. At the time, Iraq was perceived to be the greater and more likely threat in light of its larger and more modernized armed forces.[6] Accordingly, the strategic need for Riyadh to have good relations with Tehran as a potential check against possible Iraqi adventurism was logical and compelling.

Seed seven: the Muscat conference of 1976

Even so, Tehran's value as a strategic counterweight to Baghdad was limited. By itself, it was insufficient to override Saudi Arabia and the other Arab countries' unease with Iran's non-Arab identity, coupled with the implications of its multi-faceted relationship with Israel. In an effort to find a way to bridge the doubts and suspicions of Iran's international intentions, Oman's Sultan Qaboos bin Said invited representatives of all eight Gulf governments to convene in Muscat to explore such possibilities in the fall of 1976.

Despite the lofty ambitions and possibilities implicit in the strategic challenges that drew them together, the participants in the Muscat meeting were unable to agree on an acceptable set of policies. Neither were they able to concur on an institutional means by which they might systematically coordinate efforts to maintain and strengthen what they acknowledged was in their collective interest: namely, the region's defense. According to accounts shared with this writer by attendees of the Conference, Iran's and Iraq's representatives did everything they could to dominate the proceedings in ways that the other attendees found intimidating and threatening.

The reported behavior of Iran and Iraq's representatives reflected not only their respective agendas to expand their influence in matters pertaining to Gulf affairs in general. It also revealed their separate ambitions to reconfigure the region's balance of power to their benefit with little, if any, regard for the interests of the six monarchial regimes lining the shores of eastern Arabia. In the heated give-and-take between the representatives of these two erstwhile neighbors *cum* competitors, who within only a few years would become enemies, the other six countries' representatives were in effect consigned to the role of onlookers, largely unable to get a word in edgewise.

According to the Conference attendees, the Iranian and Iraqi participants were particularly disdainful of the strategic orientation of the six Arab monarchies' defense policies. In particular, they viewed the insistence of these countries' leaders on maintaining close military ties with their Great Power allies as outdated, unnecessary, and unbecoming of sovereign and independent nations. The experience of witnessing such displays of Iranian and Iraqi hubris, stridency, condescension, and disrespect toward the six east Arabian countries' strategic situations and preferences was far-reaching in its effect. Like nothing else, it gave important impetus to what in five years would be the formation of the Gulf Cooperation Council by the Gulf's six dynasties and the accompanying decision not to invite Iran or Iraq to become members.

Seed eight: the Iranian Revolution and the Iran–Iraq War

Whereas the islands issue, the Nixon Doctrine's TPS, the Algiers Accord, and the Muscat Conference all predate the ouster of the Shah, there have been many more Iran–GCC disputes and disagreements since the Pahlavi Dynasty was overthrown. Of these, the most far-reaching in its impact was the record of Iranian violations of the Algiers Accord in interfering in the domestic affairs of Iraq following the return of Iranian Ayatollah Rouhollah Khomeini from exile in February 1979. Senior Iraqi and American officials with whom this writer spoke in the course of escorting several American Congressional staff delegations to Iraq in the mid-to-late 1980s alluded to 111 additional violations of the Accord by Iran in comparison to none by Iraq.

Cumulatively, these provocations were followed by the inevitable onset of the Iran–Iraq War that would last from September 1980 to August 1988; the documentation of Iranian efforts to sow subversion in practically every GCC country; Tehran's continued refusal to submit the three islands' dispute with the UAE to peaceful international settlement; the Islamic Republic's pursuit of uranium enrichment processes that, unchecked, could eventually give it the capacity to produce nuclear weapons; Iranian government leaders' continuing call for the withdrawal of all Western defense forces from the Gulf; and Iran's insistence on being a player in inter-Arab affairs as evidenced by its support for domestic political factions in Iraq, Lebanon, Palestine, and elsewhere in the Arab world. The overall impact of this evidentiary record has sown an unbroken row of seeds for further pan-GCC distrust of Iran that exists to this day.

It should be clear that GCC country leaders insist that the reasons for their limited trust and confidence in Iranian motives and agendas regarding Gulf defense and security are grounded in fact, not myth. Pressed for proof, they cite not only the record chronicled herein but also numerous specific occasions when Iran has threatened virtually every GCC country. In contrast, they contend, Iran cannot point to more than two instances when an action by a GCC country could possibly be interpreted as having threatened Iran. One arguable exception is Saudi Arabia's ongoing strategic actions designed to ensure that international oil prices remain lower than what Iran would prefer, with Iran pointing out with arithmetical accuracy that it has three times the population of all six GCC countries combined and thus has far more people with legitimate material, defense, and development requirements that, on moral and humanitarian grounds, it is obliged to try to meet and serve.[7]

Another possible exception could be differing GCC and Iranian perceptions regarding an issue involving Doha and Tehran. In the eyes of some Iranian nationalists, Qatar has been benefiting unjustly from revenues derived from its exploitation of the offshore North Dome Field, known in Iran as the South Pars Field, which straddles the median line delineating the two countries' international maritime boundary. Qatar's position, however, is similar to Kuwait's regarding the Rumeila oil field that overlaps the border between Kuwait and Iraq. It is also similar to that of Riyadh in a situation pertaining to an oil field that straddles the border between Saudi Arabia and the UAE's Emirate of Abu Dhabi.

Qatar, Kuwait, and Saudi Arabia have been proceeding in accordance with the school of thought that whichever country develops and produces oil for export or domestic use from its side of an acknowledged international boundary—as the boundary between Iran and Qatar, Kuwait and Iraq, and Saudi Arabia and the UAE are acknowledged to be—is entitled to receive the economic proceeds of that production. Iran's complaint is therefore understandable that this approach works to its disadvantage. An unstated reason is that because Iran has been under American-led economic sanctions for more than a quarter of a century, international oil companies have refrained from assisting Iran in its goal of producing from its side of the field in question. Even so, that the GCC countries have adhered to their obviously advantageous and legally defensible position with respect to the development of the region's energy resources has hardly endeared them to Iran.

Iranian counterpoints

From the foregoing, it should not be surprising that Iran has repeatedly expressed its displeasure at the elusiveness of its quest to be the Gulf's paramount power. In turn, Tehran's displeasure has given the GCC countries' leaders reason to believe that the Islamic Republic may at some point resort to means other than peaceful political persuasion to produce outcomes more to its liking. A particular GCC concern in this regard remains Iran's continued refusal to acquiesce to the GCC's criteria for admission. The implication of the refusal is that Iran may remain intent on doing whatever it deems necessary to gain entry into the GCC, which would be a disaster in GCC eyes.[8] Indeed, Iran appears to reject outright the idea that it should take the GCC's "no" for an answer. Instead, it has continuously argued from an entirely different perspective—one that from the beginning until the present the GCC countries have found objectionable—as to why it should be included.

Most Iranian critics couch their arguments for GCC membership in the following manner. First, Iranians are undeniably heirs of one of the world's more renowned anvils of antiquity, including the classical era when ancient Persia was universally acknowledged as one of the most culturally advanced civilizations in the Middle East. Many Iranians contend further that much of their country's rich history is older and more variegated than that of the GCC. Second, Iranians posit that the deep-rooted family ties between millions of Arabs and Iranians on both sides of the Gulf are centuries-old and counting. Third, Iranian nationalists point out that Iran has been present at the creation of more international organizations than any GCC country except Saudi Arabia. For example, Iran is, among other things, a founding member of the United Nations; the United Nations

Economic, Social, and Cultural Organization; the International Court of Justice; the Organization of the Islamic Conference; the Organization of Petroleum Exporting Countries; and the earlier but subsequently disbanded Baghdad Pact, the Central Treaty Organization, and the Organization for Regional Cooperation and Development. Fourth, since the onset of the Iranian Revolution in 1979, unlike Iraq and Kuwait, and, further afield, Lebanon, Palestine, and Syria, Iran has been able to maintain without interruption its national sovereignty, political independence, and territory free of foreign intervention and control.

Tehran's leaders further contend that the GCC has consistently failed to come to a geo-strategic political and military accommodation with the reality of Iran's far more extensive Gulf coast. That alone, many in Tehran argue, ought to merit, if not Iran's membership in the GCC, then Iran's participation in any and all deliberations bearing on the defense of the Gulf as a whole. To wit: Iran's southern shoreline, which spans almost the entire length of the Gulf along its western side, is more than twice as long as the shores of any two other Gulf countries combined.

Yet another Iranian attribute that has no equivalent among any of the GCC nations is the country's demographic weight. As mentioned above, Iran's nearly 80 million citizens outnumber the six GCC member-states' citizens combined by a ratio of more than three to one. A related consideration has to do with Iran's human resources in comparison to those in the GCC. With the exception of Saudi Arabia, Iran has a comparatively larger number of citizens with advanced doctoral degrees, applied technical expertize, and professional experience— skilled labor assets in demand throughout the Gulf. Further, these numbers are over and beyond the more than one million largely middle and upper professional classes of Iranians living and working in Europe and North America, with estimates of as high as a million Iranians living in United States alone.

Yet except for the UAE Emirate of Dubai, which hosts estimates varying from 250,000 to 440,000 to 500,000 Iranian workers and business representatives,[9] the GCC countries have done little to capitalize on a ready source of fellow Gulf-skilled labor in the service of the two people's shared commercial interests. In the face of these realities, Iranians have largely concluded that GCC employers and would-be joint venture business partners are prejudiced against hiring Iranians. They believe that, despite being immediately adjacent to the GCC countries, being fellow Muslims, and in many instances being able to communicate in Arabic, GCC employers across the board have preferred to hire Western expatriates as well as South Asian and Southeast Asian laborers instead.

Further, Iran's leaders call attention to the fact that it has on several occasions provided important strategic and tactical assistance to the GCC countries' most important protector, the United States, only to receive little or nothing in return. Examples include when: 1) Iran accepted from but refused to return to Iraq the armed forces and civilian aircraft that Saddam Hussein sent to Iran in the fall of 1990 for what he hoped would be safekeeping; 2) Iran tacitly supported the United States and numerous other countries mobilizing and deploying hundreds of thousands of their armed forces personnel to Arabia with the goal of reversing Iraq's aggression against Kuwait in 1990–1991; 3) Iran offered the American oil company Conoco a $2.3 billion concession to develop the country's offshore gas reserves in the South Pars Field in 1995, only to have the Clinton administration, which was pressured by the principal American lobby for Israel, the American Israeli Public Affairs Committee (AIPAC), to veto the concession and subsequently declare that it would revisit America's relations with any country that invested more than $20 million in Iran's energy industry; and 4) Iran tacitly supported by not opposing America's attacks against al-Qaeda bases and violent extremist operatives in Afghanistan in the fall of 2001.

Even so, that Tehran has persisted in its pursuit of a nuclear development program that could enable it to eventually produce one or more nuclear weapons and the means to project them abroad has overridden these positive examples of Iranian international behavior. It has also deepened the GCC's fears regarding the Gulf's intra-regional balance of power, and has caused representatives of every GCC country to comment to this writer their dismay at the seeming irony embedded in the observation that in 2003, America attacked Iraq, and Iran won—without firing a single bullet or shedding a drop of blood—just as it also won when the United States earlier eliminated the threat that Taliban-ruled Afghanistan had posed to Iran. Instead of the GCC countries significantly loosening or otherwise diminishing related ties to their non-Gulf Great Power protectors as a result, the opposite has occurred.

As a result of this strengthening of Iran, GCC–U.S. defense ties have been consistently expanded. Further, not least among potentially ominous developments related to Iran has been the degree to which a growing number of GCC countries have moved to explore the possibilities of pursuing their own nuclear development programs. In every instance thus far, they have done so in close association with the United States, France, Great Britain, South Korea, and other powers, thereby deepening their already extensive reliance upon and defense cooperation with non-Gulf countries.

The above has documented reasons as to why in large measure the GCC's founders opted not to invite either Iraq or, more importantly, Iran to join the GCC, as well as why they remain opposed to the idea of either country joining it. An additional reason for the exclusion of Iran and Iraq was that a war was being waged between the two countries at the time. On that ground alone, admitting either country, let alone both, would have inevitably and unavoidably drawn the GCC countries into the conflict against their wishes.

GCC–Iran shared interests and concerns

In enumerating the reasons why the GCC countries have refused to extend an invitation to either Iran or Iraq to become a member, it is important to emphasize that the strategic dynamics of GCC–Iranian relations are far from being a distinguishable whole. Depending on the issue, the specific nature and extent of relations with Iran differs from one country to the next. And though the mistrust on the side of the GCC is strong, the countries have historically shared a number of commitments with Iran that may bode well for future relations.

Wars

Iran and the GCC countries share a common goal of avoiding an invasion and occupation by foreign powers. The sinews of this interest and concern are wrapped around a joint GCC–Iranian belief that such an intervention would threaten their security and stability. This concern is also anchored in another belief, namely that given what the Gulf has, what it does, where it is, and the importance of all three attributes to humankind as a whole, such a conflict and its repercussions could quickly become global in scope. In this regard, it is Iran and the GCC countries' mutual conviction that the four wars that have occurred in or near the region dating from eight months before the GCC was established have been four too many.

Clash of Civilizations

Another GCC–Iranian goal has been to counter the so-called "Clash of Civilizations" (CC) thesis propagated by writers such as Bernard Lewis and the late Samuel Huntington. The thesis of these two authors *cum* polemicists posits that the world's future wars are as likely to be caused by stark differences between and among people's cultures as by anything else. Analysts the world over have taken this to imply, among other things, an inevitable conflict between Western and Muslim countries.

The formulation, dissemination, and widespread acceptance of this thesis have been and remain troubling for Arabs and Iranians alike. The results have intro-duced a significantly greater degree of tension and mutual animosity, suspicion, and distrust not only between them, but also in Western–Muslim relations, than previously existed. Many analysts contend that this is not an accident, that it was what Lewis, if not also Huntington and the neo-conservatives appointed to key American strategic, defense, and foreign policy posts within the administration of President George W. Bush, had in mind.

Iranians, GCC citizens, and other Arabs have been in broad agreement in their response. They have contested and continuously sought to repudiate the CC postulate's implicitly negative depiction of an irreconcilable divide between Arabs, Iranians, and other Muslims, on one hand, and the Western world, on the other. Separately and at times in concert within international organizations of which they are members, the GCC countries and Iran have repeatedly rebutted the CC's prediction of a marked increase in culture-driven interstate conflicts as illustrative of future trends and indications in world affairs. They are jointly determined to do whatever is necessary to defend their cultures and diminish Western and American tendencies to demonize Middle Easterners and Muslims in general.

On this particular issue, GCC and Iranian government leaders agree that, left unchecked, such antagonistic and provocative Western sentiments could spread. They believe the impact could be devastating should this occur. Among poten-tially damaging results would be the threat of their quests to retain—or in the case of the Palestinians and Syrians obtain—their respective national sovereignties, political independence, and territorial integrity.

Energy

A third GCC–Iranian common strategic interest revolves around energy issues. In particular, it relates to the production and pricing of the region's oil and gas resources. A recent variant of this shared interest has been their concern about a growing sentiment and an emerging shift in the focus of American energy policies.

Neither Arabs nor Iranians deny that altered American attitudes about energy issues were evident throughout the 21-month 2008 U.S. electoral campaign. GCC and Iranian analysts alike charge that not only the then-incumbent Bush administration, but virtually all of the Democratic and Republican Party candidates for election, failed to acknowledge that speaking of a reliance on "foreign oil" is code for Arab and Iranian oil. In choosing not to be clear, specific, or educative, the candidates not only pandered to xenophobia and isolationism, but also catered to the baser and more crudely perceived exigencies of American domestic political electioneering.

If few others sensed what this element of American politics signaled for future United States relations with the GCC countries and Iran, none in Tehran and the GCC capitals were in doubt. The message received was one of irresponsible and potentially dire consequences, that is, divorce proceedings between the United States and the existing reciprocally rewarding relationship of interdependence between the United States and most of the countries, including those in the Arab and Islamic world in particular, that produce for export hydrocarbon fuels, the source of 80 percent of America's transportation needs. Propelling such electoral concerns to the forefront, on one hand, were pervasive worries about climate change and the environment. On the other was a combination of widespread American ignorance and prejudice against Arab, Iranian, and other Muslim oil-exporting countries.

If successfully implemented, the commitment would sever the energy-specific ties between the United States as the world's premier oil importer and the Gulf countries as the world's premier oil exporters. Left unstated but clear to many analysts was the following: in the short-term, the effort to implement such a policy would likely prove harmful to both sides.

But for those who have long been jealous of the Arab–U.S. energy relationship, the prospects for American and other Great Power policies at some point tilting away from the Arab energy exporters and closer toward Israel would be welcomed. In their view, the rupture between Washington and the capitals of the Arab oil exporters would potentially drive an enormous and much desired wedge in the overall Arab–U.S. strategic relationship. It would also help preclude the emergence of a future renewed American–Iranian strategic relationship—unless American, Israeli, and other neo-conservative strategists were to have their way in changing the regime in Tehran and replacing it with one more responsive and favorable to American, Israeli, and other Western countries' interests. Stated differently, the goal would be for regime change to lead to a new situation in which the successor government in Iran would be more amenable to the United States as well as to Israel, moderate in its approach to the Arab–Israeli conflict, less supportive of Hezbollah in Lebanon and the Assad government in Syria, and unlikely to continue supporting Hamas and Islamic Jihad in Palestine.

Maritime security

A fourth GCC–Iranian shared concern has to do with seaborne security issues, namely the prevention of disruptions to their respective ports' exports and foreign-sourced goods upon which citizens of the GCC and Iran are vitally reliant. In this regard, only Iran has threatened, albeit only rhetorically thus far, the Gulf's maritime commerce.

Whenever Iran has implied such threats, the impact has been damaging, not only to the economies of all eight Gulf countries, but to much of the world. An example is the numerous occasions when Iran attacked foreign vessels engaged in the region's seaborne trade during the second half of the 1980–88 Iran–Iraq War. In so doing, Tehran threatened the maritime safe passage of a quarter of the world's international energy exports that originate daily inside the Gulf.

The harm that Iranian forces inflicted upon foreign shipping during that period was indiscriminate and extensive. In attacking the ships of a dozen countries, including four ships carrying Iranian oil, the Islamic Republic not only heightened international anxieties regarding regional security and stability and thereby depressed the level of inward flows of foreign investment into the Gulf, but also heightened maritime insurance rates that, in turn, negatively affected the economies of every country in the Gulf.

Fast forward: the contemporary period

A sanctioned Iran

For most of the intervening years since the GCC's establishment until the present, the relationships between the GCC countries and Iran have been unsteady. The ties have been laced with the same kinds of tensions noted earlier, including Iran's robust nuclear development program, which served as a catalyst for the imposition of sanctions by the United States and then by the United Nations Security Council.

The UN Security Council justified the heightened levels of international sanctions against Iran with its charge that Tehran has failed to cooperate fully with the investigations of the International Atomic Energy Agency (IAEA) into Iran's nuclear development program. Declaring they were not persuaded that Iran had earlier been completely truthful in its declarations to the IAEA, three of the Security Council's five permanent members—the United States, France, and Great Britain—have continued their support for sanctions and other efforts to isolate the Islamic Republic in an effort to halt the enrichment of the uranium components of its nuclear program.

As China and Russia, in contrast, have emphasized the need for conciliatory measures, the UN sanctions have been narrower in scope than Washington, Paris, and London would have preferred. Without question, the GCC countries have favored using whatever means necessary to avoid the outbreak of yet another war in the region. Even so, while the GCC countries have not called for the cessation of sanctions, they have indicated their preference for the United States and the European Union to engage Iran peacefully and productively.

Threats to attack Iran

Persistent rumors that fueled GCC apprehensions about Iran provided a subtext to the international discussion of the nuclear issue prior to the election of U.S. President Barack Obama. Of particular concern was how continued American and other foreign opposition to Iran might play out in terms of Gulf security and stability. Despite continued refutation from United States and Israeli administration officials, the rumors held that the United States and/or Israel might attack Iran militarily.

Certainly throughout the second half of the Bush administration, both sides engaged in saber-rattling, with U.S. officials pointedly refusing to rule out military options, while sending two carrier battle group ships to the Gulf and staging simulated war games near Iran's territorial waters. Iranian officials did not ignore these actions. Citing what they referred to as provocative American actions designed to bring about armed conflict, they periodically issued pronouncements threatening to respond with all means available. Among the suggestions were that Iranian forces could wreak havoc on United States interests in the GCC region and beyond, with instruments ranging from support for armed groups fighting American and U.S.-trained forces in Iraq and Afghanistan to the sabotage of UAE or other GCC coastal desalination and power-generating installations.

Choosing not to limit its responses to rhetoric alone, Tehran has staged its own annual offshore war games in and around the Hormuz Strait most years since the early 1990s. These games have included: 1) demonstrations of its navy's capacity to remain for longer and longer periods at sea without the need for replenishment of supplies; 2) practicing armed forces special operations activities associated with enhancing its undersea abilities to attack or otherwise neutralize adversaries' ships, pipelines, and water intake for coastal electrical power generating and desalination plants; and 3) simulating amphibious landings, which GCC analysts conclude could only be directed toward one or more of the GCC countries. Viewed in their entirety, such actions have persuaded GCC strategic analysts and defense leaders to be on their guard less against Iranian intentions, which as with any country are oftentimes hard to fathom with clarity, and more against Iranian capabilities to inflict harm upon one or more GCC countries and/or their allies.

As the international standoff with Iran continued in the aftermath of the transition from the American presidential administration of George W. Bush to that of Barack Obama in early 2009, some analysts implied that the most propitious moment for the United States and/or Israel to attack Iran would turn on the status

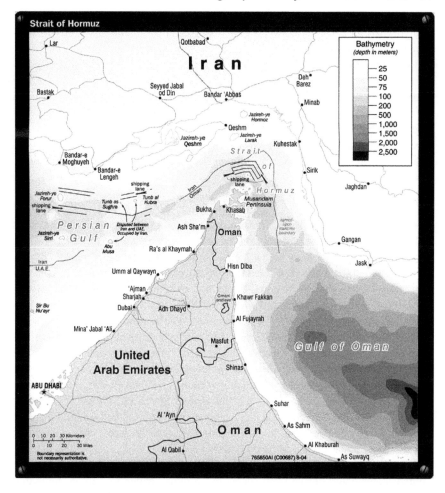

Figure 5.1   Strait of Hormuz map.

Source: Courtesy of the University of Texas Libraries, The University of Texas at Austin.

of the Iranian nuclear reactor at Bushire, situated in the southwestern part of the country in an area adjacent to the Gulf coast, with regard to its receipt or utilization of uranium fuel enrichment rods from which it could eventually produce a nuclear weapon.

Analysts in and beyond the Gulf argue that the consequences of either an armed attack on or accident or explosion at the Bushire reactor could pose a Chernobyl-like threat.[10] Such an eventuality, a prominent Kuwaiti strategic analyst indicated to this writer, would have the potential for a disaster of epochal proportions. An explosion at Bushire would immediately threaten to contaminate most of the northern Gulf's vital water supplies, to say nothing of the danger any radiation released as a result of such a catastrophe could have on shipping into and out of the Gulf of vital food supplies, medicines, and, most importantly, its hydrocarbon fuels upon which global economic wellbeing are and will long remain vitally dependent.[11]

Yet the optimum timing of that scenario disappeared as press releases issued by the Islamic Republic News Agency and official Russian statements on 30 January 2008, reported that Russia's final shipment of the remaining nuclear fuel destined for the Bushire reactor had been delivered earlier in the month. This led analysts to doubt whether either the United States or Israel would attack that particular reactor, but it did not rule out the possibility of strikes on other reactors and related facilities located in Iran at inland sites somewhat distant from the Gulf.[12]

Fear run amok

These recent events played out amidst broad fears of a resurgent Iran. The question of how to deal with Iran, not only on the nuclear issue, but in a broader strategic perspective, loomed large for the GCC, the United States, and many other countries. Opinions remained divided on the relative merits of continued international isolation of Iran versus engagement and the pursuit of conciliation and compromise.[13]

Material matters compounded the difficulties that the United States and its allies, on one hand, and the GCC members, on the other, faced in forging a unified position among so many countries. Massive and pervasive international interests remained eager to increase the level of foreign investments, trade, and the establishment of joint commercial ventures with Iran. Indeed, economic and commercial rewards were the undeniable, if unacknowledged, objectives of many foreign governments and businesses, the United States and the GCC countries included, in what all agreed could be incalculable strategic advantages and material benefits for any country able to gain significant access to Iran's massive oil and gas resources and its large consumer market.

Some analysts continued to believe that the kinds of potential benefits the United States could derive from successful regime change in Tehran, including privatizing the country's energy sector and opening it and other sectors of the economy to GCC-based American and other foreign contracts and operations, outweighed any benefits of the "spoils of war" cited by those who had earlier advocated attacking Iraq and which, in the invasion's aftermath, critics' accounts to the contrary have increasingly been obtained.[14]

If only in terms of the 2008 presidential campaign rhetoric, the change in American presidents from Bush to Obama seemed to offer relatively positive prospects for opening a new chapter in American–Iranian, as well as GCC–Iranian, relations. Certainly a less hostile and antagonistic tone to whatever dialogue might ensue between Tehran and Washington appeared likely at the onset of the Obama administration. Not to put too fine a gloss on the euphoria that accompanied the new president's election victory and his inauguration, few denied that the possibilities for civil dialogue were greater than at any point not only in the previous eight years, but dating back to 1979 when the Iranian Revolution began.

If nothing else, the new American president's promise to explore the prospect for meaningful dialogue with Iran was immediately well received throughout the GCC region. Many welcomed the diminished prospect that Washington would continue the previous administration's allusions to forcible regime change in Tehran. Those skeptical of a change in the nature of U.S.–Iranian and GCC–Iranian relations, however, took care to remind analysts that the idea of toppling the government in Tehran began not with the administration of President George W. Bush, but with the Clinton White House.

Another uncertain prospect under examination as control of the White House changed hands was whether Iran would hold fast to its long insistence that the Gulf be freed of Western or any other non-Gulf militaries. Were it to do so, it would be difficult to envision a significant thawing of either the U.S.–Iranian relationship or the GCC–Iranian relationship. Were it not to do so, few things would be more welcomed in Washington and the capitals of the GCC countries.

Further, in the absence of a major political rapprochement between Washington and Tehran, it remained to be seen to what extent, if at all, Iran could expect to consolidate its geopolitical gains in Iraq. Not the least of the GCC countries' apprehensions regarding these unknowns was how Iran and Iraq might possibly form an informal bilateral power bloc that could potentially pose threats to the governmental status quo in the GCC region.

Certainly, the GCC leaders reckoned that Baghdad and Tehran at peace and in a mutually beneficial relationship with each other might explore the possibilities of what they could achieve in tandem vis-à-vis one or more GCC countries or the GCC as a whole that neither could accomplish alone. If so, who could say they would not be hard-pressed to resist rekindling the sense of strategic oneness they achieved and maintained for almost four years following their entering into the Algiers Accord three and a half decades earlier?

The roots of such pan-GCC fears are anchored in an awareness of the Islamic Republic's intimate association with the post-Saddam Hussein government led by Iraqi Shi`as, many of whom Tehran supported during their long exile in Iran. Whether such a scenario could prove credible is questionable. Analyst Ali Ansari has written about "the overthrow of Saddam [Hussein] – through democratic elections – by a regime comprised largely of individuals who had lived in or were sympathetic to Iran." He added that "one of the major arguments working against the notion that Iran wants to destabilize a post-invasion Iraq is the fact that there has never been a more pro-Iranian government in Baghdad." This, according to Ansari, constitutes a monumentally profound reordering of Gulf strategic realities directly resulting from the U.S.-led invasion and occupation of Iraq that commenced in March 2003, has continued until the present, and shows every sign of continuing far into the future (Ansari 2006). Destabilizing Iraq would also constitute an ongoing affront to the Islamic Republic leaders' religious sensitivities, given that the location of many shrines deemed holy not only by Iran's Shi`i Muslims but by Shi`i Muslims everywhere are in Iraq, not Iran.

At the same time, since the Obama administration entered office, no Iranian leader of stature has up to the time of this writing publicly attacked a growing international consensus as to what an American withdrawal from Iraq might entail. Some feared that the decision might lead to massive instability and insecurity along much of Iran's long border with Iraq, in which case the result could produce a chaotic situation far more ruinous for the GCC region's strategic interests than the previous one. If such a situation were to occur, it would call into question how, if at all, withdrawal would further the Islamic Republic's, let alone Iraq's or the GCC's, interests.

If it remained unclear as to what further actions the GCC countries and their allies might take to forge a mutually beneficial strategic relationship with Iran, or at least what they might do to avoid a serious deterioration in the relationships between the two sides of the Gulf as they exist, it was not for lack of the GCC's eagerness, or for that matter a comparable eagerness on the part of Iran, to put such uncertainties to rest.

Notes

1 On August 25, 2009, in remarks on the record to a group at the Middle East Institute in Washington, D.C. at which this writer was present, American Ambassador to Kuwait Deborah Jones explained Kuwait's decision long ago to align itself with the United States and other Great Powers for its national defense and related interests. In so doing, she used an analogy that applies to most of the other GCC countries. "If you are smaller in size and not as powerful as someone else on the playground, you naturally tend to go out of the way not to antagonize or provoke the stronger person," she said. "In addition, as an insurance policy, you tend to associate yourself closely with whoever could protect or defend you in the event that the mightier person were to think they could threaten or harm you in some way and get away with it."

2 An account of the actions and reactions occurring during this period between the British and the people that would eventually form the GCC can be found in Anthony 2003 and Anthony 1975. This writer was the only American allowed by then British Political Agent Julian Walker to be present as an observer at the final meeting in Jumeirah, Dubai, in July 1971, when the rulers of six emirates (all but Ra's al-Khaymah) opted to form the United Arab Emirates.

3 Two examples are illustrative. One is how the perpetuation of such arrangements helped reinforce adherence to the norms of international law and interstate behavior by foreign and domestic actors alike. Another is how such certainties have tended to strengthen the defense agreements and understandings by which most of the Gulf's eight countries conduct their relations with one another.

4 It is unknown to me whether the decision of the government of Egypt to allow the Shah to be buried in Egypt was in part a gesture influenced by the Iranian monarch's having assisted Egypt financially in the 1970s. Nor am I aware of what part, if any, Egypt's decision was a way of paying homage to the fact that the Shah's first wife, Fawzia, was a daughter of Egypt's King Fouad and a sister of his son and Egypt's last monarch, King Farouk.

5 An exception when some GCC members did not adhere to this principle involved Qatar. In the aftermath of Qatari Ruler Shaykh Hamad bin Khalifa Al-Thani being overthrown in July 1995 by his son, Shaykh Hamad, Bahrain, Saudi Arabia, and the UAE all supported the short-lived efforts of the former ruler to regain his position. Qatar's new government did not take these actions lightly. One way in which it was perceived by many to have expressed its displeasure was that *Al Jazeera*, the popular Qatari satellite television news station, subsequently hosted and aired the remarks of guest speakers who criticized one or more aspects of these countries' policies.

6 Further influencing this option was that Iraq had signed a Treaty of Friendship with the Soviet Union in 1971, the very year that Great Britain had declared it would abrogate its defense and foreign relations obligations to nine east Arabian principalities. The signing of the treaty heightened Iranian, Saudi Arabian, and the Gulf Shaykhdoms' concern that Moscow and Baghdad might henceforth collaborate to advance their respective national interests in the Gulf at the expense of the Arabian Peninsula's dynastic regimes.

7 Of interest is that the counterargument would not necessarily be more logical or, for that matter, illogical. That is, countries with differently calculated strategic analyses and preferences cannot *ipso facto* be regarded in and of themselves as *prima facie* seeking to threaten another country any more than one could credibly argue the reverse.

8 This writer has attended numerous meetings in which so-called specialists of a neo-conservative bent of mind have argued from an entirely different perspective. They have advocated strongly that the GCC should allow Iran to join its ranks. The rationale advanced in support of such a recommendation has been that no regional organization can hope to be successful if it does not include all the member countries within the region where it is situated. The seductive cadence and at first glance seemingly persuasive reasoning in this instance is fallacious. It fails to recognize that a cardinal reason why the North Atlantic Treaty Organization succeeded for the better part of half a century in keeping the peace between its Western European and North American members vis-à-vis the Central and Eastern European members of the Soviet Bloc during the Cold War was the exact opposite—it was because the latter two clusters of Soviet-occupied and oriented countries in the European region were *excluded*, not included. Similarly, during most of the same span of time, regional peace in East Asia after the Korean War was maintained because such countries as China, North Korea, and Mongolia were *not* members of the region's Western-anchored de facto defense arrangement. In the eyes of GCC country representatives with whom this writer has discussed the issue, an unstated strategic objective behind the neo-conservative arguments in this regard is transparent. It is to do whatever is necessary to divert GCC and American attention away from the Arab–Israeli conflict by shifting it to the Gulf region. Were Iran ever to gain entry to the GCC, this reasoning contends, the Gulf would likely become far more laced with tension than otherwise. More specifically, the GCC's as well as America's agendas would likely be altered in such a way as to have Gulf realities replace or surmount international concerns in brokering an Arab–Israeli peace agreement that would entail Israel agreeing to permanently define its borders, end its colonization of Jerusalem and the rest of the West Bank, terminate its exploitation of Palestinian water and other natural resources, evacuate its settlements in Syria's rich Golan province, address the Palestinian and Syrian refugee problem, and unequivocally accept and help to establish a fully sovereign, independent, and territorially intact State of Palestine.

9 The two higher estimates were provided the author in separate meetings in Abu Dhabi with a senior staff member of the Abu Dhabi-based Arab Monetary Fund in early November 2008 and an editor of an Abu Dhabi-based national newspaper in April 2010. The lower number was the estimate of a senior diplomat at a foreign embassy in the UAE capital. This individual cautioned that the full-time resident Iranians in Dubai should be considered separately from the indeterminate and more fluctuating number of Iranians who travel back and forth to the emirate on short-term business visits. None of the three individuals who shared their views on this matter were allowed to speak for the record.

10 At a meeting in Kuwait on 14 December 2009 with officials of the Kuwait Fund for Economic and Social Development, this writer was provided a handout containing information about Kuwait's involvement in the aftermath of the 1986 Chernobyl nuclear reactor disaster. Beyond documenting Kuwait's 23-year concern with the implications of potential fallout stemming from accidents at nuclear power plants, the handout noted that Kuwait was the chief administrator of a special fund established within the United Nations that was tasked with helping to relocate the 200,000 people displaced by the Chernobyl accident.

11 The Kuwaiti strategist made this point at an international conference in the GCC region in 2007 in which this writer participated. Although he cannot be named, as he was not authorized to speak for the record, he emphasized that all the Gulf countries are to varying degrees vitally dependent on the intake of Gulf waters to power their electricity generating and desalination plants to meet their basic human health and economic development needs. In addition, Najmedin Meshkati, a former Iranian nuclear specialist, has called attention to a quite different reason for concern. He contends that, because of the international sanctions, "Iran has not been able to hire qualified Western contractors to conduct safety analyses and quality control inspections" at its nuclear power plants. Instead, the reactor builders, on one hand, and those tasked with ensuring that all appropriate safety measures have been and are being met at this particular nuclear installation and its facilities, on the other, are one and the same: Russians. Having the Russians supervise themselves, in Meshkati's view, is analogous to "the fox is in charge of the hen house." The implication would seem to be that, because the Russians "are supervising themselves," the inherent danger stemming from Iran's inability to access the safest possible nuclear technology available is self-evident. See Meshkati 2007.

12 Neither did it preclude a scenario where a future earthquake in Iran, of which there have been many throughout the country's history, could result in a disaster affecting the reactor at Bushire or other reactors elsewhere that could be equally devastating.

13 For an analysis of the range of arguably probable as well as uncertain regional and global consequences of an American, Israeli, or American–Israeli attack on Iran, see Anthony 2008a. See also Anthony 2008b.

14 For an account of how, contrary to popular perceptions, the neo-conservatives' and other groups' goals for changing the regime in Iraq and occupying the country have succeeded in more cases than many imagine, see Anthony 2005.

Bibliography

Algiers Accord (1975) Online HTTP: www.midseastweb.org/algiersaccord.htm (accessed May 21, 2010).

Anonymous GCC leader (2008) Personal interview, Doha, Qatar, December.

Anonymous UAE official (2008) Personal interview, Abu Dhabi, November.

Ansari, M.A. (2006) *Confronting Iran: The Failure of American Foreign Policy and the Next Great Crisis in the Middle East*, New York: Perseus Books.

Anthony, J.D. (1975) *Arab States of the Lower Gulf: People, Politics, Petroleum*, Washington, D.C.: Middle East Institute, 1–29.

Anthony, J.D. (2003) *Dynamics of State Formation: The United Arab Emirates, Abu Dhabi: Emirates* Center for Strategic Studies and Research.

Anthony, J.D. (2005) "Measuring the Iraq War's 'Accomplishments' through the Lens of its Authors: A Preliminary Assessment," address to the Voltaire Institute's International Axis for Peace Conference, Brussels, 17 November. Online HTTP : www.ncusar.org (accessed November 19, 2009).

Anthony, J.D. (2008a) "War with Iran: Regional Reactions and Requirements," 20 June. Online. HTTP: www.ncusar.org (accessed November 19, 2009).

Anthony, J.D. (2008b) "War with Iran: Regional Reactions and Requirements" (condensed version), *Middle East Policy*, 15 (3):1–29.

Meshkati, N. (2007) "Interview: Waiting for an Iranian Chernobyl," *The Nuclear Age*, 2612, 11 July.

6 Gulf cooperation council diplomatic coordination

The limited role of institutionalization

Matteo Legrenzi

Introduction

In this paper I analyze Gulf Cooperation Council (GCC) diplomatic coordination and performance in the internal and external realms in the first 20 years of its history. After an examination of several episodes in the life of the organization, I conclude that institutionalization has played a small role in the life of the GCC.

While it is possible that the GCC will become an organization possessing supranational powers, it is my contention that so far the organization has served as a useful, if loose, forum when it comes to diplomacy. In the words of Erik Peterson, "the GCC has not by any means replaced the individual foreign policies of the member states but rather has served as the vehicle for the implementation of consensus policies among them" (Peterson 1988: 56–138). Though these words were written almost 20 years ago, they remain true. The events selected to explain this point represent crucial moments or issues on which a sub-regional organization such as the GCC could have been expected to take a stand.

I focus on how the GCC reacted to the cases of the Iran–Iraq War, the Abu Musa and Tunbs territorial dispute between the UAE and Iran, and the Bahrain–Qatar border dispute. I also dwell upon the GCC's dealings with the European Union and the two entities' fruitless attempt to reach a free trade agreement. I purport to explain these situations and their overarching principles by using the method known as "narrative explanatory protocol."[1] The aim is to construct an account that is verisimilar and believable to others looking over the same events, rather than offer "if then" predictions or lawlike statements. I will supplement the deductive arguments with inductively derived insights.

The Iran–Iraq War was a protracted international conflict involving the two foremost regional powers in the Gulf. It was also instrumental in the creation of the GCC, since it allowed member-states to refuse membership to Iraq. The dispute over the Abu Musa and Tunbs islands is the perfect case in which the GCC could have displayed its joint diplomatic clout, since the UAE could have legitimately asked the organization to give the issue prominence through its unified strength. Further, the border dispute between Bahrain and Qatar seems a textbook case for the Commission for the Settlement of Disputes, whose establishment is explicitly called for in the GCC charter's sixth article.[2]

Finally, negotiations with the European Union have so far been the only case in which both organizations have engaged on a *multilateral* level to achieve a free trade agreement. Taken together, these case studies give a fair picture of the diplomatic modus operandi of the organization.

Diplomacy in the GCC

The approach to handling disputes and disagreements between GCC states has always been based on trying to reach consensus (*ijma*) through informal means. In Gulf politics, resorting to institutions to come to a binding decision is frowned upon, as is recourse to judicial settlement in business circles. Abdullah Bishara has referred to the GCC as a "gentlemen's club" in which clear, if unstated, rules of conduct are to be followed and deference accorded to more powerful players (Bishara 2000).

Hence GCC institutions have played only a limited role in facilitating the mending of fences between member-states and the adoption of common diplomatic stances. However, this is not necessarily a limitation on the part of the organization, but is rather more an indication that the GCC is rooted in Gulf political culture and its general diplomatic principles, such as how failure to reach an agreement or forge a common position is often a signal of the unwillingness to make a difference in opinion emerge. In the same vein is a lack of follow-up and limited enforcement, even within the national administrations of the GCC member-states.[3]

For all of its shortcomings, however, the GCC played an important diplomatic role during the Iran–Iraq War, as it allowed some of the smaller member-states protection vis-à-vis either or both belligerents. This is a similar process to Germany taking cover under a common European Union position vis-à-vis Middle East matters, especially the Israeli–Palestinian conflict.

Furthermore, even in the heat of intense disagreements, as when meetings are boycotted by a head or heads of state, GCC technical cooperation at the ministerial and administrative level continues unabated. This is an aspect of the GCC that is too often overlooked by critics who focus on the lack of binding agreements between member-states. It actually provides a welcome pattern that gives rise to knowledge networks between officials in the six member-states and facilitates the solution of day to day administrative problems.

Indeed, even in the UAE (which vests a greater amount of sovereignty in the federal government than other GCC members), where individual emirates take significantly different stances on major international political issues, these intense and sometimes bitter disagreements do not preclude the GCC from operating effectively and cohesively.

The Iran–Iraq War

Traditional accounts of GCC behavior throughout the Iran–Iraq War stress the progressive tilting of its diplomatic position towards Iraq as the Iranian military situation improved, particularly in the aftermath of March 1982.[4] Before looking at the behavior of the GCC as an actor, it is essential to sketch out the overall dynamic of the conflict.[5]

The war can be schematically divided into three parts if we take as a guiding principle the balance of power between Iraq and Iran. In the first phase, which dates from September 1980 to March 1982, Iraq had the upper hand on the battle-front as judged by territorial control. The new Reagan administration that took over in January 1981 and the GCC states seemed uncertain as to how to react. The United States perceived Iraq as a Soviet client and Iran as a radical regime bent on spreading its Islamist ideology throughout the Middle East. But even the Soviet Union reacted negatively to the Iraqi invasion of Iran, recognizing Saddam Hussein's regime as the aggressor and temporarily suspending weapons shipments. This reflected its irritation at not being informed.

The second phase of the war began with the Iranian counteroffensive of March 1982. This was the first of a series of successful Iranian counterattacks that brought the war onto Iraqi territory. Iranian aims also came to explicitly include the over-throwing of the Ba'athist regime in Iraq. The Iranian war thus changed from a defensive undertaking to an offensive operation aimed at punishing the aggressor, and the conflict assumed increasingly ideological overtones. On one side, Iran fash-ioned itself as the leader of revolutionary Islam, while on the other, Iraq came to be perceived as a secular bulwark and as the defender of the status quo.

In Washington the danger of an Iranian victory became more palpable and overcame American reluctance to support in any way an ally of the Soviet Union. A cautious rapprochement therefore began between the United States and Iraq. The United States started utilizing loan guarantees to provide Iraq with grain and other raw materials, and the Soviet Union, also alarmed at the prospect of an Iranian victory, resumed selling military supplies to Iraq.

From the start of the conflict, the United States had two overarching aims. It wanted to prevent the decisive victory of one of the two sides, and it aimed to prevent a spillover of the conflict that would endanger freedom of navigation and the flow of oil from the Gulf. Most GCC states shared these two goals, even if there were significant differences within the organization.

A third phase of the conflict began in 1986 with the progressive deterioration of the Iraqi military situation. From this point of view, the Iranian conquest of the Faw peninsula in February of that year marked a turning point. The peninsula's location at the opening of the Gulf overlooking Kuwait made it an extremely important strategic asset. The fall of Basra and the dismemberment of the Iraqi state came to be seen as concrete possibilities. This episode nudged the United States even closer to Iraq, and heralded a renewed commitment on the part of the Soviet Union in support of Iraq.

In 1984, the United States and Iraq restored diplomatic relations that had been suspended 14 years earlier. The United States began selling dual-use equipment, such as Bell helicopters, to Iraq as well as acquiescing to French sales of missiles and fighter jets that allowed Iraq to hit Teheran and other important Iranian centers in the so-called "war of the cities." However, the United States always encountered problems exporting weapons to Iraq because of opposition from Congress regarding direct arms sales to a country seen as a traditional enemy of Israel.

In 1986 the United States assumed an even more direct role in the escalating conflict. From the fall of the Faw peninsula, the United States began to share tactical intelligence with Iraqi armed forces. The value of this intelligence has been hotly debated,[6] but it must be remembered that even low-grade battlefield information can prove very valuable to a country that does not have access to satellite reconnaissance.

The Iranians, frustrated by Soviet and Western support of Iraq, started to attack neutral shipping in the Gulf, particularly oil tankers departing from Kuwait. After a series of Kuwaiti diplomatic moves and counter-moves, in December 1986 the United States offered to protect Kuwaiti ships by re-flagging them with American flags—a reaction to a Soviet offer to do the same.[7] The prevention of a Soviet role in the Gulf had been a long-standing foreign policy aim of the United States, and it spurred the Americans to take upon themselves, with the help of some Western allies, the burden of ensuring free navigation in the Gulf. It was, however, a risky undertaking, and on 17 May 1987 an Iraqi missile mistakenly hit the USS Stark.

From that moment on, pressure on Iran to accept an armistice increased. The United States Navy started to attack Iranian oil platforms, such as Sirri, and it organized an international embargo on the sale of any kind of weapon system to Iran. The downing of an Iranian Airbus on 3 July 1988, which killed 290 innocent civilians, as well as a new series of Iraqi offensives, finally gave the Ayatollah Khomeini the opportunity to accept UN resolution 598 and to sue for peace on 18 July 1988, a decision that he described a few days later as "more deadly than drinking poison."[8]

The war cost the two regional powers between $150 and $300 billion, according to different estimates. The number of casualties varies considerably according to the source, but it can be stated with some certainty that there were at least 350,000 Iranian casualties and around 150,000 Iraqi casualties.[9]

The GCC and the Iran–Iraq War

The attitude of the GCC states oscillated throughout the war according to the events in the battlefield. It also mirrored to some extent the attitude of the United States in that the member-states became increasingly worried about the possibility of an Iranian victory. However, variations among the states existed. In particular, throughout the course of the war, the support for Iraq by Kuwait and Saudi Arabia was at times overt, whereas Dubai and Oman can be said to have leaned more towards Iran in trying to establish a negotiated settlement. The GCC as an organization served as a useful cover for these different bilateral positions.[10]

The first phase of the conflict

In the first phase of the war, when it was hoped that the Iraqi blitz would succeed, GCC states were on the whole cautiously supportive of Iraq. However, there was no consensus on the degree of support to lend to Saddam Hussein, as everyone waited to gauge the results on the battlefield. As a stalemate set in after the first month of the conflict, the GCC's future six members articulated their position further. The main diplomatic aims became to end the war soon and to prevent an Iranian victory at all costs.

Two broad fronts came into being. The Emirates of Dubai, Sharjah, and Umm Al-Qaiwan, and even more significantly the Sultanate of Oman, maintained a neutral diplomatic stance between the two belligerents, not wanting to damage relations with Iran. The motives were mixed; in the case of Dubai, significant trade relations with Iran played an important role in addition to the presence of a sizable population of Iranian origin. For the two other emirates, the determining factor was the joint management of the Mubarak oil field on the island of Abu Musa. Finally, with regards to Oman, Gerd Nonneman highlights the fact that Sultan Qaboos always had more leeway than other Arab leaders in pursuing a pragmatic foreign policy because of the relative insulation of Oman from Arab nationalist currents. Furthermore, the geopolitical significance of the Strait of Hormuz caused Oman to deal cautiously with Iran, both under the Shah as well as the new regime of the Islamic republic.[11]

On the contrary, Kuwait and Saudi Arabia sided more decisively with Iraq at the beginning of the war. Their hope was for a successful blitzkrieg that would reverse what were seen as the more pernicious provisions of the 1975 Algiers treaty. Nonneman goes so far as to argue that Saudi Arabia was informed in advance of Iraq's plan to invade Iran (Nonneman 1986: 22–23, 78). Be that as it may, Kuwait and Saudi Arabia initially displayed full-blown support for Iraq, spurred undoubtedly by the increasingly radical rhetoric of the new leaders of the Islamic Republic.

This lack of unanimity within the newly formed GCC—even within the UAE—is reflected in the first declaration of the first regular session of the Supreme Council in Abu Dhabi on 26 May 1981. The Iran–Iraq War is mentioned only in the second to last paragraph, and the drafters studiously avoid taking sides, instead limiting themselves to expressing a vague desire for the cessation of hostilities and including no call for withdrawal to international borders, a pro-Iraqi stance by international standards. The declaration read:

> Their majesties and highnesses backed the efforts spent on putting an end to the Iran-Iraq war, as it is considered a problem which threatens the security of the area and increases the likelihood of foreign intervention in it, and they affirmed the necessity of doubling efforts to find a final solution to the conflict.[12]

> (cited in Peterson 2008)

This follows a discussion of organizational matters, such as the appointment of the first Secretary General of the organization, and a mention of the need for further economic integration. Even more tellingly, the declaration is preceded by a denunciation of Israeli actions against the Palestinians and an assertion of support for Syria. The haziness of the GCC's stance vis-à-vis a major regional conflict breaking out on their doorstep sets the tone for the diplomatic activity of the GCC throughout its history. The traditional caution of most Gulf Arab monarchies has been compounded by the difficulty in reaching a consensus on most diplomatic issues.

The second phase of the conflict

During the second phase of the conflict, the six member-states generally displayed heightened support for Iraq, but the differences in their diplomatic stances did not disappear and thus made it difficult to achieve a common GCC position. Nonneman interprets this lack of coherence by underlining how the GCC served as a forum that allowed the Six to consciously follow diverging policies, both domestic and international. In particular, Nonneman argues that the collective vehicle of the GCC allowed the two more pro-Iraqi actors, Kuwait and Saudi Arabia, to retain a possible line of communication with Iran (Nonneman 2004: 180–257).[13]

In May 1982, the Ministerial Council gathered the foreign ministers of the six GCC states in Riyadh. Their communiqué called on Iran to be more forthcoming to a peace initiative, and mentioned the Islamic Conference Organization (ICO) as a possible organization under whose aegis the two parties could resolve their differences. The choice of the ICO as the recommended venue to reach a cease-fire was a curious one, as the ICO had never served as a venue for peacemaking, even if it had hosted several important diplomatic encounters during its meetings. Thus it was felt that an *Islamic* venue would be preferable to the United Nations, as it would deter the two superpowers from exerting an overbearing influence.[14]

The GCC foreign ministers were correct in feeling that this was a crucial moment. Iran had gone on the offensive, and Saddam Hussein had agreed to withdraw to the international border. If the occasion was lost, the war was bound to continue for a very long time. Saudi Arabia and Kuwait started buttressing Iraq financially to the tune of $26 billion. As Iraq tried to internationalize the conflict by attacking Iranian oil installations, Saudi Arabia and Kuwait succeeded in producing a GCC initiative explicitly criticizing Iran (Nonneman 2004: 178–257).[15] Essentially, they finally convinced the more reluctant member-states to adopt bolder language. In May 1984, amidst fiery Iranian rhetoric directed at the GCC and the first attacks on neutral, mostly Saudi and Kuwaiti, ships, the organization sponsored a UN resolution condemning Iranian attacks on international shipping (United Nations Security Council 1984). These attacks proved to be the tipping point even for traditionally Iranian-leaning member-states such as Oman.

The downing of an Iranian F4 over Saudi territorial waters by the Saudi Air Force escalated tension among the Gulf states. That the war could not be contained and that the conflict would spread seemed more plausible. Saudi Arabia appealed directly to both the ICO and the non-aligned movement at the United Nations to help bring an end to the war. These diplomatic demarches culminated in a May 1985 visit to Teheran by Prince Saud al-Faysal, which was reciprocated by Foreign Minister Ali-Akbar Velayati at the end of the year. These initiatives did not signal the end of Saudi support for Iraq, but underscored the fear of escalation felt by the Six.[16]

On the contrary, GCC communiqués throughout this period are studiously even-handed, even if they constantly refer to the need by all parties to accept the two relevant UN resolutions, which Iran continuously refused to do. This symbolizes a certain support for Iraq, as UN Security Council resolutions were certainly biased against Iran throughout this period. They never clearly recognized that the conflict's inception was due to Iraq, and they never called for a return to the international border until the Iraqi war effort had been blunted.[17]

The four southern members of the GCC had by now recognized that neutrality was their best option, but they allowed themselves to adopt a shared pro-Iraqi tilt when acting under GCC cover. This enabled them to be good, collegiate GCC members while not antagonizing Iran bilaterally. Looking at the communiqués, it is also worth noting how denunciation of the Zionist regime and appeals to Muslim solidarity through the ICO are more prominent and more starkly conveyed when compared to references to the Iran–Iraq War, thus demonstrating that the matter remained too sensitive and too close to home for the GCC to take a definitive stance. On the contrary, declarations denouncing the occupation of Palestine and proclaiming the need for Islamic unity vis-à-vis the Zionist threat could be dispensed more liberally, as they did not risk exposing the fault lines running through the foreign policies of the Six. On the contrary, they acted as solidarity promoters.

The third phase of the conflict

A third phase of the conflict can be said to have started in February 1986 with the capture of the Faw peninsula by Iranian forces. This event sent shivers down the backs of GCC rulers as well as American decision-makers, and it increased the direct and indirect support of Saudi Arabia and Kuwait for Iraq while making the position of the "neutral" GCC states more difficult.

From a military point of view, the fall of the Faw peninsula represented a prominent setback for Iraqi forces and posed a direct threat to Kuwait Bay. Iraq decided to escalate the tanker war by attacking Iran's oil terminals in the southern Gulf to make international intervention to end the war more likely. The dissolution of the National Assembly in Kuwait in 1986 made the reflagging operation easier to achieve, as it had previously been blocked by Kuwaiti nationalist deputies. The operation duly began on 21 July 1987, the day after the passage of UNSC resolution 598 that eventually formed the basis to end the war. Only 10 days later, hundreds of pilgrims died in Mecca following violent demonstrations by Iranian pilgrims (Nonneman 2004: 180–182, 257).

After these events, the Iran–Iraq War still did not feature prominently in Supreme Council communiqués, but the tone became increasingly stern vis-à-vis Iran. In March 1986, GCC foreign ministers condemned Iran collectively, something that had never before taken place (Nonneman 1986: 78). Even more strikingly, the Supreme Council in its 29 December 1987 declaration noted:

> with great regret Iran's procrastination regarding accepting the resolution [UNSC resolution 598] and urged the international community led by the Security Council to shoulder its responsibility to adopt the necessary steps to implement Resolution 598 as soon as possible.

It further expressed its hope that:

> Iran will take an attitude responding to the will of the international community and to answer the appeal of the Islamic nation by ending the war, establishing peace, halting the bloodshed of Muslims, and conserving its energies in order to confront the enemies of the Islamic nation.

These were harsh words when compared with previous statements by the Supreme Council, and they point squarely to Iran as the party responsible for extending the war.

The events of Mecca did indeed play a significant role in stiffening Saudi attitudes, and they were coupled with grievances over other hostile acts. At the same meeting, the Council

> discussed the events in Holy Mecca and the sedition which the Iranians aroused at the House of God; what the State of Kuwait has encountered – shelling by missiles and Iranian aggressions against Kuwait's security and stability; the Iranian aggressions against the embassies of the State of Kuwait and the Kingdom of Saudi Arabia in Teheran; the striking at oil tankers and commercial ships sailing to and from the ports of the GCC member states in Gulf waters; and what such aggressions represent in terms of violating international law and the UN Charter.

Finally, the Council called on Iran to "adhere to the principles of mutual respect in a manner that guarantees the reestablishment of security and stability in the region." It must be reiterated that these stern calls come in the form of a six-page-long communiqué that tackles many issues in the region as well as the internal workings of the Council. However, these are expressions of unprecedented harshness vis-à-vis Iran.

The atmosphere had indeed changed, and while Iran tried to divide the Six by singling out Saudi Arabia and Kuwait as propaganda targets, the GCC functioned as an umbrella to express a more severe condemnation of Iranian actions. From this point of view, the GCC served a useful purpose during this last phase of the war.

The last year of the war, marked by further escalation of the conflict, still sees the GCC as a useful forum through which collective messages were conveyed while single member-states pursued individual initiatives. In June 1988, a communiqué of a foreign ministers' meeting reiterated a call for Iran to accept

UNSC resolution 598 while actually *congratulating* Iraq for its military victories, chiefly the recapture of the Faw peninsula that had been completed on 18 April. During the same period, Saudi Arabia broke off diplomatic relations with Iran over Teheran's refusal to accept a quota of 45,000 pilgrims for the Hajj. Other member-states, however, still maintained relations with the Islamic Republic. For example, Qatar, Oman, and the UAE received envoys during the same month who presented evidence of Iraq's use of chemical weapons (Nonneman 2004: 185–257). Finally, after Iranian acceptance of UNSC resolution 598 in July of 1988, the GCC, led by Saudi Arabia and in a sudden role reversal, played a useful part in convincing Iraq to accept a cease-fire on 6 August.

It is important to remember that throughout the war, the GCC conducted diplomatic démarches towards the warring parties and throughout the Arab world, mostly through its Secretary General, Abdullah Bishara. These had to respect a consensus among the Six, and therefore they were not always incisive; however, they proved useful in presenting a common front at events such as Arab League summits. They also increased in number and deepened in substance during the last phases of the conflict. However, the institution never developed a supranational role in foreign policy matters. Though the Secretary General acted as an emissary, an attempt to forge a common foreign, let alone security, policy did not occur.

Abu Musa and the Greater and Lesser Tunb

In relation to the dispute over Abu Musa and the Greater and Lesser Tunb islands, the GCC as a body did not behave differently from the League of Arab States. In other words, it was a forum in which to air grievances and express common positions, but, as during the Iran–Iraq War, it did not have a truly independent role as an institution.

In his exhaustive study of the dispute, Thomas Mattair, who embraces and exposes the Emirati position, concludes that "the consistent message has been that Iran can only improve its relations with the Arabs if it resolves this dispute" (Mattair 2006: 18, 261).[18] While this is probably an overstatement, it is worth analyzing the evolution of the dispute to ascertain whether GCC support for the UAE ever translated into a reorientation of the foreign and security policies of single member-states.

Geopolitical and geoeconomic factors as well as events in the global political context were still driving the foreign policies of individual GCC states vis-à-vis Iran. We have seen, for example, how the Iran–Iraq War did not prevent single GCC states from acting as mediators between the two belligerents when they deemed it in their interest to do so. Likewise, after the Lebanon war of July 2006, the dispute over the islands had no discernible effect on Saudi Arabia and Iran's dealings. Friction has always been determined by diverging interests on issues considered much more relevant, such as the situation in Iraq after the regime change in 2003 or the balance of power within Lebanon.

As such, the intermittent surfacing of the dispute over Abu Musa and the two Tunbs is more a symptom of troubled relations vis-à-vis other issues than an actual cause of friction. It could be said that it is something that the GCC states, with the notable exception of Ras al-Khaimah, bring up when they want to raise the temperature of relations with Iran. Otherwise, the GCC, in this as in other matters, with the notable exception of Palestine, has always tried to maintain a moderate tone. It is worth noting, for instance, that at the outset of the dispute the Emirate of Sharjah—which claims territorial sovereignty over Abu Musa—continued to share revenue from the jointly owned Mubarak oil field with Iran throughout the Iran–Iraq War and beyond (Cordesman 1997: 59, 298–299). Further, throughout the 1970s, the reactions of Arab League members, such as Iraq and South Yemen, to the Iranian occupation of the islands can be said to be more bellicose in tone than anything uttered by the GCC.

In May 1983, after the first wave of Iranian military successes in the Iran–Iraq War, other GCC members gave the UAE and Kuwait a mandate to try to mediate on behalf of all six states. The attempt came to naught, but it is worth noting how the dispute over the islands did not prevent the UAE from trying to act as an intermediary. This episode shows that from early on, the GCC delegated the handling of difficult disputes to the diplomatic offices of single member-states or individuals. Indeed, the organization has never taken upon itself the task of tackling a really difficult dispute involving either member-states or regional powers.

The war actually led to further militarization of the three islands, particularly the Greater Tunb. The islands served as bases for regular Iranian armed forces and for the naval branch of the Iranian Revolutionary Guard Corps (Mattair 2006: 261–286). Particularly during the war's last two years, an increasing number of attacks were launched from the islands against shipping in the Gulf. In spite of these strategic considerations, the GCC states, let alone the organization itself, did not make their relations with Iran dependent on the issue of the islands.

As Thomas Mattair concludes, "While maintaining sovereignty over the islands throughout the war, the UAE and its GCC partners were mostly preoccupied with the larger issues of the war" (Mattair 2006: 261–287). The issue of the islands continued to be muzzled around the time of Desert Storm and in the aftermath of the liberation of Kuwait in the early 1990s. Likewise it did not surface in Arab League deliberations. And as the League's president, Hashemi Rafsanjani, signaled his intentions to establish a more pragmatic relationship with the GCC states, it did not feature explicitly in the final communiqués of the Supreme Council. Saudi Arabia and Iran reestablished diplomatic relations in March 1991, and the issue certainly did not constitute an obstacle to this climate of renewed collaboration. Indeed, the closing statement of the twelfth Supreme Council meeting in Kuwait in December 1991 did not mention the issue, and it expressed "its satisfaction about the positive and concrete development of relations and its desire to push forward bilateral relations" (Gulf Cooperation Council 1998).

The issue began to surface in GCC collective statements only after Iran violated the Memorandum of Understanding (MoU) with Sharjah in 1992. On that occasion, Iran started to require visas of Egyptian teachers sent there to teach at the local school in the southern part of the island. Some have speculated that the

Supreme Leader decreed this move and the Iranian Revolutionary Guard Corps (IRGC) enacted it to sabotage the new conciliatory line of President Rafsanjani.

Irrespective of the motives behind the decision, it sparked a long series of GCC diplomatic protests that lasted throughout the 1990s and into the twenty-first century. It is worth noting that these protests did not affect the bilateral relations of single GCC states with Iran, and after the initial reaction to the Iranian breach of the MoU on Abu Musa, reactions to it became almost ritualized, appearing only as footnotes in various GCC communiqués.[19]

Yet, despite the somewhat hidden nature of the information, since 1992 the final communiqués of the Supreme Council have for the most part drawn attention to the islands dispute. Furthermore, the UAE has become bolder in the last decade, reminding the outside world that the 1971 MoU did not imply a recognition of Iranian sovereignty even on the northern half of Abu Musa, and that the UAE still claims sovereignty on all three islands. The UAE is ready to bring the case to the International Court of Justice (ICJ). What is interesting from a GCC point of view is how the three serious attempts to resolve the dispute since 1992 have not been led by the GCC as an institution or even by its Secretary General. The UAE and Iran conducted negotiations twice on a bilateral basis and, more significantly, the single mediation attempt was conducted by a tripartite commission of GCC member-states with the endorsement of the organization but without resorting to its offices.

The first bilateral attempt occurred immediately after the breaching of the MoU when it was thought that the dispute could perhaps be solved expeditiously. This first attempt failed, as Iran made it clear that it did not intend to revert to the *status quo ante*. Significantly, even this bilateral attempt was broached by a third party, in this case Syria, which enjoyed close relations with Iran, endorsed UAE rights, and had an interest in Gulf stability (Mattair 2006: 261–292). This reinforces a pattern of resorting to third parties to mediate disputes in the Gulf; there thus appears to be a need to resort to leaders with their own power base when broaching serious and delicate matters.

In the following three years, the GCC resumed its usual role of a collective forum that allowed smaller states, such as Bahrain and Qatar, to support the UAE position without endangering their crucial relations with Iran. Then in September 1995, a second set of bilateral negotiations was jumpstarted to try to reach an understanding between Iran and the UAE. The talks were again broached by a third party, in this case a GCC leader acting individually—the Foreign Minister of Qatar, Shaykh Hamad bin Jassim bin Jabir Al-Thani—who hosted a round of talks in Doha in November (Mattair 2006: 261–300).

The negotiations failed when Iran refused to accept the UAE agenda for the talks, which had broadened to include the possibility of a referral to the ICJ on the issue of the sovereignty of all three islands. This demarche made a possible resolution more difficult to achieve and was perhaps spurred by the solidarity that the UAE had encountered both within the GCC and at the League of Arab States. The idea of a referral to the ICJ was first broached by the new Secretary General of the GCC, Shaykh Fahim bin Sultan Al-Qasimi, a UAE national from the Qawasim tribe of Ras al-Khaimah, in December 1993, and was then incorporated in the final communiqué of the GCC Supreme Council Fifteenth Summit at Manama in Bahrain in December 1994. However, collective support in a GCC setting should not be confused with the willingness of other GCC states to spend valuable political capital when their national interest is at stake.

Further proof of the Gulf's preference for third party mediation is the attempt to settle the dispute in 2000. Saudi Arabia had been chafing at the inclusion of ritual statements condemning Iran in final GCC communiqués. President Khatami of Iran had visited Saudi Arabia in mid-May 1999, and Saudi Arabia clearly saw it as an opportunity to resume calm relations. Therefore, at a ministerial council meeting in June 1999 in Riyadh, Saudi Arabia insisted that the ritual condemnations in GCC statements be toned down. The UAE officials were furious, and they let it be known that the UAE was ready to forego membership in the GCC over the matter (Mattair 2006: 261–315). This reaction demonstrates that some individual member-states conceive of the GCC as a forum that can be abandoned or at least boycotted in case of diplomatic strife. It is very different from an organization such as NATO or the EU, in which membership is never in doubt and in which states boycott meetings in only the most dramatic circumstances.

In response, the GCC Secretary General, by then Shaykh Jamil Ibrahim Al-Hujailan, began touring the capitals of GCC members to end the public row. A tripartite committee composed of Saudi Arabia, Qatar, and Oman was also created, and the body was to report by May 2000 on a mechanism to resolve the dispute. The communiqué issued by the Supreme Council meeting in late November 1999 in Riyadh was unusually conciliatory vis-à-vis Iran in apprehension of the deliberations of the tripartite committee. The committee failed in its task, and the UAE currently seems to be determined to make the issue of the islands a central one in GCC–Iran relations. In the years since 2000, however, it has been clear that the other GCC governments are not willing to make their bilateral relations with Iran hostage to this issue. In particular, the symbolic importance of the three islands seems to take a back seat to the tensions emanating from the escalation of the Iranian nuclear program.

In terms of the workings of the GCC, one theme emerges clearly: GCC rulers, in the case of a dispute with a preeminent regional power such as Iran, preferred mediation, conducted through the usual rules of "shaykhly exchange," to reliance on the GCC as a multilateral organization charged with solving the dispute.[20] For a number of reasons, including the nature of the domestic regimes of member countries, the GCC is not seen by its members as an institution that can be entrusted to act autonomously on the regional stage. GCC functionaries are always seen as subordinates charged with specific tasks and not as counterparts. Hence the GCC Secretariat is not perceived as an independent actor by the leaders of the member-states, and indeed, he does not act as one.

The Bahrain–Qatar border dispute

It is now useful to review an intra-GCC dispute to ascertain how the organization fared in mediating issues among its member-states. As noted previously, the GCC charter provides for a "Commission for the Settlement of Disputes" that is supposed to adjudicate. However, the commission was never activated, and intra-GCC disputes have been settled outside the GCC institutional framework.

It should first be noted that traditionally in the Arabian peninsula, sovereignty was exercised over peoples and not over territory. This led to a host of disputes when territorial borders became suddenly very important in the granting of oil concessions. Furthermore, GCC states are particularly jealous of their sovereignty and sometimes even disputes that are not endowed with a financial component spiral out of control. The process of settling border disputes continues apace but some are still left unresolved.[21]

The border dispute between Qatar and Bahrain is a longstanding one, and it involves a number of islands lying between them and crucially, for the purposes of oil exploitation, the exact line of the maritime boundary.[22] In fact, it was the need to proceed with oil exploration that prompted the British to intervene in the matter in the 1930s. The dispute became the object of mediation efforts and finally of a British adjudication in 1939 that satisfied neither party and left tensions simmering.

While the dispute involves a large number of smaller islands and shoals, it is essentially as follows: the Bahraini ruling family claimed a piece of land on the northern coast of the peninsula of Qatar, basing its claim on the fact that the area had been the ancestral home of the Khalifa family before their conquest of Bahrain in 1783. A Qatari counterclaim asserts that the Bahraini Hawar islands should be Qatar's on the grounds that it is extremely close to the Qatari peninsula (al-Makhawi 1990: 129–256).[23]

While the British were present to enforce their adjudication and continuously carry out mediation efforts, the dispute remained dormant. But after independence in 1971 it started causing enough dissension that in 1976 the Saudi government—particularly King Khalid bin Abdul Aziz Al-Saud—took up the mediating role that the British had relinquished (Al-Arayed 2003: 250–326).

Five principles were established on which negotiations to reach a comprehensive settlement were to be based.[24] The preference for a mediated agreement was clearly expressed, but, importantly, one of the principles stated that if this failed, the entire gamut of disputes would be submitted to arbitration. The mediation efforts continued after the establishment of the GCC, but they were conducted under "the continuing patronage of Saudi Arabia" (Al-Arayed 2003: 250–326). The pivotal role of Saudi Arabia was never in doubt, as the GCC did not constitute much more than a venue for the tripartite meetings of Bahrain, Qatar, and Saudi Arabia.

Further, all the subsequent mediation efforts on the part of the GCC should be seen as a continuation of the Saudi attempts. They did not emanate from GCC institutions themselves and did not imply an autonomous initiative by the GCC Secretary General. Even this is a generous interpretation, since the other GCC leaders were not consulted on the subsequent mediation efforts undertaken by Saudi Arabia.

The dispute flared up again in March and April 1986 during a particularly sensitive period of the Iran–Iraq War. In April 1986, after Bahrain named a navy vessel "Hawar" and announced military exercises, Qatar on 26 April attacked construction crews sent to build a coastguard station on the reclaimed coral reef of Fasht Al-Dibal located between Bahrain and the Qatari mainland; 29 workers were arrested. Qatar then proceeded to declare an "exclusion zone" around the disputed area.

Despite this escalation, the situation returned to the *status quo ante* within a month. Both parties agreed to freeze the situation to avoid an escalation at a delicate time of the Iran–Iraq conflict. Saudi Arabia took the lead as King Fahd dispatched his defense minister to the two capitals and tasked GCC Secretary General Abdullah Bishara to mediate the dispute. It is perhaps noteworthy that the GCC Secretary General was chosen for this role, but it must be stated that he did so on behalf of King Fahd of Saudi Arabia. As such, he was not acting in an independent role as GCC Secretary General when he negotiated a settlement. In his own words, "My power emanated from King Fahd, because I went on his behalf and I had to report to him. I only implemented his instructions" (Priess 2000: 138–237).

It was at a meeting during the 1987 GCC Supreme Council meeting in Riyadh that the dispute was put on course for eventual resolution. On that occasion, both Qatar and Bahrain agreed to submit the dispute to the ICJ at The Hague for a final ruling in case mediation efforts failed. This followed a dispatch of letters by King Fahd to the Emirs of Bahrain and Qatar setting up a specific roadmap for a solution. A tripartite committee formed, and it met six times between January and December 1988 to prepare for a joint submission to the ICJ (Al-Arayed 2003: 250–328). More mediating attempts ensued to no avail, and in the December 1990 GCC Supreme Council meeting in Doha, the basis was laid for Qatar's unilateral submission of the case to the ICJ in 1991. The ICJ ultimately resolved the dispute with a final judgment issued in March 2001 slightly more favorable to Bahrain, particularly in terms of the maritime boundary, than the British adjudication of 1939.[25]

Though this major border skirmish was discussed by the tripartite committee on the sidelines of Supreme Council meetings, it was not mentioned in communiqués. And the crucial decision to submit the dispute to the mandatory judgment of the ICJ was made in a similarly informal way. The fact that the dispute could not be solved through the mechanisms specified in the GCC charter may be read as a failure for the organization. A more benign interpretation would posit that the way the dispute was solved demonstrates that the low degree of GCC institutionalization is in fact a positive characteristic, as it allows the organization to weather major crises between its constituent states, thus shielding it from making decisions that would potentially lead to its breakup.

EU–GCC negotiations: dialogue of the deaf?

Another interesting case study to gauge the nature of the GCC diplomatic persona is to retrace, albeit briefly, its conduct during negotiations regarding a free trade agreement (FTA) it has entertained with the European Union for more than

20 years. While such an agreement may be out of reach after Bahrain, Oman, Qatar, and Kuwait concluded bilateral FTAs with the United States from 2004 to 2007, the long history of negotiations is indicative of the diplomatic behavior of the GCC. It is thus useful to review the subject from the point of view of GCC diplomatic cohesiveness and the difficulty the General Secretariat has encountered in mustering up a united front.

Gulf states had been part of the Euro-Arab dialogue, launched in 1974, that achieved little and came to an end in 1989 (Nonneman 2006: 14, 269). The EU-GCC Cooperation Agreement, signed in 1988, was supposed to herald a new era in the relations between the then European community and the Gulf. European officials were hoping to achieve the first FTA negotiated by Europe on a multilateral basis and therefore attached particular symbolic importance to this relationship. The 1988 Agreement went into effect on 1 January 1990 (Baabood and Edwards 2007: 164–271), and it has provided a fairly institutionalized setting whose premier expression is the annual Joint Ministerial Council meetings. The political dialogue stemming from the Agreement yielded a long series of rather vacuous communiqués expressing common positions on the political issues of the day, save for really contentious issues. From this point of view, the two organizations found common ground, but crucially the trade aspect that required painful domestic compromises remains unresolved.

It is particularly interesting that the European Union feels it has a lot to offer in terms of its experience as a peacemaker and purveyor of confidence building measures "in the framework of cooperative and collective regimes on regional security" without a willingness to provide any military guarantees.[26] Indeed, it leaves the field chiefly to the Americans, and even to the United Kingdom and France, who operate on a bilateral basis.

This ambivalence on the part of the European states—wanting to preserve their lucrative bilateral links while pushing the multilateral framework for declaratory purposes—has been one of the main obstacles to a functioning multilateral EU–GCC relationship. However, the GCC's difficulty in presenting a united front in trade negotiations has been throughout the years an even greater deterrent. The GCC Secretariat's limited institutionalization and lack of supranational powers have proved a formidable obstacle.

A few milestone dates demonstrate the meager pace at which the General Secretariat was able to muster a mandate for the EU–GCC negotiations. After the cooperation agreement in 1990 came into force, GCC countries were able to agree on a negotiating mandate for the FTA only in 1997. The customs union, a precondition for a multilateral FTA with the European Union, was finalized only in 2003 and was soon thrown into disarray by the wave of rapidly concluded bilateral FTAs with the United States mentioned above.[27] And it was not until 2004—16 years after the signing of the Cooperation Agreement—that the European Union opened a delegation in Riyadh with an ambassador accredited to the six GCC states,[28] a fact that has to do with the reluctance of the Europeans to deal with the Gulf on a multilateral basis but also with the low priority that GCC institutions command in the international arena.[29]

The European Union put what will possibly be the final nail in the coffin of this negotiating saga. Up to this point, outstanding disputes have been concentrated in four areas: market access, rules of origin, government procurement (a particularly crucial one in a place like Saudi Arabia), and investment protection and guarantees criteria (Nonneman 2006: 19, 269). These are fairly usual, if in this case quite thorny, areas of negotiation when aiming at a trade deal. However, probably influenced by contemporary American initiatives, the European Union decided to introduce human rights and good governance clauses in its negotiating stance, drawing the ire of the GCC delegation. The joint EU–GCC communiqués have so far touched upon political notions but always at the regional and international level without touching on domestic concerns. The actual incorporation of these clauses in the trade deal has proven unacceptable to the GCC delegation, which noted that these issues did not arise in its parallel negotiations with China.

Another issue that highlighted the institutional, and in this case even societal, mismatch between the European Union and the GCC is the European Union's insistence on a parallel process of "decentralized cooperation" to involve civil society actors in the Gulf in business, academia, and the arts. This process of track two diplomacy was interpreted by the GCC and Saudi Arabia in particular as interference in the domestic affairs of its member-states and was eventually dropped.[30] These episodes highlight the limited role that GCC institutions can play in carrying out multilateral negotiations, even when they are headed by capable functionaries. In sum, the lack of supranational authority is an obstacle that is very difficult to surmount.

Conclusion

By analyzing how the GCC has dealt with key internal and external disputes as well as its extenuating dealings with the European Union, we can conclude that the GCC acts as a loose forum on the diplomatic scene. In other words, in the first 20 years of its existence, the GCC has not developed independent agency, and likewise it cannot be said to shape the interests of its member-states. However, the GCC's looseness is the key to its strength, as closer, concerted diplomatic action would cause the differences between the national interests of the constituent states to come to the fore.

Regime security is the foremost priority in the foreign policy of the six member-states. If there is no common threat to bring them together, GCC states revert to competition, and GCC institutionalism is certainly not enough to keep them from doing so. As such, GCC member-states do not constitute a security community.

Perhaps the only instance of GCC unity is in the economic area, in which the Secretariat personnel pushed the rulers for many years to herald the customs union. However, as we have seen, the fate of the customs union hangs in the balance as a result of the bilateral FTAs concluded with the United States by single member-states. This only reinforces my previous conclusion.

In general, smaller GCC states display a greater tendency to defy the traditional "rules of shaykhly exchange" that have characterized intra-GCC relations for the first 20 years of its existence. For example, they are more likely to defy notions of Saudi leadership, the bilateral FTA issue being only the most egregious instance. This new tendency can be partially attributed to a perceived waning of American soft power in the region following the regime change in Iraq in 2003, as well as a more general "hollowing out" of the regional level as the Iran–U.S. confrontation is increasingly played out globally. Under these circumstances, smaller GCC states feel that the imperative of regime security can probably be attained while carving out a more autonomous role for themselves.

Notes

1 For a full explanation of this scholarly method, see Finnemore 2003: 13–253. She takes inspiration from Ruggie 1998: 254 and Peirce and Buchler 1978: 256.

2 Its rules of procedure are further spelled out in a 13-point document approved by the Supreme Council. See GCC Secretariat 1985: 290.

3 For elucidation on the administrative culture prevailing in some of the GCC member-states, see Davidson 2008: 274 and Tétreault 2000: 247. An illuminating case study of a major government organization is also in Tétreault 1995: 279. Finally, for a look at another international organization, see Tétreault 1981: 280.

4 See, among others, Gause 1994: 23, Peterson 1988: 56, and Nakhleh 1986: 61. A more nuanced and comprehensive treatment can be found in Nonneman 2004: 257. For general histories of the Iran–Iraq War, see Chubin and Tripp 1988: 289 and Karsh 2002: 287. Even more readable is Hiro 1990: 286. A good bibliographic guide is Gardner 1988: 288.

5 For a more comprehensive account of the balance of power dynamics in the Gulf in the last 200 years, see Legrenzi 2006: 258.

6 See the long running discussion on the topic in the *Gulf 2000* academic list, available at www1.columbia.edu/sec/cu/sipa/GULF2000/index.html (after registration).

7 For two excellent accounts of this aspect of the conflict, see Navias and Hooton 1996: 259 and el-Shazly 1998: 260.

8 For an interesting account of how the decision of the Ayatollah Khomeini took even his own lieutenants by surprise, see Milani 1994: 214–215.

9 For an exhaustive discussion of the issue from an Iranian point of view, please see the discussion on the *Gulf 2000* academic list in September 2004 that can be found at www1.columbia.edu/sec/cu/sipa/GULF2000/ (after registration).

10 As Gerd Nonneman points out, the technique of sending different messages to different audiences can be noticed in the domestic realm by scrutinizing the differences between governmental policy and the permitted expression of alternative views in the media (Nonneman 2004: 168–257). These were two sophisticated methods of sending messages to both belligerents throughout the war without breaking diplomatic cover.

11 See Nonneman 2004: 169–257. For a military analysis of the significance of the Strait of Hormuz, see also Cordesman 1997: 59. In particular, it is now debatable whether Iran nowadays could be contained as effectively as it was during the Iran–Iraq War. The procurement of Chinese "Silkworm" missiles seems to have added to the insidiousness of the Iranian military in the Gulf. These same missiles, undoubtedly supplied by Iran, were utilized to great effect by Hezbollah in its 2006 conflict with Israel against its navy.

12 For an English text of the communiqué, see Peterson 1988: 56–286. For the Arabic text, see Government of Bahrain 1983: 142.

13 This assessment is borne out by an analysis of the diplomatic demarches of the different GCC members throughout this phase of the conflict.

14 To this very day, the ICO plays a role in world politics, but it would be interesting to see it emerge as an even more significant diplomatic actor in the twenty-first century.

15 See also Cordesman 1987: 281. A more technical, military analysis is found in Karsh 1987: 282. For a more polemical stance on this issue, see Cass 1994: 285.

16 A number of sources also point to Iran–Saudi negotiations during this period and the facilitation of American weapon sales to Iran as well as Iran supplying the United States with refined oil products as another indication of the fear of escalation (Nonneman 2004: 179–257). Nonneman calculates that by the beginning of 1986, Gulf aid to Iraq amounted to about $40 billion. Of this sum, all but $3 to $5 billion came from Saudi Arabia and Kuwait (Nonneman 1986: 78, 102–104).

17 For a list of most of the communiqués, see www.gcc-sg.org. The remaining ones are available in printed form at the GCC Secretariat. Some of the closing statements of the GCC Supreme Council since 1981 are now available at www.gcc-sg.org/closingsessions.html. For an English translation of the Supreme Council communiqués throughout this period, see also Peterson 1988: 56, 286–309.

18 For an account that is more sympathetic to the Iranian position, see Amirahmadi 1996: 116. See also Schofield 1997: 117.

19 For an exhaustive analysis of the MoU, see Schofield 2003: 268.

20 The "rules of shaykhly exchange" is a particularly felicitous expression that encapsulates the habits of political mediation in the Gulf. It can be traced back to Gerd Nonneman. See exchange on the *Gulf 2000* academic list, available at: www1.columbia.edu/sec/sipa/GULF2000/ (after registration).

21 For a very good overview of border disputes in the Gulf, see Schofield 1997: 117.

22 For an illuminating discussion, see Said Zahlan 1998: 58.

23 The dispute is discussed in detail in Said Zahlan 1998: 58, and it gave rise to a wide literature. See, for example, Cordesman 1997: 59 or Joffé 1996: 266. The most monumental account is the one based on the documents presented by Bahrain to the ICJ. See al-Arayed 2003: 250. Here the topic is tackled only in relation to the GCC (in)action on the issue.

24 These were later amended in 1983. They can be found in al-Arayed 2003: 250.

25 The case interestingly involved the alleged forgery of several documents and the intervention of Dr. John Wilkinson, Tutorial Fellow at St Hugh's College, Oxford, who was called upon to judge the veracity of the suspected documents. It is also interesting to note that Bahrain and Qatar, after their disputes had been satisfactorily settled, tried to build a bridge between them. Saudi Arabia, the erstwhile mediator, attempted to prevent them from doing so because of concerns that the bridge would pass over its territorial waters. It is difficult to imagine such disputes arising within other multilateral organizations that are nominally committed to ultimately achieving unity among its members.

26 For some recent examples of communiqués, see: www.eu2005.lu/en/actualites/communiques/2005/04/05uegolfe/0504uegolfe.pdf; www.consilium.europa.eu/ueDocs/cms_Data/docs/pressdata/en/er/89619.pdf For a more general account of the reasons for the lack of credibility of the EU in the Gulf in defense matters, see Baabood and Edwards 2007: 270.

27 In addition, European misgivings about free access of GCC petrochemical products to its markets have made for what Baabood and Edwards quite aptly label an "institutional mismatch" (2007: 270–276).

28 The opening of the delegation and the renewed emphasis by the EU in bringing about the conclusion of an FTA was probably due to the successful completion of the EU-Saudi agreement of August 2003 regarding the Kingdom's accession to the WTO (Nonneman 2006: 13, 18, 269).

29 It must be noted, with the experience of the GCC customs union in mind, that the signing of an eventual agreement would only be the first step. Practical implementation would

be very arduous given the lack of supranational powers on the part of the General Secretariat.
30 NATO is experiencing similar problems with its track two efforts in the Gulf, even if it wisely chose to carry out its Istanbul Cooperation Initiative on a purely bilateral basis. For the problems encountered by the EU, see Baabood and Edwards 2007: 270. For the similar ill-fated attempts by NATO that are in fact made easier by the exclusion of Saudi Arabia, see Legrenzi 2007: 272.

Bibliography

al-Arayed, J.S. (2003) *A Line in the Sea: The Qatar v. Bahrain Border Dispute in the World Court*, Berkeley, CA: North Atlantic Books.

al-Makhawi, R. (1990) "The Gulf Cooperation Council: A Study in Integration," Ph.D. dissertation, University of Salford.

Amirahmadi, H. (ed.) (1996) *The Gulf Cooperation Council: A Model of a Regional International Regime*, Madison, WI: University of Wisconsin Press.

Baabood, A. and Edwards, G. (2007) "Reinforcing Ambivalence: The Interaction of Gulf States and the European Union," in *Eighth Mediterranean Social and Political Research Meeting*, Montecatini: European University Institute.

Bahrain, Government of (1983) *Cooperation Council for the Arab States of the Gulf*, Bahrain: Bahrain Government Printing Press.

Bishara, A. (2000) Personal interview, Kuwait City, November.

Cass, S.J.R. (1994) "The U.S. Takes Sides: U.S. Policy Toward Iraq During the Iran-Iraq War," University of Oxford.

Chubin, S. and Tripp, C. (1988) *Iran and Iraq at War*, London: I.B. Tauris.

Cordesman, A.H. (1987) *The Iran-Iraq War and Western Security 1984-1987: Strategic Implications and Policy Options*, London: Jane's.

Cordesman, A.H. (1997) *Bahrain, Oman, Qatar, and the UAE: Challenges of Security* (CSIS Middle East Dynamic Assessment), Boulder, CO: Westview Press.

Davidson, C.M. (2008) *Dubai: The Vulnerability of Success*, New York: Columbia University Press.

European Union Communiqués. Online HTTP: www.eu2005.lu/en/actualites/comm uniques/2005/04/05uegolfe/0504uegolfe.pdf and www.consilium.europa.eu/ueDocs/ cms_Data/docs/pressdata/en/er/89619.pdf (accessed May 2006).

Finnemore, M. (2003) *The Purpose of Intervention: Changing Beliefs About the Use of Force*, Cornell Studies in Security Affairs, Ithaca, NY: Cornell University Press.

Gardner, J.A. (1988) *The Iran-Iraq War: A Bibliography*, Boston, MA: GK Hall.

Gause, F.G. III (1994) *Oil Monarchies: Domestic Security Challenges in the Arab Gulf States*, New York: Council on Foreign Relations Press.

GCC Secretariat (1985) "Rules of Procedures Commission for the Settlement of Disputes," Riyadh: GCC Printing Press.

Gulf Cooperation Council (1998) Closing Statements of the Twelfth Supreme Council Meeting, Riyadh, 108–267.

Gulf Cooperation Council Communiqués. Online HTTP: www.gcc-sg.org (accessed May 2006).

Hiro, D. (1990) *The Longest War: The Iran-Iraq Military Conflict*, London: Paladin.

Joffé, G. (1996) "Arab Frontier Disputes: The Consequences for Arab Security," *Geopolitics and International Boundaries*, 1 (2), pp 159–177.

Karsh, E. (1987) "The Iran-Iraq War, a Military Analysis," *Adelphis Papers*, 220, London: International Institute for Strategic Studies.

Karsh, E. (2002) *The Iran-Iraq War, 1980-1988, Essential Histories*, Oxford: Osprey.

Legrenzi, M. (2006) "Iraq, Iran E Arabia Saudita Come Triangolo Scaleno: Per Una Storia Degli Equilibri Di Potenza Nella Regione Del Golfo," in M. Nordio, M. Torri and G. Vercellin (eds.) *Grande Medio Oriente*, Milan: Bruno Mondadori.

Legrenzi, M. (2007) "NATO in the Gulf: Who is Doing Whom a Favor?" *Middle East Policy*, 14 (1).

Mattair, T.R. (2006) *The Three Occupied UAE Islands: The Tunbs and Abu Musa*, Abu Dhabi: Emirates Center for Strategic Studies and Research.

Milani, M.M. (1994) *The Making of Iran's Islamic Revolution*, Boulder, CO: Westview Press.

Nakhleh, E.A. (1986) *The Gulf Cooperation Council: Policies, Problems and Prospects*, New York: Praeger.

Navias, M.S. and Hooton, E.R. (1996) *Tanker Wars: The Assault on Merchant Shipping During the Iran-Iraq Conflict, 1980-1988*, London / New York: I.B. Tauris.

Nonneman, G. (1986) *Iraq, the Gulf States and the War*, London: Ithaca Press.

Nonneman, G. (2004) "The Gulf States and the Iran-Iraq War: Pattern Shifts and Continuities," in L. Potter and G. Sick (eds.) *Iran, Iraq, and the Legacies of War*, New York/Basingstoke: Palgrave Macmillan.

Nonneman, G. (2006) "EU-GCC Relations: Dynamics, Perspectives, and the Issue of Political Reform," *Journal of Social Affairs*, 23 (92), pp 13–33.

Peirce, C. and Buchler, J. (1978) *The Philosophy of Peirce: Selected Writings*, New York: AMS Press.

Peterson, E.R. (1988) *The Gulf Cooperation Council: Search for Unity in a Dynamic Region*, Boulder, CO: Westview Press.

Priess, D. (2000) "Alliance Durability: Why Breaking Up is Hard to Do," Ph.D. Dissertation, Duke University.

Ruggie, J.G. (1998) *Constructing the World Polity: Essays on International Institutionalization*, London / New York: Routledge.

Said Zahlan, R. (1998) *The Making of the Modern Gulf States* (2nd edition), Reading: Ithaca Press.

Schofield, R.N. (1997) "Border Disputes in the Gulf: Past, Present, and Future," in G. Sick and L. Potter (eds.) *The Persian Gulf at the Millennium: Essays in Politics, Economy, Security, and Religion*, Houndmills and London: MacMillan.

Schofield, R.N. (2003) *Unfinished Business: Iran, the UAE, Abu Musa, and the Tunbs*, London: Royal Institute of International Affairs.

el-Shazly, N.E.-S. (1998) *The Gulf Tanker War: Iran and Iraq's Maritime Swordplay*, New York: St. Martin's Press.

Tétreault, M.A. (1981) "The Organization of Arab Petroleum Exporting Countries: History, Policies, and Prospects," *Contributions in Economics and Economic History*, 40, Westport, CN: Greenwood Press.

Tétreault, M.A. (1995) *The Kuwait Petroleum Corporation and the Economics of the New World Order*, Westport, CN: Quorum Books.

Tétreault, M.A. (2000) *Stories of Democracy: Politics and Society in Contemporary Kuwait*, New York: Columbia University Press.

United Nations Security Council (1984) Resolution 552, 1 June.

Section III

Labor constraints and migration issues

7 Dependence, disdain, and distance

State, labor, and citizenship in the Arab Gulf states

Gwenn Okruhlik

Political elites and private financiers seem to have unbridled optimism about the progressive nature of globalization in the Arab Gulf. Entire new cities are under construction, each devoted to an endeavor such as medicine, technology, science, education, or petrochemicals. In Bahrain, Kuwait, Oman, Qatar, Saudi Arabia, and the UAE, the value of infrastructural projects planned or currently underway totals around $2.1 trillion dollars (Kuwait National Bank 2009) and, by the decade's end, they may reflect up to $3 trillion in investment (de Boer and Turner 2007). With thousands of cranes dotting the landscape, the frenzied pace of construction is reminiscent of the 1970s. The current meta-construction and industrialization is thus sometimes referred to as Boom #2.[1]

This chapter is about state, labor, and cultural identity in the midst of such developments. I focus on the sociopolitical meaning and the implications of the ways in which foreign labor is treated. This matters in all of the Gulf Cooperation Council (GCC) states because foreign labor constitutes the vast majority of the private sector labor force and a substantial proportion of the overall population, sometimes even comprising the majority of residents. Foreign workers are essential to the success of the industrialization projects now underway in the Peninsula. They are the backbone of the dizzying infrastructural boom; without them, it would collapse. Yet the state uses an extensive system of sponsorship and oversight to deny these workers basic rights and protection and to marginalize them from civil associations. Sponsorship also allows the state to protect its capacity to control and deport significant portions of the labor force. Labor migration rarely leads to naturalization or permanent settlement, no matter how long a worker has lived in a country or how much he/she has contributed. They are truly "excluded essentials" (Okruhlik 1999).

Theoretical bridges: citizenship, foreign labor, and new spaces

It is analytically fruitful to look at new globalized spaces such as economic cities, Free Trade Zones, and construction sites in the Arab Gulf where the labor force is structurally disadvantaged, expatriate, and essential to the success of those very endeavors. Questions about the integration or distancing of foreign labor are especially provocative in these new spaces because local populations and governments are still struggling with the substance of rights of national citizenship in a territorial state even as new globalized spaces and actors are evolving beyond it. The distinctions accorded to foreign labor tell us something about the contours of citizenship and belonging to a community. While the oil states are integrated into the global capitalist economy through oil and labor, they remain internally fragile in many ways.

I demonstrate how overwhelming dependence on foreign labor fosters layers of confrontations and multiple modes of distancing. In a larger sense, the way in which foreign labor is treated is intimately related internally to ideas about gender and ethnicity and externally to global markets. An analytical focus on foreign labor can ultimately build bridges between debates about citizenship and the growing research on new, globalized spaces of contestation. One could connect the rich work of, on the one hand, Nils Butcheson, Uri Davis, and Manuel Hassassian, Suad Joseph, Yasmin Soysal, and David Jacobsen and, on the other hand, Saskia Sassen, Arang Keshavarzian, and Waleed Hazbun.

Citizenship anywhere is multidimensional. It provides membership in a community, empowerment, privilege, and rights, but for those excluded, it is a catalyst for subordination, vulnerability, and marginality. This is especially marked in the GCC states that have dual dependency on income derived from oil and on an expatriate labor force.

During the first oil boom, millions of foreign laborers inundated the GCC seemingly overnight before the territorial national state and its attendant ideas of citizenship were consolidated. There was not yet deep coherence or political meaning to being Emirati or Saudi or Qatari. Yet, the bureaucratic apparatus of the state mushroomed in a rapid and massive transformation in order to distribute the windfall profits of oil. Ideas of "being local" were primarily codified using a negative referent. It was a way to differentiate locals from whom they were not, namely waves of foreign workers. Citizenship was defined largely in terms of social privilege (familial status, behavior, community) and economic privilege (access to the welfare benefits of the state). Political rights were incorporated, to greater and mostly lesser degrees, only much later.

Foreign workers were largely excluded from all of these rights. Over time, the state codified, legalized, and institutionalized physical segregation, labor exploitation, and socioeconomic inequality. Unskilled workers from the developing world suffer disproportionately. Indeed, the most salient identity in the Peninsula is simply whether one is a local citizen or a foreign laborer. This has long inhibited organization along class lines. Identity based on class is relatively recent; the state was long able to effectively substitute the local-foreign cleavage for the more problematic class cleavage that would otherwise develop, thus avoiding the emergence of a sizeable, local, and organized underclass.

The demographics of confrontation and distance

Both confrontation and distance are related to the confluence of hyper-investment, inflation, and dependence. I briefly contextualize labor politics in population demographics because it is the larger demographic context that makes foreign labor a politically salient issue. To greater and lesser degrees, these countries share a difficult, if not paradoxical, situation: local unemployment, limits on women's full participation in the economy, and dependence on foreign labor. Gender, class, ethnicity, and citizenship intersect in especially provocative ways.

As a percentage of the total population of a GCC country, foreign workers range from a low of 19 percent in Oman to a high of roughly 85 percent of residents in the UAE and Qatar. There are almost 14 million foreign workers in the GCC; they constitute 33.7 percent of the combined population of 41.5 million and the vast majority of the workforce.[2]

The problems that unskilled foreign laborers encounter in the Peninsula are well known. These include exorbitant fees charged by recruitment middlemen, bait-and-switch schemes once in the host country (i.e., contract substitution), inability to change jobs or to return home, lack of payment, restrictions on physical mobility, intimidation and violence, inadequate housing and health care, long hours, rape, and isolation. Domestic and rural workers are the most vulnerable. There is little procedural redress for worker grievances, and they remain at the mercy of their sponsors. In many cases, conditions are perilously close to indentured servitude. In the end, the treatment of migrant workers is the underbelly of globalization.

Table 7.1 The demographic context of labor politics in the GCC

	Bahrain	Kuwait	Oman	Qatar	Saudi Arabia	UAE
Total population	1,046,814 2008 est.	3,399,637 2008 est.	3.2m	1,448,446 2008 est.	28m 2008	4.4m 2007
Nonnationals	517,368	2.34m	618,500[a]	~1,231,179	5.6m	~3,630,000
% Population that is foreign	49.4%	68.8%	19.3%	85%	20%	80–85%
Total labor force	352,000 2006 est.	2.093m 2007 est.	920,000	508,000 2006	6.49m	2.968m 2006
% of Labor force that is foreign[b]	44%	80%	~67%[c]	90%	71%	93%

Source: U.S. Department of State Background notes accessed on December 14, 2009. NB: These data are provided to discern general patterns only. Specific data vary by source. For example, the World Bank, the CIA World Factbook, the United Nations Human Development Reports, the Gulf Investment Corporation and the Ministries of the GCC countries provide quite different data.

Notes
a The same report provides two figures for the number of nonnationals in Oman (660,000 and 577,000). I use the average of the two.
b It is important to note that the State Department reports do not distinguish between public and private sectors. The percentage of foreigners in the private sector is always higher than in the public sector.
c The report did not provide the percentage of the labor force that is foreign. This figure may contain some dependents of foreign laborers.

Furthermore, the massive development now underway is coupled with a seemingly out of control inflationary spiral. Official inflation rates range from a low of 7 percent in Bahrain to highs of 20 percent in the UAE and 15.1 percent in Qatar (CIA World Factbook 2008 est.). Such rates are 19- and 27-year highs for inflation. Unofficial estimates are markedly higher. Still, it is "perceived inflation" that matters politically. Perceived inflation refers to the cost of daily basics, such as food and rent, and it reflects how much harder people think it is to get by on a daily basis. Perceived inflation is 22 percent in the UAE.

Governments have responded with a variety of measures to blunt the impact of inflation. State policies differentiate between public and private sector employees and between local and foreign workers (in implementation, if not in the text). Measures include, for example, freezes on rents, cuts in tariffs, and significant salary increases for public sector workers. In 2008, the UAE raised public sector salaries by 70 percent, and Oman raised them by 43 percent (Worth 2008). This is important to note because most foreign labor is employed in the private sector, and hence it remains untouched by such relief measures.

Another problem is that inflation is coupled with new taxes (indirect and direct) to fund the infrastructural development. Foreign workers are pinched by this dual hit without a corresponding pay raise. Health care services that were free now come at a price to the foreign worker. Some states instituted a road congestion charge. There are high utility bills (electricity, water, and sewage), entertainment taxes, and a municipality tax. The GCC is considering a sales tax.

The Gulf may simply not be as lucrative a workplace for foreigners as it was previously. The reality today is that the decline of the dollar makes labor migration less attractive (*Bahrain Tribune* 2008; Cummins 2007). The workers are paid in currencies that are pegged to the dollar, and the value of their salaries—translated into Indian rupees, for example—has dropped significantly. The wage differential between home and host country is shrinking. Thus, it is simply less cost-effective to work in the Gulf, and this may prompt an exodus of the very expatriates who are necessary to the construction and industrialization boom. Indians in particular are returning home to their own thriving economy. In sum, the confluence of a weak dollar, surging inflation, new indirect taxes, and booming home economies means it is not worth staying in difficult conditions.

Layers of confrontation

My first argument is about confrontation. Different actors in the Gulf have long used foreign labor to postpone painful domestic confrontations. For the past 40 years, states studiously avoided a confrontation with the private sector over the hiring of more expensive national labor. Such a confrontation would lead to sticky political issues that princes would prefer to avoid, such as accountability, regularity, predictably, and the rule of law. So, the state turned a blind eye to the transgressions of the private sector, which registered ghost companies to obtain extra worker visas and then used the foreign workers in their real companies instead of hiring more expensive locals.

The Gulf private sector, in turn, allowed others to fight the really complicated political battles. On the one hand, World Trade Organization (WTO) negotiators pressed the hard economic and financial issues, such as the stock market, transparency, and investments. On the other hand, Islamists and other social forces pressed the messy political issues, such as corruption, royal land grabs, and deviation. In the meantime, entrepreneurs avoided their *own* messy issues, such as hiring locals or establishing labor standards. Essentially, the private sector was a "free-rider" and avoided confrontation with the state. Likewise, labor exporters to the oil countries, both Arab and Asian, used migration as a means to avoid the implementation of serious and painful political and economic reforms at home, effectively buying time by sending their workers abroad. This collusion worked well for everybody, except, of course, for millions of foreign workers and for citizens who wanted more accountable governance.

Though states and private sectors have studiously avoided confrontation for self-serving reasons, a series of impending confrontations—both brewing and overt—have recently been propelled to the front burner. The terms of the old bargain have shifted in light of dependence, inflation, and hyper-building. These include confrontations among:

- *Local recruiters and foreign embassies that try to protect their nationals abroad.* Sri Lanka instituted a mandatory health insurance scheme in 2003 for its workers in the GCC that requires Gulf employers to obtain the policy before submission of any contract to the Sri Lankan Embassy (Rizvi 2003). Indian policy seeks higher wages abroad for its nationals, and the ambassador to Bahrain said that no Indian would be permitted to leave India for less than $265/month (in Fadhel 2008). Several countries seek especially to protect their citizens who work as domestic servants in the Gulf. A Gulf recruitment agent said, "The new rules of embassies are affecting our businesses, imposing minimum wages and costly paperwork [for us]" (*Khaleej Times* 2008).
- *Retailers, suppliers, importers, and ministries over pocketed subsidies.* This may be illustrated by an occurrence in Saudi Arabia. In light of high inflation, King Abdullah gave an order to subsidize the cost of baby milk. After several months, however, the price of milk on the store shelves remained unchanged, with no trickle down to the consumer, who continued to pay the same inflated price for an essential product. Someone in the supply chain apparently pocketed the subsidy. A blame game ensued, as there is no accountability about who flagrantly ignored the king's order.
- *Contractors and real estate developers over diminishing profit margins.* They will butt heads over profit if the workers get the basic raises they now demand, which would increase construction costs. Contractors will try to shrug off their higher costs to developers. This is notable in the UAE.
- *Individual states, the GCC, and the private sector over new policies.* In 2006 the GCC Labor Ministers jointly recommended a limitation of six years of uninterrupted residency for any foreign worker, tougher recruitment

conditions, the deportation of surplus labor, and visa permits that are more difficult to obtain. However, the maximum stay limitation was sidelined, apparently very late in the process, due to intense private sector pressure. A Labor Minister singled out the Gulf commercial lobby and, specifically, the Riyadh Chamber of Commerce for the failure to impose the residency limit. For its part, the Chamber insisted that the workers were needed indefinitely to fulfill the states' development plans. Of course, all of this begs the question of failed localization efforts.

- *Corporations over interstate poaching for highly skilled workers.* Gulf corporations can no longer recruit highly skilled Asian workers as easily as before, so they now actively poach foreign workers such as engineers and technicians, especially in oil, gas, and petrochemicals, from Saudi Arabia. Reports describe Gulf corporate representatives meeting with already employed, highly skilled workers in five star hotel lobbies in Saudi Arabia, during which the representatives offer the workers higher wages, perks, and better living conditions if they switch employers (Avancena 2008). Whether called pirating, poaching, competition, or sabotage, the workers recruited from Saudi Arabia go directly to a new position without going home to get visas. This intra-Gulf confrontation is new.
- *Global imperatives and protection of local jurisdiction.* By virtue of their commodity, the oil countries are active participants in the global capitalist economy. They are also intensely protective of their domestic jurisdiction, signing on to international conventions with multiple reservations and exceptions about applicability and enforcement. The tensions between global economic and rights imperatives, on the one hand, and national sovereignty, on the other, will continue to play out in the treatment of foreign labor. For example, a Saudi Arabian official said in 2001 that it would dismantle the sponsorship system as part of joining the WTO. Years later, and after becoming a member in 2005, it has not.
- *Foreign laborers and Gulf employers.* Foreign workers are increasingly assertive.[3] Below are some prominent recent examples of worker strikes in the Arab Gulf; far more go unreported.

Bahrain

In July 2007, workers at Batelco, the principal telecommunications company of Bahrain, engaged in a work slowdown to protest the firing of two union organizers. Though Labor Minister al-Alawi said the firings were unjustified, the workers have not been reinstated.

In February 2008, about 1,300 mostly Indian migrant workers who were building a luxury coastal development, the Durrat Al Bahrain, demanded higher wages by walking off the development. Economist Khalid Abdullah explained that the strike shakes their image as compliant workers. "In the past they were obedient because their remittances were sizable. The slump in the value of the dollar has eroded their purchasing power and they are feeling the pinch" (in Fadhel 2008).

Kuwait

In April 2005, Bangladeshis stormed their embassy in Kuwait to call attention to local work conditions, which they called "slave-like." In July 2008, more than 200 Bangladeshi workers, mostly cleaners and rubbish workers, were deported following a major demonstration outside Kuwait City that turned violent. They returned to Dhaka with harrowing descriptions of their ordeal. The Kuwaiti government is said to have acknowledged that the abuses by employers were responsible for the strike in the first place (*BBC News* 2008). Ongoing strikes by Filipino nurses in Kuwait over their work conditions have also occurred.

Qatar

In 2005, workers walked out of their jobs because they were not being paid. In 2007, foreign workers staged at least 10 strikes to seek redress and better conditions. In most of the instances, the strike organizers were summarily deported. Immediate deportation indicates the power of the sponsorship system. In October 2007, there were also reports of 200 Asian workers stranded with no water, food, or electricity. Fellow expatriates tried to care for them with their own meager resources (Bibbo 2007).

Saudi Arabia

In early 2009, 200 construction workers from the Sichuan province of China protested that they were paid far less than the promised wages. Twenty-three workers were arrested and were later deported. The arrests only came to light after several workers sent text messages about the incident to their families in China. An official at the Chinese Embassy in Riyadh said that Saudi authorities prevented the media from reporting the incident due to fears of damaged relations with Beijing (*BBC News* 2009). This is indicative of the international diplomatic dimensions of foreign labor.

The UAE

The UAE is the site of the most intense construction projects, and it has, by far, the most reported strikes. At the end of 2007, the U.S. State Department reported that in that year alone approximately 67,000 foreign workers participated in 30 strikes in the Emirates (in Habib 2007). The issues at stake are usually unpaid wages and hazardous or abusive working conditions.

In September 2005, about 1,000 workers walked off the Palm Jumeirah Project to protest that they were not being paid (*Arabic News* 2005). The artificial islands that together create the shape of a trunk and fronds of a giant palm tree are a public symbol of the glory and tragedy of globalization and labor, not to mention the destruction of the coral reefs on which they were built.

In March 2006, between 2,500 and 3,000 construction workers walked off the job, blocked traffic, and smashed parked cars near the construction site of the Burj Dubai, now the tallest building in the world. The occurrence was described as a riot or a rampage, and *Gulf News* reported that the men were angry that they were not paid for the two and a half hours per day that they spent on buses to and from work. It also took them over an hour each day to punch the time clock because only nine machines were available for 3,000 workers. Further, their wages were low: laborers earned $4/day, while skilled carpenters earned $7.60/day. They also wanted improved medical care and better treatment from their foremen (March 2006 reports from *BBC News*, the *Guardian, Gulf News* in Henderson, and the *New York Times*).

In July 2006, the government ended a four-day strike at a gas processing plant by sending in the armed forces. In August of that year, 500 foreign construction workers sought to protest their wages. Twenty-four men were deported for the attempt to strike. Also in August, 600 workers walked off the job to protest high deductions from their salaries to cover food allowances. Two months later, when workers protested at Dubai's Jebel Ali Industrial Zone, the Ministry of Labor cancelled their visas, and they received a lifetime ban from working in the country.

In October and November of 2007, huge protests at a labor camp in Jebel Ali and at a construction site in the Al Qusais residential neighborhood took place. Workers demanded better pay, housing, and transportation. They threw stones at riot police and damaged police cars. A police spokesman said 4,000 workers were temporarily detained.

Also in November 2007, workers went on strike to demand higher wages from Arabtec Holding, a contractor building a hotel on the Burj Dubai site. Arabtec paid skilled workers about $163/month and unskilled workers about $109/month. Multiple reports state that between 30,000 and 40,000 foreign employees protested unlivable wages for 10 days. More than 200 individuals were deported. Arabtec had been hired by Emaar Properties, the largest real estate company in the Middle East. Emaar, of which Dubai's ruling family owns 30 percent, denied any such strike.

Cultural threat, national identity, and distance

My second argument is about distance. Foreign nationals may be incorporated into the economic organization of the Gulf states, albeit in a subordinate position, but they are largely excluded from social and organizational structures. Dependence on the other for one's own prosperity plays out in interesting ways in the Gulf.

In her explanation of the sponsorship system *(kafalah)*, Anh Nga Longva explains the sense of external threat felt by Kuwaitis, calling it "besieged empowerment" (Longva 2005: 125). Since the 1970s, the number of foreign workers has been consistently higher than that of the local population. A minority in their own country, Kuwaitis live with a feeling of being permanently under siege, not vis-à-vis political power, social prestige, or business, but in what is called "cultural integrity." This threat coexists with an experience of control over subordinate groups, resulting in a dual process of vulnerability and empowerment. In addition, Paul Dresch, writing about marriage debates in the UAE, discusses how Emiratis complain that their culture is being swamped by foreigners (Dresch 2005: 140). A salient urban myth, for example, claims that local children are growing up speaking Tagalog or Tamil, not Arabic. Similar conversations occur in Saudi Arabia.

Fears of being swamped or threatened by outsiders are no longer just articulated by private individuals or only at social and familial gatherings. In recent years, it is ministers of state, usually Ministers of Labor, who publicly express such fears and vulnerabilities. These comments sometimes border on the alarmist.

The UAE has articulated a "cultural diversity policy" derived from a fear of reliance on a single nationality. Proposed residency limits apply only to non-skilled workers rather than teachers, lawyers, and accountants. The Labor Minister, Ali al-Kaabi, said, "[The GCC states] have agreed that Asian workers are contracted workers, not what some call immigrant workers" (in Janardan 2006). The states thus emphasize that most expatriate workers are strictly temporary, with not even an imagined possibility of naturalization over time. Al-Kaabi explained, "We want to protect the minority - which is us" (in DeParle 2007).

Bahrain's Labor Minister, Majid al-Alawi, has also been outspoken. He said in an interview,

> The majority of foreign manpower in the region comes from different cultural and social backgrounds that cannot assimilate or adapt to the local cultures. In some areas of the Gulf, you can't tell whether you are in an Arab Muslim country or in an Asian district. We can't call this diversity and no nation on earth could accept the erosion of its culture on its own land.
>
> (al-Alawi 2007)

Al-Alawi expressed the fear that expatriate workers are eroding "the national character of states in the Gulf." In an interview with *Asharq Al Awsat*, the Minister went so far as to speak of an "Asian tsunami," and urged Gulf governments to watch out for it. Foreign workers, he continued, represent "a danger worse than the atomic bomb or an Israeli attack.... I am not exaggerating that the number [of foreign workers] will reach almost 30 million in 10 years from now" (al-Alawi 2008).

Finally, in Saudi Arabia, Labor Minister Ghazi al-Ghosaibi warns there could be international pressure to force the states in the Gulf to grant foreign workers a political voice. He told the economic daily *Al Eqtisadiah* that "we do not want the day to come when we are forced to allow the [foreign] workers to be represented in our parliaments or municipal councils" (al-Ghosaibi 2008). He also expressed fears that expatriates in the GCC will themselves demand political rights.

A political analyst of the GCC, Ayed al-Manna, confirmed that "there is certainly a concern in the GCC states that they may be forced to accept something they don't want.... like granting more rights or maybe citizenship to migrant workers" (al-Manna 2008). Today, there are research surveys that tap into the unease locals feel; scholarly forums on threats to national identity; and programs in educational institutions and the media designed to heighten one's national and cultural identity (Toumi 2009).

Multiple modes of distancing

The way this perceived threat plays out for foreign workers is through multiple modes of distancing. Rogers Brubaker, writing about migration writ large, suggests that a significant trend in coming decades will be the strengthening of internal controls in order for states to maintain relatively free entry into their territory, while at the same time limiting access to their settlement institutions. Indeed, in recent years, an increase in the regulations that constrain foreigners and, more interestingly, a change in the content of such regulations have been seen in the Gulf.

I note seven modes of distancing enforced by the state or employers. Segmentation and differentiation are becoming more rigid, rather than less rigid as some globalization literature suggests. Economic and legal distinctions between groups are heightened by physical and social space.

- *Social Distance*. Marriage to foreign men has always been curtailed, as citizenship passes through the patrilineal line. The countries have also imposed tighter regulations on marriage to foreign women. An individual must seek the written permission of the state, usually from the Ministry of the Interior, to marry a foreign woman, and such permission is less and less forthcoming. Some states have introduced outright prohibitions on such marriages. Saudi Arabia, Qatar, and Oman all have laws that stringently regulate this.
- *Costume Distance*. Foreign workers are discouraged from donning the national dress. For example, the UAE considered a law that would prohibit a foreigner from wearing the *kandura* or *dishdasha*, the long white kaftan that is the daily dress for all Emirati men. Such innovations can only serve to heighten the distance between locals and foreigners.
- *Gendered Distance*. There are restrictions on jobs foreigners can hold. Specifically, Saudi Arabia announced in 2002 that foreign men are not allowed to work in jewelry shops or gold markets or as lingerie retailers or tailors—all jobs traditionally filled by foreign male labor. These restrictions are not intended to help Saudiize the private sector, as would be expected, but to distance foreign men from local women. Certainly, Saudi men are not allowed to fill these positions, as all of these targeted activities cater to a female clientele.
- *Spatial Distance*. Housing compounds provide physical distance between nationals and expatriates. Compounds are self-contained units that, by and large, workers rarely leave except to travel to their jobs.[4] Reports exist of construction workers living in a camp in Qatar's large industrial area who do not even know the names of their employers or the companies for which

they work. They only know that a bus picks them up every morning to take them to a mega construction site and brings them back to the labor camp at night (Bibbo 2007).

Recent international attention has been directed toward a massive worker slum located between the emirates of Dubai and Sharjah (reports by Ellis 2008; DeParle 2007; Dagher 2006). Called Sonapur, or "the golden place" in Hindi, it houses a minimum of 150,000 foreign laborers who are mostly illiterate and impoverished South Asian villagers. Some estimates are far higher. The compound is described as a sand-swept plain of four-story dormitories as far as the eye can see. Open sewers weave through sand and gravel streets. Small stores sell ghee, naan, and curry. Company buses shuttle the workers to Dubai's faraway building sites, where they earn $8/day.

There are new and better worker compounds called Residential Cities, such as the Abu Dhabi Model City. Such compounds are a positive development in that they must maintain certain standards and housing conditions. Nevertheless, even model compounds still physically separate the majority of the population from the urban environment in which they make a life, often for many years, and from the people for whom they work.

- *Financial and Legal Distance.* Foreign workers are distanced through wage scales, as expatriate salaries are notably lower. Along these lines—and as mentioned above—they are distanced by recent state efforts to blunt the impact of inflation by instituting salary increases for public sector workers, who are overwhelmingly local.

  Parallel sets of laws are also being enacted, some for Western, wealthy, and skilled expatriates, and others for poor Asian migrants. This demonstrates the codification of stratification, not only between foreign and local, but among foreigners. Such laws are an expression of nationals' variable perceptions of cultural and class threat, depending on worker nationality. For example, a foreigner can obtain a residency permit to retire in Bahrain if he has worked in the GCC for 15 years and if he owns a home worth around $130,000 or has investments worth around $260,000. This is a narrow pool of the foreign worker population.

  Further, while naturalization for foreign workers has been introduced, the requirements are so onerous that they cannot be met except by the most highly skilled foreigners. For example, Saudi Arabia announced in 2004 that foreigners could apply to become naturalized citizens of the country. At first, there were long lines of workers waiting for this opportunity. But then the requirements were made clear. Applicants need to be Muslim, have a 10-year residency in the country, be fluent in both spoken and written Arabic, and have an advanced degree in the field of science, medicine, or engineering. Other countries are also considering such a "loosening" of naturalization. Expatriates who meet such qualifications do not appear to constitute a threat to cultural integrity, as do unskilled laborers.

- *Institutional Distance.* In the booming states of the Arab Gulf, some nascent forms of unions or worker associations are allowed, but strict lines of demarcation are constructed between foreign and local workers within them.[5] Hence the overall effect is that labor is not represented in the labor associations.

Kuwait

Workers are permitted to join unions, but less than 5 percent of the labor force belongs. All must be affiliated with the Kuwait Trade Union Federation, whose budget is 90 percent subsidized by the government. The government inspects financial records of the unions and monitors all activities. Citizen workers benefit from the unions, though foreign workers continue to face restrictions on their participation. Foreign workers must reside in Kuwait five years before they can join. Even then, they are not allowed to vote in elections or hold official positions. The law also requires that any new union include at least 100 workers, of whom 15 must be citizens. This discourages union formation in construction and much of the private sector. Domestics, who are fully one-third of the foreign workforce, are explicitly prohibited from joining.

Qatar

The law allows workers to associate, but in practice makes it difficult. Foreign workers are prohibited from forming worker committees; they can only be members of something called "joint labor-management committees," in which they must serve with management. In reality, no worker committees, joint labor management committees, or even a single labor union exists.

Saudi Arabia

Workers, whether foreign or national, have no right to strike, to join unions, or to collectively bargain. In 2002, the Ministry of Labor and Social Affairs did approve *citizen only* worker committees, albeit with severe restrictions. For example, minutes of worker committee meetings must be given to the employer. As always, the most vulnerable workers are those completely excluded from any labor law—domestic workers, farmers, herdsmen, and workers in family-operated businesses. Foreign workers comprise 88 percent of Saudi Arabia's private sector labor force (U.S. Department of State Country Reports 2007).

UAE

The 1980 Labor Law does not explicitly permit or prohibit unions, strikes, or disruptions. In the past, such things were dealt with by swift deportation. Even if unions did exist, and none did in 2007, they would be subject to general restrictions on the right of association. The law gives the employer the right to fire an employee for striking. It also allows some "professional associations," but they are comprised of mostly citizen workers. While foreign workers may "join" them, they are denied all voting rights and are not allowed to sit on the board. In March 2007, the Ministry of Labor instituted stern measures against workers who instigate strikes, including the cancellation of labor cards, end of service benefits, and permanent work bans.

The final two cases do not appear to differentiate explicitly between national and foreign labor.

Bahrain

Workers in non-vital sectors are permitted to form and join unions. Bahrain has allowed migrant workers to join trade unions and vote since 2002, when it established a trade union law. Public sector unions are not allowed. As an example of collective bargaining, in early 2008, unskilled labor demanded a salary raise from $151 to $265 a month, and skilled labor demanded a raise from $183 to $319 a month. Their representatives informed the federation of labor unions that the workers accepted a basic raise of $40 (Fadhel 2008). So, while there is not explicit protection for foreign workers, there is at least a process available. In that way, Bahrain appears to discriminate less than its neighbors.

Oman

In November 2006, the state approved collective bargaining between labor unions and employees or between union representatives and the general federation of laborers. It allows workers the right to peacefully strike for the purpose of improving work conditions, but it also requires a three-week prior notice in writing to the employer that states the employee's intention to go on strike. The strike period is leave without pay, and the employer is given the right to partially or completely close down the establishment to defend his interests, also with a three-week notice. There is a certain irony in this.

The trend in Qatar, Kuwait, Saudi Arabia, and the UAE is important. These states are approving "labor unions" and "worker committees" in order to meet the standards of the International Labor Organization. The stickler is that the vast majority of their labor force is not represented in the new worker organizations.

Beginning reform and protection

There is much that can be done to protect foreign laborers, including international exposure from the media (e.g., *Al Jazeera*, YouTube, Human Rights Watch); the public "naming and shaming" of companies and families that violate labor standards[6]; and the inclusion of domestics and rural workers in labor laws. Transnational forums, such as the GCC Common Market, may provide an opportunity to codify and enforce common standards to govern the conditions of foreign labor. Protection of foreign laborers also means recognition that the problems extend far beyond the Arab Gulf private sector. Foreign companies doing business in the Gulf and making a healthy profit are also complicit in this problem.

By far, the most immediate way to effect change is by reforming the system of oversight and sponsorship of foreign workers. The current system leaves workers at the mercy of their employers, who control, among other essentials, their paychecks and passports.[7] Workers have no viable grievance procedure and no protection. The International Labour Organization mandated that the sponsorship system in the GCC be scrapped by June 2008.

Bahrain, for its part, has made laudable efforts to begin to reform sponsorship. To his credit, the Labor Minister said that "...the sponsorship system...does not much differ from slavery" (al-Alawi, 2009). Al-Alawi also announced that the government would assume sole responsibility for issuing work permits on 1 August 2009, effectively transferring authority from the employer to the state. Thus far, however, business interests have effectively lobbied against implementation of the reform, saying that it would hurt the economy and disrupt social agreements and that it is merely a ploy to satisfy international pressure. Foreign workers do now have the right to change jobs without letters of permission from their employer.

Kuwait's Labor Minister, Mohammad al-Afasi, quickly announced that Kuwait too would reform sponsorship, saying, "The Ministry plans to scrap the sponsorship system for certain categories of expatriates provided they have a clean security record for two years of residency" (al-Afasi 2009). Importantly, he did not specify which expatriate groups. At this early stage, the reform appears to apply to owners of commercial companies and foreign partners who own 49 percent of the company. It is unclear if the bulk of the labor force will be affected.

Qatar has made no commitment regarding reform, but has said it is monitoring developments and that employers can no longer hold workers' passports. While this is significant, permit and sponsorship rules remain almost unchanged from 45 years ago (Pandit and Salem 2009).

Saudi Arabia has no plans to modify the sponsorship system per se. Rather, the government is putting together proposals that change how unskilled foreign workers are recruited and trained; it will likely transfer that authority to privately run recruiting companies, and employers will remain the sponsors of their laborers (Murphy 2009).

Neither Oman nor the UAE have explicitly addressed the sponsorship issue.

Let us be clear about this debate. When people talk about "scrapping the sponsorship system" or "abolishing the sponsorship system," they are not advocating the free flow of labor across borders. The debate is not about a loss of control over foreigners. Rather, the debate is about who will control foreigners—the state, individual employers, or private agencies.

Conclusions: foreign labor in the shadows of citizenship

Globalization is not producing homogenization or McDonaldization in the Arab Gulf, but new expressions of distinction. These are somewhat informed by a correlation between population ratios and distance. Distinctions are striking in the UAE, where foreigners are a higher percentage of the total population, whereas in Oman, where foreigners are a lower percentage of the total population, distancing appears less.

Globalization and membership in the WTO have certainly not led to more political freedom, protection, or opening from the oil states of the Arabian Peninsula. If anything, segregation, exploitation, and inequality have grown more pronounced. Through constructions of citizenship, oil states have variously deprived the unskilled labor force on which they depend of social status, economic benefits, adequate housing and health care, legal protection, and mobility. Were it not for the voices of a few, the plight of millions of foreign laborers would go unnoticed. It is, as a Bahraini sociologist noted, "the other Gulf Syndrome" (Khalaf 2002).

In conclusion, a focus on labor yields a rich research agenda. Foreign labor provides a window from which to evaluate the bargaining power of states as they attempt to control borders and postpone confrontations with the private sector. It also highlights the potential limitations of states, especially when foreign laborers constitute a majority or significant minority of a state's population. In addition, questions about the integration or distancing of foreign labor are especially provocative in the new spaces of globalization such as the Free Trade Zones, in the burgeoning industrial and economic "new cities," and in service hubs. Scholars can also systematize the novel ways in which class consciousness develops, congeals, and manifests itself, or alternatively, is squashed or co-opted.

Further, labor migrants are symbolic markers of even larger issues. The way in which foreign laborers are treated tells us something about being and belonging. It provides a window to perceptions of cultural security, and it is central in demonstrating linkages between citizenship, gender, and ethnicity. Above all, a focus on foreign labor tells us about the human condition.

Notes

1 There are, however, important distinctions. In a general sense, Boom #1 was an effort to take advantage of oil and to circulate the influx of revenues. The current boom is generally an effort to prepare for a more diversified economy, less dependent on the simple export of crude oil. The contours of the private sectors are different as well. It remains to be seen how the late-2009 financial crisis in Dubai will affect the pace of infrastructural construction.
2 Another source states that there are 13 million foreign workers in the GCC; they constitute 37 percent of the combined population of 35 million and 70 percent of the workforce (*Agence France-Presse* February 2008).
3 The assertion of labor is interesting when viewed longitudinally. Evidence from my own research demonstrates significant attitudinal changes. In 1989, during my first long-term field research in Saudi Arabia, the level of latent fear and anger among foreign workers was palpable but unspoken. Workers were acquiescent and quiet in their relations with nationals. In later return trips, certainly by 2003 and 2005, I heard workers using sarcasm, derision, and joking when speaking about their national employers

in venues such as shops and cafes. The public strikes by large groups that we witness today are a striking contrast to the recent past.

4 I lived in a compound for foreign workers for about two and a half months in 1989. The compound was unhygienic, isolated, and surrounded by walls topped with barbed wire, with a single entry manned by armed guards. Residents were unable to go anywhere except on compound buses, which go to a set place at a set time and whose drivers confiscated the *igama* (legal residency permit) of the workers until they board the bus to return to the compound. Daily life was fraught with anxiety and vulnerability.

5 Data on the rights of foreign workers to associate, organize, or bargain collectively are taken from the individual Country Reports on Human Rights Practices, U.S. Department of State, Bureau of Democracy, Human Rights and Labor (2007) and from Human Rights Watch reports (2004, 2006).

6 In the UAE, for example, the Ministry of Labor fined a prominent construction company $2 million and froze all new hires because the company violated labor standards.

7 Particularly troubling reports speak about the recruitment of South Asians to work in the Arab Gulf, especially in Kuwait. Upon arrival, and after the customary confiscation of passports, they are instead smuggled to war-torn Baghdad, where they work in squalid and unsafe conditions that include building the massive U.S. Embassy (CorpWatch 2006).

Bibliography

"1,300 Migrant Workers Strike in Bahrain Over Pay" (2008) *Gulf Research Center*, 11 February.

"$30 Billion in Remittance Annually by Foreign Workers in Gulf" (2005) Gulf Regional Economic Section, *Arabic News*, 23 September.

al-Afasi, M. (2009) Interview with the *Saudi Gazette*, "Kuwait Mulls Dropping of Sponsorship System," 9 August.

al-Alawi, M. (2007) Interview with *Gulf News*, posted on *Agence France-Presse*, "Bahrain Presses for Six-Year Residency Cap on Expats," 20 October.

al-Alawi, M. (2008) Interview with *Asharq Al Awsat*, posted on *Agence France-Presse*, "Bahrain Labor Minister Warms of Asian Tsunami," 28 January.

al-Alawi, M. (2009) Quoted in "Sponsorship Scrapped," *Gulf Insider*, July-August.

Avancena, J. (2008) "Skill Poaching," *Saudi Gazette*, 11 February.

"Bahraini Businessmen Await Indian Decision on Minimum Wage" (2008) *Khaleej Times*, 3 March.

al-Baik, D. (2007) "Gulf States Suffer Erosion of Culture," *Gulf News*, 1 October.

"Bangladeshi Workers Return Home" (2008) *BBC News*, 31 July.

Bibbo, B. (2007) "Scores of Workers Left with no Food/Supplies in Qatar," *Gulf News*, 16 October.

de Boer, K. and Turner, J. (2007) *The McKinsey Quarterly*, 31 January.

Brubaker, R. (1991) "International Migration: A Challenge for Humanity," *International Migration Review*, 25 (4): 946–957.

Butcheson, N., Davis, U. and Hassassian, M. (eds.) (2000) *Citizenship and the State in the Middle East: Approaches and Applications,* Syracuse, NY: Syracuse University Press.

CIA World Factbook (2008) Country Studies. Online HTTP: www.cia.gov/library/publications/the-world-factbook (accessed May 23, 2010).

CorpWatch (2006) "U.S. Embassy in Baghdad Built by Trafficked Workers in Squalid Working Conditions," 17 October.

Crystal, J. (1990) *Oil and Politics in the Gulf: Rulers and Merchants in Kuwait and Qatar*, Cambridge, UK: Cambridge University Press.

Cummins, C. (2007) "Falling Dollar, Inflation Feed Dubai Strife," *Wall Street Journal*, 5 November: A8.

Dagher, S. (2006) "Sonapur Camp - Dubai's Dark Side," *Middle East Online*, 12 April.

Davidson, C. (2008) *Dubai: The Vulnerability of Success*, London: Hurst & Co.

DeParle, J. (2007) "Fearful of Foreign Labor, Dubai Eyes Reforms," *New York Times*, 6 August.

Dresch, P. (2005) "Debates on Marriage and Nationality Laws in the United Arab Emirates," in P. Dresch and J. Piscatori (eds.) *Monarchies and Nations: Globalisation and Identity in the Arab States of the Gulf*, New York: I.B. Tauris.

Ellis, E. (2008) "Dubai's Rags to Riches Miracle Built on Toil of Exploited Foreign Workers," 9 February. Online HTTP: www.theage.com.au/business/dubais-ragstoriches-miracle-built-on-the-toil-of-exploited-foreign-workers-20080208-1r4p.html (accessed May 23, 2010).

Fadhel, M. (2008) "Expatriate Workers Strike as Earnings are Hit," *Gulf Times*, 18 February.

Fattah, H. (2006) "In Dubai, an Outcry for Worker Rights, *New York Times*, 26 March.

al-Ghosaibi, G. (2008) Interview with *Al Eqtisadiah*, posted on *Agence France-Presse*, "Saudi Arabia Backs Limit on Foreign Residency," 12 February.

Graz, J.-C. (2001) "Beyond States and Markets: Comparative and Global Political Economy in the Age of Hybrids," *Review of International Political Economy*, 8 (4): 739–748.

"Gulf Inflation to Fall if Dollar Peg is Dropped" (2008) *Reuters*, 26 February.

Habib, M.A. (2007) "Emaar's Alabbar Denies Labor Strike at $1B Burj Dubai," *Zawya Dow Jones*, 12 November.

Hazbun, W. (2004) "Globalisation, Reterritorialisation and the Political Economy of Tourism," *Geopolitics*, 9 (2): 310–341.

Henderson, S. (2006) "High Rises and Low Wages: Expatriate Labor in Gulf Arab States," *PolicyWatch*, 27 March.

Human Rights Watch (2004) *Bad Dreams*, July. Online HTTP: www.hrw.org (accessed May 23, 2010).

Human Rights Watch (2006) *Building Towers, Cheating Workers,* November. Online HTTP: www.hrw.org (accessed May 23, 2010).

Human Rights Watch (2007) *Exported and Exposed*, November. Online HTTP: www.hrw.org (accessed May 23, 2010).

Jacobsen, D. (1996) *Rights Across Borders: Immigration and the Decline of Citizenship,* Baltimore, CO: Johns Hopkins University Press.

Janardan, N. (2006) "Redefining Rules of Engagements for Expats," *The Peninsula*, Gulf Research Center, October.

Joseph, S. (ed.) (2000) *Gender and Citizenship in the Middle East*, Syracuse, NY: Syracuse University Press.

al-Kaabi, A. (2006) "Redefining Rules," in N. Janardan, *The Peninsula*, Gulf Research Center, October.

Keshavarzian, A. (2010) "Geopolitics and the Genealogy of Free Trade Zones in the Persian Gulf," *Geopolitics*, 10 (2): 263–289.

Khalaf, A. (2002) "The Other Gulf Syndrome," *The Daily Star*, 12 March.

Kingdom of Saudi Arabia, Ministry of Labor (2006) *Guidebook for Expatriates Recruited for Work in the KSA*, Second edition. Riyadh, Saudi Arabia.

Kuwait National Bank study reported in "GCC's $2.1tn Worth of Projects Set to Create Job Opportunities" (2009) *Oman Daily Observer*, 10 August.

Longva, A.N. (2005) "Neither Autocracy Nor Democracy but Ethnocracy: Citizens, Expatriates and the Socio-Political System in Kuwait," in P. Dresch and J. Piscatori (eds.) *Monarchies and Nations: Globalisation and Identity in the Arab States of the Gulf*, New York: I.B. Tauris.

al-Manna, A. (2008) Quoted in "Calls Mount for Cap on Expatriates in Gulf," *Saudi Gazette*, 16 February.

McCarthy, R. (2006) "Revolt Stirs as Dubai Aims High," *The Guardian*, 29 March.

"More Dubai Labor Strikes" (2007) *In Pursuit of Justice*, 1 November.

Murphy, C. (2009) "Saudis to Concentrate on Hiring of Laborers," *The National*, 24 May.

Okruhlik, G. (1999) "Excluded Essentials: The Politics of Ethnicity, Oil and Citizenship in Saudi Arabia," in P. Batur-Vanderlippe and J. Feagin (eds.) *The Global Color Line: Racial and Ethnic Inequality and Struggle from a Global Perspective*," Stamford, CT: JAI Press.

Ong, A. (2006) *Neoliberalism as Exception: Mutations in Citizenship and Sovereignty*, Durham, NC: Duke University Press.

Pandit, M. and Salem, M. (2009) "Qatar Sponsorship Law Gets Nod," *The Peninsula*, 27 February.

"Qatar Feels Pinch as Expats Leave" (2008) *Bahrain Tribune*, 5 February.

Rizvi, M. (2003) "Compulsory Insurance Scheme for Migrant Sri Lankans," *Khaleej Times*, 30 October.

Russell, S.S. (1989) "Politics and Ideology in Migration Policy Formulation: The Case of Kuwait," *International Migration Review*, 23 (1): 24–47.

Sassen, S. (2002) "The Repositioning of Citizenship: Emergent Subjects and Spaces for Politics," *Berkeley Journal of Sociology*, 46: 4–25.

"Saudi Arabia Backs Limit on Foreign Residency in Gulf" (2008) *Agence France-Presse*, 12 February.

"Saudis Deport Chinese Laborers" (2009) *BBC News*, 15 January.

Soysal, Y.N. (1994) *The Limits of Citizenship: Migrants and Post-National Membership in Europe*, London: University of Chicago Press Ltd.

Spender, T. (2006) "Sonapur - Home to Dubai's Battery Humans." Online HTTP: http://freelanceontheroad.blogspot.com, 4 April.

"Strike Halts Work at Dubai Tower" (2006) *BBC News*, 23 March.

Toumi, H. (2009) "Scholars Warn of Increasing Threats to Gulf Identity," *Gulf News*, 17 April.

United States Department of State (2007) Country Reports on Human Rights Practices. Online. HTTP: www.state.gov/g/drl/rls/hrrpt/2007/ (accessed December 14, 2009).

United States Department of State (2009a) Background Notes. Online HTTP: www.state.gov/r/pa/ei/bgn/> (accessed December 14, 2009).

United States Department of State (2009b) Country Reports on Human Rights Practices. Online HTTP: www.state.gov/g/drl/rls/hrrpt/.

Whitaker, B. (2006) "Riot by Migrant Workers," *The Guardian*, 23 March.

Worth, R. (2008) "Rising Inflation Creates Unease in the Middle East," *New York Times*, 25 February.

8 Great expectations

Western-style education in the Gulf states

Mary Ann Tétreault

Introduction

The 2003 *Arab Human Development Report* (AHDR)[1] singled out educational systems in Arab states for their failure to create the "knowledge societies" necessary for a transition to sustainable development. While this essay concentrates on higher education, the AHDR is unsatisfied with Arab education at every level. Its authors point to the dominant style of child-rearing in the Arab world, which they criticize as both authoritarian and over-protective. Social strictures block the education of women so thoroughly that "high rates of [female] illiteracy persist," and neither state nor private-sector resources are sufficiently channeled into education: "Many children still do not have access to basic education. Higher education is characterized by decreasing enrollment, and public spending on education has actually declined since 1985" (UNDP 2003: 3). The AHDR also criticizes universities in the developing world for deficiencies in their capacity to produce knowledge (AHDR 2003: 35). Its authors look toward the development of institutions that lead to "collective learning" that is useful rather than harmful (AHDR 2003: 36), knowledge that "can contribute to finding solutions to problems affecting society at a particular time" (AHDR 2003: 37).

These criticisms highlight sometimes incompatible images of the university as an institution. If we think of universities as social bodies, we can imagine how they are perceived by their various constituencies. For students and parents the university is a place where students come to learn. It also is a space, perhaps a collection of spaces, where young people discover their capacities to create and perform on a larger stage than family and neighborhood, and form life-long friendships with peers and mentors. Students enter as adolescents, bursting with potential; they depart three or four years later, young adults with the tools they need to embark on their life journeys.

This first image of "bright college days" fits comfortably with a second image viewed from inside the university by faculty and administrators. This second image is an imagined community of learning and knowledge production, where experts make discoveries and develop skills and techniques to exploit these discoveries for the good of society. In this image of the university, students are junior partners—they learn from their teachers how information is produced, organized, and made to yield new information. They contribute as autonomous agents to the accumulation of what is already known and help produce new knowledge. The production of information and new ways to use it are as integral to this vision of the university as transmitting what is already known from one generation to the next. From this perspective, universities are more than mere repositories of knowledge—they are cosmopolitan collections of ateliers where knowledge is transformed by scholarship and skills are honed that enable educated persons to continue to contribute throughout their lives.

The second image is democratic in its emphasis on effort and performance, but everyone who lives and/or works at a university knows that these institutions retain important elements of their medieval past. Alongside their democratic elements, there exist parallel and cross-cutting hierarchies marked by the characteristic patterns of status and deference evident in the larger society. Consequently, the ability of universities to spearhead fundamental social change depends on support and protection from outside.

The third image to consider is how the university is viewed from outside. From this perspective, it should be a producer of respectful citizens and trained workers ready to take their places in modern political economies. Its graduates are expected to be competent and reliable, although perhaps a few exceptional graduates and faculty members will be able to rise in the various hierarchies in which they live and are employed. The third image diverges sharply from the second in its estimation of the university as an institution, because it is not valued for itself but rather for how well it fulfills external expectations and demands. Applied science takes precedence over basic science. Critical thinking is discouraged if it challenges the status quo. Even parents occasionally see universities this way. This is why the real-world fulfillment of most first- and second-image functions of universities depends on their insulation from those who dwell in the land of the third image. "Ivory tower" describes the protected spaces universities are granted in exchange for knowledge, techniques, and workers useful to the governors of the third-image world whose contributions to education include building and protecting those ivory towers.

These three images approximate three sets of expectations about what universities should be and should do. Variations on them exist in every culture that has universities. How and how well an actual university functions in its particular social and political economy depends on the specific content of these images and how they are articulated. Within the same culture, all three images reflect aspects of the local society, from how respect and disapproval are earned and conveyed to the ways the ethnic/national, gender, and class status of persons are expressed and viewed. Consequently, resolution of the educational deficiencies in the Arab world that are highlighted in the AHDR may begin as changes in Arab versions of the second image, but they will succeed or fail depending on how well or poorly they are echoed in Arab behavior in the first and third.[2]

Where we are

In a recent survey of "American-style" higher education in Arab countries, Shafeeq Ghabra and Margreet Arnold concentrate on the second-image university. Their critique highlights deficiencies in indigenous institutions of higher education, comparing "Arabic" colleges and universities to newer schools that apply American practices (Ghabra and Arnold 2007). They also incorporate insights from the histories of a few transplanted universities whose role in the Middle East is fairly venerable—examples include the American University of Beirut (formerly the Syrian Protestant College) and the American University of Cairo. Most transplants are new, however, especially in the Gulf. In between the Abbasid universities, whose glories in their heyday lay mainly in mathematics, science, and engineering (AHDR 2003: 43), and these American(ized) schools, whose specialties vary, are the mostly state-owned and -penetrated institutions whose narrow curricula, institution-centered practices, and focus on job skills have been identified by some as being responsible for lagging intellectual performance in Arab countries (Ghabra and Arnold 2007: 2–3).

The advantages of American-style education for the development of a "knowledge society" are said to rest on four key pillars: open curricula; life-long learning "to develop talent and character through interaction inside and outside the classroom"; making the student the first priority and a partner in education and knowledge-production; and a professional faculty (Ghabra and Arnold 2007: 3). Together, they promote curiosity, questioning, engagement, and activism—a nearly perfect antithesis of what authoritarian governments and social groups would like to see in their universities. Indeed, as Ghabra and Arnold show, even the most "American" of these institutions—the ones with American curricula, English-language education, U.S.-educated faculty, low faculty-to-student ratios, financial support for low-income students, and connections to the local community—are vulnerable to outside intervention that limits their effectiveness. It comes from the state, from powerful social groups and, with respect to private schools, from their owners (Ghabra and Arnold 2007: 4–5). Given the unity of the cultural frame that surrounds all three images of the university in any particular culture, we can observe from national examples how closely these images articulate in practice, and how that articulation assists or impedes national educational systems as they strive to fulfill their various responsibilities.

One example

Both the promise and the problems of American-style institutions are visible in Kuwait where, looking at three universities, we can conclude that the news from the front is mixed. Kuwait University is the state-owned and -run institution; the Gulf Institute for Science and Technology (GUST) is the first privately owned university opened in Kuwait (in 2002); the American University of Kuwait (AUK) is also privately owned and specializes in liberal arts, a rarity in the Arab world (Ghabra and Arnold 2007: 14).

Kuwait University has been plagued by policies oriented more toward satis-fying the demands of citizens and powerful constituency groups than toward producing graduates able to meet national needs for economic and social devel-opment. Islamist value s and goals are reflected in recurrent conflicts over gender issues, from veiling to limiting female enrollment in majors like engineering and medicine (Tétreault 2000: 162–164). University education is widely seen as an entitlement; consequently the best Kuwaiti male students typically study abroad, leaving a far more normal distribution of abilities among female students whose parents prefer that they be educated at home. These young women then have to adjust to the gender demands and expectations of their male peers, most of them poorly prepared and insecure—classmates who see them, quite rightfully, as formidable academic rivals.

Kuwait's private universities started off with an advantage because they opened after United States visa policies had been tightened following 9/11. Muslim men of almost any age and nationality encountered great difficulties getting visas to travel to or study in the United States. Some were denied entry even when they did have visas. One incensed Kuwaiti parent, having been treated harshly by United States immigration officials when he came to visit his eldest son, told me that, although he was allowing that son to continue his education in the United States, the rest of his children would be required to study in Europe or at home. Shafeeq Ghabra, then-president of AUK, said that United States policies were the main reason why the initial cohorts of students accepted at AUK were gender-balanced, producing in that and other ways a student body more similar to what is found in liberal arts institutions in the United States (Ghabra 2004).

The first two Kuwaiti private schools specialize in different areas. GUST was established to offer a high-quality technical education that its founders felt was lacking at Kuwait University (Buhamrah 2004). AUK offers a more rigorous training in liberal arts than was available at Kuwait University, one that empha-sizes critical thinking skills (Ghabra 2004). Both of these attempts to compensate for deficiencies in state-provided education reflect a perceived incompatibility in values and goals between the second and third images of the university in Kuwait.

Yet all universities in Kuwait are equally vulnerable to third-image intrusions. For example, all universities in Kuwait are subject to the state's 1996 gender-segregation law.[3] The law's proponents also hope eventually to increase geo-graphic separation between the sexes in part by instituting sex-limited access to particular majors and campuses. Until recently, however, classes remained integrated in most majors on most Kuwaiti campuses. Segregation was limited to sitting on different sides of classrooms, lecture halls and, at Kuwait University, cafeterias, as well as on the appropriate color-coded benches outside (Ghabra 2007).[4] As law enforcement tightened, however, segregation began to be applied in private schools as well. At first, it was loosely enforced in classrooms (instruc-tors kept duckboard panels that could be placed down the middle of the rooms to divide male and female students when the inspectors came around), but common areas at AUK and GUST remained unsegregated—they were not even color-coded. Because men and women shared classrooms, teachers, and common areas, the quality of the intellectual interchange between them was only marginally affected by the segregation laws.

This situation changed as the result of a January 2008 back-stairs compromise whereby then-Education Minister Nouria al-Subeih agreed to extend and strengthen the enforcement of gender segregation in exchange for enough support to survive a vote of confidence in the parliament. In early February, civil libertarian MP Ali al-Rashed challenged this agreement, submitting a bill to rescind gender segregation in all Kuwaiti universities. The MP received a death threat almost immediately afterward, although most of the people I interviewed in Kuwait later that year thought it was made for effect. Within weeks, however, the rancor among factions in parliament bitterly opposed on this and a number of other issues reached such a height that the government resigned, and the amir dismissed the parliament and called for new elections. Gender segregation in universities was a minor issue at best in the campaign but, regardless, students' first-image experiences of university life have been tarnished by the willingness of third-image dwellers to treat them as instruments rather than as responsible persons with rights of their own. A small group of elite women vowed to campaign for gender integration at private schools, itself a measure of their resignation to what they see as immutable policy for Kuwait University, and there is no evidence that their efforts have had any effect. Even more disquieting, the autonomy of all the second-image communities was jeopardized by the return of an Islamist-tribalist parliamentary majority opposed to the critical thinking and egalitarian principles advocated by the authors of the AHDR.

The struggle to impose repressive gender policies at Kuwaiti universities may well be a last-gasp effort to reverse the most obvious manifestations of modernization, something the transplant universities, with their dedication to the universalist principles and methods able to produce a knowledge society, embody. For example, gender segregation did not stop student activism. Mixed-gender groups composed of students and recent graduates of Kuwait-based universities met in homes to organize events (including field trips abroad) in connection with the student-led movement for electoral reform in 2006 (Anonymous Kuwaiti students 2006). A ready-made and tested-in-the-field cohort of young people, their social networks differed from those of the core group of young reform activists because, unlike the core group, virtually all in this larger group had been or were being educated in Kuwait.[5]

Ghabra and Arnold criticized American-style universities in the Arab world for being detached from their communities (Ghabra and Arnold 2007: 16). In Kuwait, however, the political activity I've described demonstrates the community orientation of university students in public and private schools. The Kuwaiti university group was not formally sponsored by any of their schools, yet their activities depended on access to university-provided virtual space in the form of Wi-Fi and intranet communication (Dollman 2007),[6] primary avenues for the contemporary exchange of ideas (Wheeler 2006). Mobile phones and the Internet were indispensable in the activist campaigns for women's rights before May 2005, and blogs kept Kuwaitis informed about the politics of the amiri transition the following year. The Orange movement that brought down the government a year later organized and ran a series of anti-government demonstrations via text messaging (Tétreault 2006).

Other shortcomings in Kuwaiti transplant universities stem from private ownership and shareholders keen to realize financial returns on their investment. Faculty and staff turnover is high because most university personnel work on short-term contracts. Few resources are devoted to hiring full-time staff, and there are no tenured faculty. A staff employee at one of the Kuwaiti private schools told me that reluctance to increase full-time employment reflected the owners' desire to keep costs low. Yet high turnover and job insecurity limits personal and professional relationships among students and faculty; reduces the quality of mentoring; and impairs institutional stability. At the same time, demands on faculty at these universities are extensive, leaving little time to conduct research. This violates a core value of second-image thinkers. Interestingly, support for faculty research seems to be increasing at Kuwait University where, until very recently, publications in international peer-reviewed journals were regarded as insignificant in faculty evaluation and promotion. Although this attitude has changed, books and monographs are still treated as of little importance (anonymous Kuwait University professors 2005–2006).

In spite of their difficulties, the new universities operating in Kuwait have had notable positive effects. Structurally, they constitute direct competition to Kuwait University. Since plans for the private schools began to take shape, Kuwait University has added facilities, programs, and faculty. Its institutional personality also appears to be moving toward one that is less rigidly hierarchical and more academically demanding. These changes do not appear to have cut into demand for education at the new institutions, however, whose success is attracting more competition inside Kuwait and across the Gulf as a whole. Economics drives some of this—private schools look like good business propositions from the Gulf perspective and to the administrators of foreign university partners (Willoughby 2008). The problem with unregulated competition is that it produces a Hobbesian world that promotes a rush to the bottom. It is here that other Gulf countries may have superior national models to offer.

Another example

"Education City" in Qatar offers degrees in several fields at a range of American-style universities featuring unusually strong linkages between home and host institutions.

> At Education City in Doha . . . [students] can study medicine at Weill Medical College of Cornell University, international affairs at Georgetown, computer science and business at Carnegie Mellon, fine arts at Virginia Commonwealth, engineering at Texas A&M, and soon, journalism at Northwestern.
>
> (Lewin 2008a)

Education City is entirely state-funded, and no expense seems to have been spared to acquire the best facilities, partners, programs, and professional relationships. As the "gold standard" of education in Qatar, students are willing to let their acceptance to one (or more) of the five institutions there determine their field of study, effectively surrendering some authority over their own careers.

> When Dana Hadan was a student at Doha's leading girls' science high school, she wanted to be a doctor and applied to Cornell's medical school. But Cornell rejected her, and her parents did not want her to go to a medical school overseas. So Ms. Hadan enrolled instead in the business program at Carnegie Mellon. Now, as a third-year student, she is happily learning macroeconomics and marketing... She never considered the locally run Qatar University: "I knew I wanted Education City."
>
> (Lewin 2008b)

The esteem with which Education City is regarded comes both from the rigorous admissions standards, faculty policies, curricula, and degree requirements established and demanded by the overseas partners, and from the standards expected by the government paying the bills. As Charles Thorpe, the dean of Carnegie Mellon in Qatar put it, "This *IS* American education" (Lewin 2008b). In contrast, AUK does not apply the same admissions and performance standards that its partner, Dartmouth University, applies at home. Student and faculty exchanges between Salmiyya and Hanover (and even between Kuwait and the United States) are limited. What we don't know is whether this is a problem or just a fact of life: should resources be channeled from other uses to promote student and faculty exchanges, or are AUK students doing just fine without them?

Education City appears to combine the best of both worlds: the deep pockets and long time horizons that only the state can offer, along with a spirit of innovation more often associated with the private sector. But it is too early to assume that superior resources equate to superior results. In fact, the Kuwaiti transplants are nearly as new, while neither country has enough "history" to assess with confidence how well any of these innovative institutions is performing. As transplants continue to pour into the Gulf, however, this seems to be an excellent time to begin gathering the information necessary for a rigorous assessment of their contributions to the creation of the knowledge societies their stakeholders want.

Taking stock

Perhaps the first step in assessment is to acknowledge that the many education stakeholders look at the university from each of the perspectives generating the images I have described. In that light, it seems useful to begin by determining what each constituency in both home and host countries expects from the transplants. Only then can we evaluate how well they are doing.

From the first image, we must determine what students and parents expect. For example, what were Dana Hadan and her parents looking for when they decided that she should study at Carnegie Mellon in Qatar? What other alternatives were considered? How is she doing as a student? After she graduates, what kind of job will she get? Will she be able to marry and juggle home and work as her American counterparts expect to do?

From the second image, it is important to assess the quality of the faculty and the amount of support for faculty development and research that each institution provides. Are faculties multinational? Even if all the faculty in the transplant do not come from the host institution, do they meet the academic and professional standards of that institution? Are they good mentors and colleagues? Do they maintain relationships with Gulf students and peer professionals after they return to their home countries? Do they bring academic recognition to their host institution while they are overseas? Do they give papers, publish, and organize conferences that bring new information, techniques, and other resources to their students, colleagues, and communities?

From the third image, we would like to know how satisfied employers are when they hire new graduates. Do they have the expected skills? Are they energetic, creative, and able to perform well in a variety of situations? What about their attitudes toward the more mundane aspects of work—are they productive, or do they come late and leave early? Perhaps one measure of success could be assessed as employers' increased willingness to hire nationals educated in home-country institutions.

Assessment is a buzzword in the United States, but its ubiquity also reflects a real desire to determine the results of large investments in higher education and, as much as possible, to understand why career and life-trajectory outcomes vary so widely among students whose education is presumed to be similar in content, if not in style. To assess the contributions of transplants in the Gulf countries, it is not enough to examine the students at American-style universities in isolation. Experiences and outcomes should be compared with students from several groups. One useful comparison base would be students who studied abroad in actual American institutions. A second consists in students who studied at home-country state universities. Still another would be graduates of regional private and public institutions. If, as John Willoughby puts it, a thousand educational models are blooming in the Gulf, the reason might well be that "one size" is no more likely to "fit all" in Kuwait or Qatar than it does in Texas or California (Willoughby 2008).

In addition to looking at outcomes, it is also important to consider such things as differences in the characteristics and backgrounds of students and student cohorts who study at home or overseas, their courses of study, and their academic "generations." Academic preparation should be evaluated in terms of the signals prospective university students received from their families and the economy, including their expectations about finding work after graduation and the likelihood that they will lose their jobs if they do not perform well. State support for Kuwaiti students studying abroad was offered only to those majoring in fields that the state decided would be needed by the economy into which they would be graduating. Student assistance was one half of a social contract that also guaranteed a job when the graduate returned home. Students changing their majors found that financial support would be withheld and reclaimed, and that there would not be a job waiting for them.[7]

As I noted earlier, at Kuwait University female students were discouraged from taking majors in medicine and engineering, two fields where demand for well-trained workers is strong. This dominance of the third-image world over first-image choices is organized differently now. Students in private universities—and their parents—are paying in part to be able to make such decisions themselves. Even so, investment in an education that does not result in satisfying work is a questionable use of limited resources, including the life chances of young persons cheated out of their expected adult autonomy.

Transplants and the knowledge society

Some of the allure of transplants comes from their relative freedom from social strictures—girls are welcome; grades do not depend on the status of family or clan; standards of performance emphasize characteristics seen as "modern," perhaps even daring. It is impossible to capture in mere academic prose the heady feelings conveyed by the twenty-somethings of the Orange movement when they toppled a corrupt government and were still hopeful that their actions would succeed in moving their country forward. It is equally difficult to capture what I am sure the amir and his family felt when they realized this movement was not going to go away quietly.[8] But there are other feelings that are even harder to imagine. How do parents feel when their children are criticized for their hard work and the acquisition of skills that are meaningless—even threatening—to family elders and long-time friends?[9] As opportunities for "American" education proliferate in the Gulf, these examples of distances yawning between generations can only increase.

The authors of the AHDR realized that some of the biggest obstacles to developing a knowledge society in the Middle East come from economic poverty and the impoverished spirits of the millions left behind. In poor countries, resources for education come at the expense of very basic services, food, and shelter. But populations in rich countries also may see the allocation of resources as a zero-sum game. They may believe that spending on "elite" education is unfair to them—even if it benefits their children. This is why campaigns to block choice in Kuwaiti higher-education institutions are framed as defenses of religion and tradition. These authorities are the bulwarks of Kuwaiti society. As such, they can become powerful weapons against what their wielders see as the social and moral dangers inherent in foreign-influenced social change.

The capacity of autonomous universities to create knowledge is especially dangerous to such persons. It challenges the permanence of revealed truth while the status accorded to science undermines the domination of hierarchies resting on traditional epistemologies. Perhaps most threatening of all, equal education for women undermines the masculine domination rooted in particular interpretations of religious values (Roy 1994). Transplants that are successful in achieving what their proponents hope they can offer in improved first- and second-image experiences of national universities are likely to attract a backlash from some denizens of the third-image world. As Gulf countries accelerate the transfer of education technology, they will have to take care to assuage the trepidation of individuals and groups who fear that this process will erode cherished values, and take even more care to protect their nation's ivory towers from destruction by the uncompetitive and the envious.

Notes

1 See United Nations Development Programme and the Arab Fund for Economic and Social Development 2003—hereafter AHDR.
2 This model of parallel imaginaries and their interaction within a given society is derived from Wolf 1982: 385–391.
3 Universities were given five years to comply, but the private universities—GUST, which opened in 2002 and AUK, which opened in 2004—made little effort to do so until they were threatened with "legal penalties" if they continued to resist (Ghabra and Arnold 2007: 7).
4 Ghabra 2007 is available through diwaniya@jusoorarabiya.com. Students I spoke to at Kuwait University said that they thought the color-coded benches were ridiculous and that they and their friends ignored the codes and sat wherever they liked (anonymous Kuwaiti students 2006). I should say, however, that I did not observe any mixed-gender seating on benches of any color.
5 See Tétreault 2006. The core of the "Orange Movement" was composed of students whose degrees were earned at U.S. institutions.
6 Internet access is available on all three campuses, although there is a shortage of technical staff and access is limited due to differing levels of computer literacy among students, faculty, and staff.
7 This information was gathered through interviews I conducted in Kuwait and the United States over the past 20 years.
8 According to one of the activists, when about 200 young Kuwaitis wearing orange t-shirts and waving orange flags showed up in front of the palace, government ministers driving in for a meeting were startled. "The prime minister waved to us," he reported. "And we heard in *diwaniyyas* [regular open meetings held in private homes] that they kept asking why was everyone wearing orange."
9 One of my Kuwaiti friends, whose father was intensely proud of what his son had achieved at his American university, was repeatedly treated to old men at *diwaniyyas* bringing him their broken radios. "Here, Engineer," they would say. "Can't you fix this?"

Bibliography

Anonymous Kuwaiti students (2006) Personal interviews, Kuwait, March. (Some interviews were conducted at the home of Nadia al-Sharrah.)
Anonymous Kuwait University professors (2005-2006), Personal interviews, Kuwait, December-January.
Buhamrah, K. (Trustee of GUST) (2004) Personal interview, Kuwait, December.
Dollman, S. (2007) "A Model of American Higher Education in the Middle East," *Educause Quarterly*, 3. Online HTTP: http://connect.educause.edu/library/abstract/AModelofAmericanHigh/44840 (accessed November 14, 2007).

Ghabra, S. (2004) Personal interview, Washington, D.C., July.

Ghabra, S. (2007) "Coeducation an Segregation in Kuwaiti Colleges," *Weekly Diwaniya*, 10 September.

Ghabra, S. and Arnold, M. (2007) "Studying the American Way: An Assessment of American-Style Higher Education in Arab Countries," Policy Focus #71, Washington, D.C.: The Washington Institute for Near East Policy, June. Online HTTP: http://www.washingtoninstitute.org/pubPDFs/PolicyFocus17FinalWeb.pdf

Lewin, T. (2008a) "Universities Rush to Set Up Outposts Abroad," *New York Times*, 10 February. Online HTTP: http://www.nytimes.com/2008/02/10/education/11global.html (accessed February 10, 2008).

Lewin, T. (2008b) "Oil Money Cultivates a Mideast Ivy League," *New York Times*, 11 February. Online HTTP: http://www.nytimes.com/2008/02/11/education/11global.html (accessed February 11, 2008).

Roy, O. (1994) *The Failure of Political Islam*, London: I.B. Tauris.

Tétreault, M.A. (2000) *Stories of Democracy: Politics and Society in Contemporary Kuwait*, New York: Columbia University Press.

Tétreault, M.A. (2006) "Kuwait's *Annus Mirabilis*," *Middle East Report Online*, 7 September. Online HTTP: http://www.merip.prg/mero/maro090706.html/

United Nations Development Programme (UNDP) and the Arab Fund for Economic and Social Development (2003) *The Arab Human Development Report* (AHDR), New York: The United Nations.

Wheeler, D.L. (2006) *The Internet in the Middle East: Global Expectations and Local Imaginations in Kuwait*, Albany, NY: State University of New York Press.

Willoughby, J. (2008) "Let a Thousand Models Bloom: Forging Alliances with Western Universities and the Making of the New Higher Educational System in the Gulf," unpublished article, 14 March.

Wolf, E. (1982) *Europe and the People without History*, Berkeley, CA: University of California Press.

Section IV

The role of women in industrialization

9 Saudi women

Modernity and change

Hatoon Ajwad al-Fassi

Introduction

The oil boom of the 1970s affected the Gulf countries immensely in terms of social structure as well as political and economic formations. In Saudi Arabia, modernity came at a remarkably fast pace, and industrialization became the declared goal of the country, with change and development that had not been known before in both society and government. Najd, the country's central and most conservative area, was able to exercise an influence on the rest of Arabia and the Gulf through its new oil wealth.

Saudi women were particularly affected by the shift in the country's economic fortunes. In just three decades, female literacy rates rose sharply, and today female students outnumber male students. This jump in the number of educated women generated a demand for work outside the home, though the workplace was not developed enough to receive women. Segregation, a practice less strictly followed before modernization,[1] was gradually institutionalized until it became a new reality. Thus the main challenges occupying conservatives in Saudi Arabia have been how to maintain and regulate the veil and how to prevent women from working alongside men.

Technology provided this traditional community with ways to solve those problems. To preserve women's privacy and separation from men without preventing them from studying or working, the country adopted closed-circuit television (CCTV) and modern communication facilities. CCTV allowed women to observe male teachers on television without being observed in return, and an internal telephone made communication possible between the two sides. This process of securing segregation is a key element in understanding and assessing the development of Saudi women's social and economic life in the past three decades.

Modernity

The increased revenue brought in by the oil boom allowed more schools and universities to open, but it also whetted appetites for modern luxuries. Signs of modernity proliferated, as Saudis began to see and experience more cars, bigger and better houses, and advanced communication systems, including television stations.

Projects mushroomed everywhere. Multinational companies, foreign workers, diplomats, and politicians from around the world became interested in Saudi Arabia. Studies have been exhaustive in this area, and books about Saudi Arabia were bestsellers in many countries for years. The government also embarked on a renewable five-year development plan in 1970 to expand the civil service and through which all governmental sectors were modernized and entered into international agreements, among other activities.

As Saudi Arabia entered the third millennium, the lifestyles of its citizens became even more globalized through such conveniences as satellite television, the Internet, and mobile phones. Such an environment was conducive to CCTV and technologized segregation.

Education

King Saud (1953–1964), who was under the constant demands of intellectuals and notables, issued a declaration for women's education in October 1959. Two years later, some 20 years after the development of men's schools, Saudi women's education expanded from a limited number of private schools to a wide array of public regular schools. Launching this project was not easy. Society and religious leaders, especially in central Saudi Arabia, fiercely resisted the initiative. As a compromise, the government entrusted women's education to the clergy, who justified it by making its main objective the training of good mothers and obedient housewives. Religious leaders also preserved the proper segregated study environment for girls in conformity with local traditions and narrowly interpreted Islamic rules (al-Bakr 1997: 14–15).

Segregation and proper clothing for women were maintained through a completely separate system of education for them. This system, called "The General Presidency for Girls' Education," ran women's education facilities from primary school to the university level between 1961 and 2003. The Ministry of Education, on the other hand, ran boys' and men's education, which followed a different curriculum and different policies.[2]

As a result of King Saud's policies, in 1970 there were only 378 elementary schools for girls, but by the end of 1975, 881 elementary schools for girls were in operation—an increase of 133 percent (al-Bakr 1997: 48). The gap between boys and girls was narrowing. In 2006, there were 6,714 public and private elementary schools for girls in the Kingdom, compared to 6,603 public and private elementary schools for boys (Saudi Ministry of Education 2006). In addition, the percentage of women enrolled in higher education rose from 47.5 percent in 1990 to 66 percent in 2002 (Saudi Ministry of Economy and Planning 2005–2009: 430), exceeding that of male students. Female graduates now outnumber male graduates, representing 56.5 percent of the total graduates in higher education (diploma, college, and graduate schools) (Saudi Ministry of Economy and Planning 2005–2009: 360).

One can argue that technology such as CCTV helped women's education expand through its maintenance of segregation, which prompted more families to allow their daughters to pursue their studies all the way up to higher education. Indeed, some scholars attribute the rapid growth in women's education to the fact that the standards of education and curriculum content are consistent with Saudi society's deeply rooted values, making education appealing to parents. They also point out that women find in education an area of self-realization that improves their social status, while men prefer to work rather than study (al-Bakr 2005).

However, modern Saudi society is still not at peace with the changes its women have experienced, as women are considered guardians of tradition and the first line of defense against a Western "intellectual invasion." Although technology has helped increase the number of women joining schools and universities, which has resulted in changing and elevating their social status, it has also helped to endorse traditional norms that preserve the isolation and invisibility of women as much as possible.

This can be seen in the prevention of female students from enrolling in certain subjects that allow them to mix with the other sex later in life, such as engineering, architecture, archaeology, geology, politics, and journalism. Indeed, the Ministry of Education's 1999 report indicates that, out of a total of 174,876 female students who joined the universities in the same year, 44 percent of them were admitted to the College of Education, 5.8 percent to the College of Arts & Humanities, 2.7 percent to Islamic studies departments, 1 percent to medical science specialties, and none to engineering, while the distribution of 129,889 men who were admitted in the same year showed more balance among the different specialties (Saudi Ministry of Education 1999: 133). In similar fashion, in 2007 the female students registered in the humanities at King Saud University (KSU), a public women's university in Riyadh and the largest in the Kingdom, numbered around 17,000 students, whereas only 4,000 female students were enrolled in the sciences.

In 2005 King Saud University established a law school, though some private colleges had already opened law departments for women that had produced a few graduates.[3] However, the law students of KSU who will soon graduate are concerned, as their future career and where they will work have not yet been settled by the Ministry of Justice, which regulates legal practice.

Vocational education was also closed to women for a long time. It was only in 2007 that a women's institute was established within the Technical and Vocational Training Corporation (TVTC), and four branches began to accept female students in limited numbers (fewer than 1,000 women). This endeavor will expand to 23 institutes in the coming years. To that effect, the TVTC has accepted 1,886 female students out of a total of 22,354 applicants for the 2008–2009 academic year (Technical and Vocational Training Corporation 2008).

In looking at the disciplines offered to women students in Saudi colleges and universities, it is clear that the emphasis is on theoretical subjects, which is exactly the opposite of what the labor market needs. This limitation has affected women's job opportunities, and has led to high rates of female unemployment.

Work

Article 160 of Saudi Arabia's 1969 labor law states that "women should not, by any means, mix with men in workplaces or its utilities, or any other place (Government of Saudi Arabia 1969)." This article, which is based on a strict reading of gender relations in Islam (Zaid 2000: 81–87) shaped the formation of women's participation in the labor market. What work women do, where they do it, and how they do it were major issues that needed to be settled before women could work with the permission of their families. The article was wholly implemented in the governmental sector and to a lesser degree in the private sector. Since 1969, certain authorities have monitored and reinforced this rule, including the General Presidency of Promotion of Virtues and Prohibition of Vices (i.e., the religious police).

For 35 years, Article 160 and its tenet on segregation shaped women's work. It also reflected the social attitude towards women working outside the home and was a hot topic for debate in Saudi society and media of the 1960s and 1970s. A return to this debate also took place from the 1990s through the new millennium in regard to school textbooks (Doumato *et al.* 2003: 247) and university books (al-Fassi 2003), where references to the value of women staying at home and rearing children as opposed to working outside the home and mixing with men abounded. Today, the religious movement's very conservative position regarding women's work outside the home is experiencing a revival, and what was thought to be a settled matter is again unresolved (Zaid 2000: 78–80).

In September 2005, the Ministry of Labor replaced Article 160 with Article 4, which states: "When implementing the provisions of this Law, the employer and the worker shall adhere to the provisions of *shari`a*" (Saudi Ministry of Labor 2005). This article, which refers to the private sector only,[4] does not single out women in the observation of *shari`a*; rather, it commands both men and women to adhere to its provisions, thus slightly loosening the tight segregation law. Strangely, this innovation was not taken up by the media or by women's groups, and it was not publicly implemented at its inception. The following two examples demonstrate how segregation continues to be implemented at women's expense and show the contradiction between law and practice in the Kingdom.

The first instance occurred in June 2007, when female bank professionals were scrutinized in their work environment. Segregation rules were strictly enforced by creating different entrances, elevators, and even buildings for women, thus preventing them from participating in daily meetings and limiting communication to telephones and email. These measures have made women vulnerable to the loss of leadership positions, which are then filled by men (Associated Press 2007; Reuters 2007).

The second instance took place in January 2008. The Grand Mufti, Shaykh Abdelaziz Al-Sheikh, was reported to have insisted in a keynote conference speech on the necessity of preventing male doctors from mixing with female doctors in hospitals, which are both public and private in Saudi Arabia. He then asked for reports of any such incidents (*Al-Khaleej* 2008). His comments had a very strong impact, and such ideals often determine the Kingdom's male/female relationships.[5]

However, powerful princes in the royal family have delicately challenged some of these ideals. Prince Khalid Al Faisal Al Saud, the governor of Makkah, issued a circular that was published in the local papers in April 2008 highlighting Article 4 and naming the Ministry of Labor as the only reference for women's terms of work (e.g., al-Zayed 2008). He sent a copy of his order to the General Presidency of Promotion of Virtues and Prohibition of Vices. The implementation of this law is now taking place in the Makkah governorate, which includes Jeddah and Taif. No changes have been noted in Riyadh yet, and it is still too early to assess the law's impact.

Despite such changes, working outside the home is still a challenge for Saudi women. Yet they continue to do so—albeit in small numbers—and technologies such as CCTV allow such work by maintaining a segregated education and a subsequent work environment separate from men. How did CCTV come about, and what are the implications of segregated education and work?

Closed-circuit television (CCTV)

When CCTV was introduced in Saudi Arabia, it was given a different function from its original uses, which included distance learning, surveillance, and entertainment. King Saud University first used CCTV in the late 1970s under the direction of Rector Abdulaziz al Fadda (1973–1979). The faculty of education introduced the technology through their department of educational methodology, and later, in the mid-1980s, a more official department called the Audio & Video Distribution Center was established.

The system became a medium through which women would learn under men by observing male teachers on television without being observed by them. Communication occurs between the sexes through an internal telephone. The teacher sits in a small studio furnished with a television camera aimed at his face, a white board, a light projector, and the telephone. Other supervision rooms take care of monitoring the studios and fixing any technical problems with sound, image, or light (King Saud University 1999: 436–437). The teacher is dependent on a female supervisor to tell him when the women are present and ready for him to start. The supervisor also keeps order in the class and proctors exams.[6]

In its first iterations, the system was not very efficient. When it failed to work, the teacher would come to the class and give his lecture face to face with the female students. This was especially true in the science departments (Anonymous KSU professor 2008; Samarkandy 2008). It was also hard to maintain CCTV between male and female campuses because of constant financial challenges due to the expense of doubly installing the technology. But the system improved little by little via the newest technology available on the market, and it eventually guaranteed a maximum degree of segregation and efficiency. And despite financial setbacks, Saudi Arabia's economic affluence has helped this happen in a permanent, institutionalized way.

CCTV's main positive outcome has been its social acceptability. Because women needed a male guardian's permission to study and work outside the home, conditions for doing so must be acceptable to him. CCTV thus paved the way for more women to enter into the public sphere—albeit in a segregated way. Segregation did not solely rely on CCTV, however; universities implemented "softer" segregation techniques, such as a dark glass partition. Women would sit in a minimally lit room with phones on one side of the partition, and the professor would teach in a well-lit room with a phone on the other side of the partition.

Segregation is strictly maintained in the colleges run by the religious establishments and in many parts of other universities. KSU completely conformed to the system in 1995, when it began to require its female graduate students to use CCTV to defend their M.A. and Ph.D. theses. Prior to 1995, graduate women studied and defended their dissertations face to face with their professors.

Fowziyah Abu Khalid, a sociologist and KSU staff member who wrote one of the first academic studies about gender and power relations on KSU's campus, considers education through CCTV to be the first officially recognized instance in Saudi Arabia's conservative area of Najd in which female students interacted with male professors in an academic setting. It also fosters communication between male and female staff members there. Abu Khalid calls the practice a "penetrative potentiality" (Abu Khalid 2001).[7]

Today, the complex system of CCTV that includes a sound system, wired and wireless types of communication, and the latest mobile phones, has helped to empower women who either welcome or critique segregation, and has allowed them a relative degree of participation in meetings, conferences, and lectures.

Criticism of CCTV has been evident, though not widespread. The media has not been quick to censure the technology, and it has thus remained a sanctioned means of maintaining segregation. A few student publications have expressed negative views of it, particularly *Ḥiwār* magazine, in which male and female undergraduates debated equality between the sexes, the limits of mixing and Islam's role in it, and other relevant issues (al-Hamlawi and al-Rayyis 1983: 11–13). The views expressed ranged from conservative to less conservative, but the magazine was suspended in 1984 when it grew too critical (*Ḥiwār* 1981–1984). Such publications of the 1980s, in addition to public criticism in general, highlighted how the system controls communication and enforces women's public exclusion. In later decades, public criticism became more directed at how the use of CCTV in conferences and public lectures denies women an equal voice. In such environments, men control the technology, which they use to favor male audience members over physically absent female ones (al-Fassi 2004).

Recently, an academic critique has questioned the excessive use of this technology. Badr al-Salih, a professor of education at King Saud University, calls CCTV a means by which education "hangs," or rests, its flaws. He points to the importance of full interaction for learning via CCTV to be successful, and considers video conferencing that shows only the male speaker to be misleading and inefficient (B. al-Salih 2006; 2008: 70–72).

Saudi women have also shown resistance to women's "public exclusion" (Women for Reform 2008) by wearing the veil to guarantee their participation in the public domain. As Abu Khalid writes

> This invisible presence was the female students' own way to encounter the social pressure that was launched against their public presence in the attempt to deprive them of one of their basic human rights. Medical female students who kept the full face cover have chosen to penetrate the existing system of gender relations by trying to find a new mechanism in facing this uneven power struggle in an attempt to develop a new scale of power relations inside the newly established institution of higher education.
>
> (Abu Khalid 2001: 186–187)

> Female students have also challenged the gender apartheid they experience in the educational system by joining fields that are traditionally exclusively male, such as medicine and pharmacy. In addition, an Islamist female writer and activist recently rejected the assumption of an Islamic order of segregation of the sexes in many articles and interviews.
>
> (H. al-Salih 2007; al-Abedeen 2008a and 2008b)

The expansion of education in the 1990s has resulted in a new class of qualified women who join their predecessors in demanding that the government promote a higher level of women's participation in economic, social, political, and religious arenas, despite the fact that criticizing segregation remains a difficult and taboo act of resistance.

Implications of segregation

These forms of resistance demonstrate that while segregated work environments, such as those fostered by CCTV, have expanded women's choices, they have also limited them. By preventing women from getting the required qualifications for the market, segregated school and work spaces hinder women from joining many sectors. This has raised the rate of unemployment among women, impoverished and weakened them, minimized their rate of economic participation, and raised the cost of work and education for them.

Specifically, limiting the fields of study for women in universities and vocational institutes has led to the rise in unemployment among female university graduates. The majority of graduates are trained in the educational and health sectors and, as a result, the Saudi education and health ministries (particularly education) are the main employers of women. Most of the job opportunities in the country, however, are in different sectors that require technical and communication skills unavailable to women through their schooling. Thus, women's specialties do not fulfill the demands of the labor market.

Even female university graduates from fields such as computer science and accounting remain unemployed, primarily because these professions cannot be conducted in an environment separate from the rest of the work team. Policies preventing women from working such jobs have become more widespread, often leading to a closed labor market for women, which simultaneously opens itself up to foreign male labor, which has increased from 6 percent of labor in 1979 to 52 percent in 2003. Seven percent of this labor is female.[8]

Also, adhering to Article 160 by duplicating every institution is obviously expensive, and only a small part of the private sector, such as banks, can afford to do so. The public sector has thus been the one to take on segregation requirements and provide them as needed. As a result, women join the public sector at higher rates than they join the private sector.[9]

As such, segregation has allowed for the creation of many jobs for women in government ministries, such as the aforementioned ministries of education and health. Furthermore, the number of women working in the education field as teachers has increased from 113 teachers in 1962 (al-Bakr 1997: 47, plan 5) to 190,641 elementary, intermediate, and secondary level teachers in 2006, compared to 160,711 male teachers for boys' private and public schools at all levels in the same year (Saudi Ministry of Education 2006). These figures show the vast difference in attitude towards work for women, especially in those areas in which women are completely segregated from men.

Yet, because of the glut of women trained in the education sector, high unemployment rates occur for women in the field. Recent statistics show the excess: 83.4 percent of women working outside the home worked in education in 2003, while 5.4 percent worked in health fields (Saudi Ministry of Economy and Planning 2005–2009: 353).

According to official estimations by the Public Statistics Division, the rate of unemployment for both men and women in Saudi Arabia was 8.34 percent in 2003, and it increased to 16 percent in 2004.[10] The 2005–2009 five-year development plan estimated an unemployment rate for women at 21.7 percent (Saudi Ministry of Economy and Planning 2005–2009: 372), and recently the Deputy Minister of Labor submitted a rate of 24.7 percent (al-Morky 2008). Other unofficial sources estimate it at 32 percent. This is one of the highest rates in the world, given that seven million jobs are available to foreign workers and that the high percentage of unemployed women includes many that are highly qualified. Indeed, according to the plan, 76 percent of unemployed women are university graduates, and 22 percent are high school graduates (Saudi Ministry of Economy and Planning 2005–2009: 193).

Furthermore, the population of Saudi Arabia is 16 million, with approximately 3.5 million women of working age. According to statistics from the Ministry of Labor in August 2007, the number of working women in both the public and private sectors is only 502,456, leaving three million at home. This constitutes a participation rate of 5.5 percent, the lowest in the world. Again, this waste is usually compensated for by the presence of foreign labor, whether male or female, and mostly unqualified.

The number of women in need who are not allowed to work is thus increasing. Many such women experience hardship due to the difficulty of executing family law verdicts found in their favor (al-Shubaiki 2004: 17–20). Instead of working, they beg in the streets or wait for social security, if they can prove their need with or without a male supporter. But even once women receive social security, it is never enough.

Women can also become impoverished through guardianship. Because a woman must avoid mixing with men, she cannot represent herself in government agencies and other public places freely. If she does not have a male guardian, or if she is a businesswoman in the private sector, she has to assign a male "authorized representative" who officially and legally conducts business on her behalf. This has led to many cases of financial loss and fraud. Luckily, the recent campaign to contest that rule—led by businesswomen and activists from Jeddah, Riyadh, and Eastern Province, was fruitful, and the condition was removed—to a point. Women whose businesses are completely segregated are exempt from having a male legal representative, but if the environment is not entirely segregated, a woman must assign a male manager. This new position has less authority than the previous one, but it can still cause issues for the female owner.[11]

Indeed, in the May 2003 Saudi Arabian General Investment Authority (SAGIA) report on "the obstacles to the female investment businesses in Saudi Arabia," the authors find that one of the major roadblocks facing women is that, because of this system of male representation, they do not have direct access to the sectors necessary for their businesses to run and prosper. It can be very difficult for a woman to find a trustworthy man to represent her business in the government and deal officially with other businesses run by men and foreign investors (SAGIA 2003: 68–69, 72–73). Another problem is that of importing male labor for their businesses, because women are not allowed in the male labor import offices (SAGIA 2003: 74).

In addition, using a male representative prevents women from gaining the experience and skills needed to run and develop their businesses (Ba-Isa 2007). It also goes without saying that a segregated woman cannot represent herself or her business on any leading boards or decision-making committees. She is not allowed to be a public figure in a leading position or sit in the Cabinet or on the Shura Council. According to businesswoman M. al-Ajroush

> Segregation of men and women in Saudi society cuts women off from the most well established leaders in the business community. It makes it difficult for women-owned businesses to enter into affiliations with other firms and to cooperate as contractors on major projects. The most successful businesswomen tend to come from families where there is a strong business background. These women capitalize on their families' networks and connections to succeed. Such a situation is not helpful to society in general. Success in business should be determined by ability, not gender.
>
> (Ba-Isa 2007)

Thus, although there are thousands of women willing to work and in need, the reasons outlined above demonstrate how they are often prevented from joining the labor force. Because of some of these same reasons, economic waste in the government is substantial.

According to statistics from the Ministry of Education, the government spent 25.9 billion Saudi riyals on girls' education in 2004, one and a half billion more than the amount of money spent on boys' education that year. Wastes include the following:

- Money spent on schools and teachers for women who will not use their education for work outside the home.
- Building duplicate departments, offices, libraries, labs, etc.
- The handicapping of half of society, replacing them with seven million foreign workers who transfer over 40 billion dollars out of the country a year.

All of this has resulted in the rise of a labor market with abnormal characteristics: on the one hand, women's participation in education is greater than ever. On the other hand, another (foreign) labor market has risen that does not follow the well-known market laws of supply and demand.

Update: a co-ed university

On 23 September 2009, King Abdullah inaugurated the King Abdullah University of Science and Technology (KAUST) in the city of Thuwal in western Saudi Arabia. KAUST is the first co-ed university in the Kingdom, and as such is a revolutionary step. It has evoked an intense debate about the mixing of the sexes, and what is forbidden (*harām*) or allowed (*halāl*) in Saudi society.

Many in the religious establishment are unhappy with the founding of KAUST. One such figure, Shaykh al-Shathri, expressed his views on the Islamist satellite television station Al-Majd, saying that gender mixing is forbidden in Islam and that the university should change its policy (al-Shathri 2009). Shortly after, the Shaykh was dismissed from his position on the Council of Senior Scholars; since then, critics of KAUST have been careful in how they express their opinions.

On the other hand, many religious scholars have begun to give new interpretations of gender segregation and have concluded that it is allowed. These scholars emphasize the difference between mixing (*ikhtilāt*) and being alone with a stranger (*khulwah*), allowing the former and forbidding the latter. Major Islamic figures, such as Justice Minister Muhammad al-Issa, have supported this interpretation (*Al-Riyadh* 2009).

This new position has brought about a great deal of confusion. Men and women are questioning the credibility of religious scholars and the meaning of *harām* and *halāl*, as well as asking themselves about their lifelong effort to remain segregated. What opportunities of marriage, experience, and work have been missed, they ask, in order to meet the obligation of segregation? Hundreds, if not thousands, of articles have been posted on the Internet both in agreement with and opposed to these new societal interpretations. One example of those opposed are the fatwas issued on Ana al Muslim website (Ana al Muslim 2009).

No other university in Saudi Arabia has attempted to become co-ed, though some private schools in Jeddah, such as Effat University, allow a semi-mixed setting during official events. At these events, speaking panels are mixed, and men and women sit together in the audience with a partition between them. Other institutions, depending on the courage of their leadership, offer symbolic gestures such as mixing men and women at official openings or conferences or decreasing the level of segregation in a particular space.[12]

Conclusion

In light of these developments, the future may bring new norms and standards in regard to the rules of segregation in Saudi society. In the meantime, methods like CCTV will continue to be used. The use of this technology to facilitate segregation has to an extent helped expand the areas of work available to women. For example, the percentage of women working as teachers is very high; around 85 percent of Saudi working women are employed in this manner.

Still, the total percentage of Saudi women who are employed is one of the lowest in the world. This is not because they do not want to work or because they are not qualified. Rather, it is because segregation techniques limit women to certain jobs, such as teaching and clerical work. Jobs in such fields as engineering, law, or retail cannot be totally segregated, and are therefore closed to women. Until norms change or science and technology advance to the point of allowing women to work in such sectors while remaining segregated, strong forces in society will continue to bar women from these opportunities.

Industrialization has thus brought two contradictory effects to the women of Saudi Arabia. It has strengthened and institutionalized the local customs that prefer to hide and protect women through segregation, while at the same time allowing women to enroll in schools and colleges at record numbers and to work in a secluded environment.

Notes

1 In the pre-boom period, gender relations were different. Women in central Arabia who were totally or partially veiled sat and talked with men and sold their wares in the market, whereas in such areas as the Aseer region, they did so with an exposed face.
2 In 2003, girls' education came under the supervision of the Ministry of Education as well. Many efforts are trying to bring about equal curricula for both sexes, but they are not yet realized. In 2006, the 102 Girls' Colleges, which were formerly part of the General Presidency for Girls' Education that accredited women with M.A.s and Ph.D.s, merged with universities in different cities. In Riyadh, they form the nucleus of Riyadh University for Girls, recently renamed Princess Norah bint Abdelrahman University and headed for the first time by a woman.
3 One woman lawyer has broken the ice in Jeddah. She is a graduate of the Effat Private College of Law program and was trained under the lawyer Omar al-Khooly. She has

been able to litigate in favor of some women even without a license. The story was reported by *Arabian Business* on 7 June 2008, and is available at www.arabianbusiness.com/arabic/521323.

4 The public sector, which includes schools and universities, continues to adhere to the more traditional laws regarding gender mixing.

5 Usually the religious authorities enforce their own understanding of regulations based on religious interpretation if the official law is not on their side, as is seen in this example.

6 I played this role when I was a professor's assistant as part of my duties in the history department of KSU from 1989 to 1992. I was then the director of CCTV at the women's campus in 2002.

7 Male/female staff communication did not occur through CCTV during the first decade of women's university education at KSU, that is, from 1976 through 1986. See Abu Khalid 2001: 179–182.

8 See al-Rashid 2003; the article relates how 400 Saudi women who were discharged from a dairy products factory after one day of being appointed out of fear they were not sufficiently segregated. See also the long debate on feminizing the lingerie shops between the Ministry of Labor and the conservatives, who won the battle and kept the industry in the hands of foreign men instead of Saudi women for fear of not observing complete segregation (Women for Reform 2008: 9–10, 45–46). Dr. Abdelaziz Abu Hamad Aluwaisheg, Director General of International Economic Relations for the Gulf Cooperation Council (GCC), also shed light on this topic in a personal interview in Riyadh on 1 July 2008.

9 However, quality in women's workplaces in this sector has not been guaranteed, as most women's sections and departments are situated in the old buildings of the institution previously occupied by men. Constructing new buildings for women from scratch is rare. Examples include the campuses of the all-female King Saud University and Imam Muhammad bin Saud University as well as the women's departments of the Ministry of Education and the Ministry of the Interior, all in Riyadh.

10 These rates, however, are imprecise due to the methodology the Division of Statistics follows. A study dated August 2007 that was later omitted from the site showed that the number of unemployed women had reached 164,787. This figure included only the number of women who had applied for jobs and did not succeed in obtaining one.

11 I was the representative of the above campaign in the Riyadh region, and wrote many articles on the issue. The leader of the campaign was Ms. Alia Banajah, a businesswoman from Jeddah who was forced to close her company until the condition was removed on 3 May 2009. See al-Fassi 2009; Mokhtar 2009; al-Shareef 2009.

12 For example, the opening of the Institute of Public Administrations' Jubilee Celebration at the Intercontinental Hotel in Riyadh, 1 November 2009.

Bibliography

al-Abedeen Hammad, S.Z. (2008a) "Mafhūm lā yakhluwann rajul be imra'ah illa wamaʿdī maḥram," *Al-Madinah*, 3 July.

al-Abedeen Hammad, S.Z. (2008b) "Baʿd kull hādhihi al-mushārakāt yaʿtī Dr. Bāḥārith bijarrat qalam yanfī ay wilāyah aw āyat mushārakah siyāsiyyah li-al-mar'ah," *Al-Madinah*, 10 August.

Ana al Muslim website (2009) 4 October. Online HTTP: www.muslm.net/vb/showthread.php?t=361310&page=2 (accessed January 8, 2010).

Anonymous King Saud University (KSU) professor (2008) Personal interview, Riyadh, Saudi Arabia, 11 July.

Arabian Business (2008) 7 June. Online HTTP: www.arabianbusiness.com/arabic/521323 (accessed June 29, 2010).

Associated Press (2007) "Segregation Rules Hit Saudi Bankers," 26 June. Online HTTP: www.kuwaittimes.net/read_news.php?newsid=ODEzMDM2MDk0 (accessed June 29, 2010).

Ba-Isa, M. (2008) "Guardianship Issue Must Be Solved," *Arab News*, 7 March. Online. HTTP:archive.arabnews.com/?page=1&section=0&article=107594&d=7&m=3&y=2008&pix=kingdom.jpg&category=Kingdom (accessed June 29, 2010).

al-Bakr, F. (1997) *Al-mar²ah al-su'ūdiyyah wa al-ta'līm*, Second edition, Cairo: al-I'lāmiyyah.

al-Bakr, F. (2005) "Al-mar²ah al-su'ūdiyyah: al-ta'līm wa al-'amal: tahaddiyāt matrūhah," Paper presented to Saudi Women in the Millennium, United Nations Development Programme, Riyadh, Saudi Arabia, December.

Doumato, E., Posusney, A. and Pripstein, M. (2003) *Women and Globalization in the Arab Middle East; Gender, Economy and Society*, Colorado: Lynne Rienner Publishers.

al-Fassi, H. (2003) "Saudi Women: New Perspectives and Visions for Reforms," *Arab News*, 19 June. Online HTTP: <www.arabnews.com/?page=7&section=0&article=27647&d=19&m=6&y=2003> (accessed June 29, 2010).

al-Fassi, H. (2004) "Al-multaqayāt al-thaqāfiyyah wa-al-intikhābiyyah, limādha al-hudūr al-dhukūrī al-tāghī," *Al-Iqtisadiah*, 27 September.

al-Fassi, H. (2009) "Sayyidāt al-a'māl al-su'ūdiyyāt yarfudna al-mudīr al-'ām," *Al-Riyadh*, 3 May.

Abu Hamad Aluwaisheg, A. (Director General of International Economic Relations for the Gulf Cooperation Council (GCC)) (2008) Personal interview, Riyadh, Saudi Arabia, 1 July.

al-Hamlawi, M. and al-Rayyis, S. (eds.) (1983) "Mixing," *Hiwār*, 42, 11 April.

Hiwār (1981–84) Riyadh: The Cultural and Art Committee, Administrative Studies Faculty, King Saud University.

Al-Khaleej (2008) "Muftī al-su'ūdiyyah yushaddid 'alā man' al-ikhtilāt," 18 January.

Abu Khalid, F. (2001) "Exploration of the Discourse of Saudism: Gender Relations and Relations of Power (Case Study of the Women's Center of King Saud University)," Unpublished thesis, University of Salford, United Kingdom.

King Saud University (1999) *King Saud University (KSU) in a Hundred Years*, Riyadh: King Saud University.

Mokhtar, H. (2009) "Why Should Men Run Our Business, Ask Women Entrepreneurs," *Arab News*, 8 March.

al-Morky, F. (2008) "Nā²ib wazīr al-'amal yu²akki tarāju' al-batālah ilā 11%," *Al-Hayat*, 19 January.

al-Rashid, N. (2003) "Īqāf 400 su'ūdiyyah 'an al-'amal fī masna' li-al-albān ba'd yawm wāhid min ta'yyinahunn," *Al-Riyadh*, 22 March.

Reuters (2007) "Saudi Arabia to Segregate Men, Women in Bank HQs." Online HTTP: www.thepeninsulaqatar.com/Display_news.asp?section=World_News&subsection=Gulf%2C+Middle+East+%26+Africa&month=June2007&file=World_News2007062532635.xml.

Al-Riyadh (2009) 24 October. Online HTTP: <http://www.alriyadh.com/2009/10/24/article468615.html>.

al-Salih, B. (2006) "Al-ta'allum al-elektrōnī shammā'at al-mujtama' al-tarbawī," *Al-Riyadh*, 30 November.

al-Salih, B. (2008) "Al-ta'allum al-elektrōnī 'an bu'd fī al-jāmi'āt al-su'ūdiyyah," *Al-Ma'rifah*, 153.

al-Salih, H. (2007) "Hal al-ikhtilāt bayn al-rijāl wa al-nisā² muharram kulluhu," *Asharq Alawsat*, 24 May.

Samarkandy, M.K. (Chairman of the Technical Committee for the Specification of Girls' College Electronic and Broadcasting Studios between 1984 and 1996, King Saud University) (2008) Personal interview, Riyadh, Saudi Arabia, 21 June.

Saudi Arabia, Government of (1969) Labor and Workmen Law. Online HTTP: www.saudiembassy.net/about/country-information/laws/Labor_and_Workmen_Law-3of4.aspx.

Saudi Arabian General Investment Authority (SAGIA) (2003) "The Obstacles to the Female Investment Business in Saudi Arabia," Riyadh: SAGIA, May.

Saudi Ministry of Economy and Planning (2005–2009) *The Eighth Development Plan*, Saudi Arabia: Ministry of Economy and Planning.

Saudi Ministry of Education (1999) *The Ministry of Education's Report*, Riyadh.

Saudi Ministry of Education (2006) Education statistics. Online HTTP: www.moe.gov.sa/stat/final1427.htm#a7.

Saudi Ministry of Labor (2005) Article 4 (labor law).

al-Shareef, M. (2009) "Al-tijārah tulzim furūʿaha bi ilghāʾ al-wakīl li sayyidāt al-aʿmāl," *Al-Madinah*, 4 May.

al-Shathri, Shaykh. (2009) Appearance on Al-Majd Satellite Television.

al-Shubaiki, I. (2004) "Al-mushkilāt al-ijtimāʿiyyah li al-marʾah al-faqīrah fī al-mujtamaʿ al-suʿūdī," *Papers of the Third National Dialogue*, Medina: King Abdulaziz Center for National Dialogue.

Technical and Vocation Training Corporation (2008) Technical and Vocational Training Corporation Statistics, Saudi Arabia. Online HTTP: www.tvtc.gov.sa/Downloads/Reports/TadreebReport%5B56pages%5D.pdf and www.gt.gotevot.edu.sa (women's branch).

Women for Reform (2008) *CEDAW Shadow Report*, January. Online HTTP: www2.ohchr.org/english/bodies/cedaw/docs/ngos/womenreform40.pdf.

Zaid, B.A. (2000) *Ḥirāsat al-faḍīlah*, sixth edition, Riyadh: Dār al-ʿāṣimah.

al-Zayed, M. (2008) "Wazīr al-ʿamal fī khiṭāb li-amīr manṭiqat Makkah muḥaddidan ḍawābiṭ ʿamal al-nisāʾ," *Al-Watan*, 2 April.

10 The role of women in industrialization in the Gulf

The case of Bahrain

Munira Fakhro

The changing role of women in the GCC countries

The changing role of women has recently received more attention on the local, regional, and global level, especially from the UN and human rights organizations. International conferences now focus on women's empowerment and gender equality. This topic takes a prime position in the Gulf region, as its societies have recently modernized, particularly since the advent of oil in the 1940s and 1950s. Some attribute this modernization to an earlier time, though rapid development did not occur until after the discovery of oil.

In the early years of the last century, Gulf women lived a traditional life dominated by old practices. In Bahrain, for example, one scholar classifies the pre-oil society as consisting of two main socioeconomic groups dominated by men, the first being the elite made up of the ruling family, the land owners, the pearl merchants, and the traders, and the second comprised mainly of the majority who lived at a subsistence level, whether they were fishermen, peasants, or pearl divers (al-Rumaihi 1984: 163). The discovery of oil and its exploitation contributed to the development of education and employment, which strengthened family and society. All Gulf states transformed from traditional beginnings to societies with varying levels of openness to new concepts.

With the flow of oil and the new opportunity of work for both sexes, an increasing number of women joined the workforce for an income. However, while men's traditional role has inevitably shifted, women still manage domestic responsibilities. Moreover, though some laws have changed in favor of a more equitable relationship between men and women, societal norms have not changed with them.

The most important legislation that supports women's new roles and achievements is the Personal Status Law, or family law, which regulates and promotes equality in affairs such as betrothal, marriage, dowry, and spousal rights, as well as separation and divorce. Gulf states such as Bahrain and Saudi Arabia have yet to pass such legislation, though other states have instituted the law in varying degrees of application. The challenge is that these laws must derive from both the essence of *shari`a* and Islamic jurisprudence as well as the laws issued by international and human rights organizations, such as the UN charter. All Gulf states, except for Qatar, have signed gender equality agreements with these organizations, such as the Convention of Elimination of All Forms of Discrimination Against Women (CEDAW). However, not only do societal norms lag behind these changes; the states themselves have reservations regarding these agreements, such as vis-à-vis issues of inheritance, monogamy, and adoption (Nazir and Tomppert 2005: 244), and as such, do not always implement them.

Education and women in the Gulf

Education has always been the most important factor in the development of society, and it seems clear that education and employment have played a major part in changing the status of women in the Gulf. Indeed, education has been the main feature of social and cultural development in the region for both men and women, but it has been more pronounced for women due to their new ability to work outside the home. The more education women achieve, the better chances they have in employment. Thus, the aim of education has not been mere literacy and teaching women to perform simple clerical tasks, but to provide professional expertise that industry and services require. As a result, secondary and higher education have been expanded to respond to the demand of the business and industrial sectors.[1] However, while education has helped in this regard, it often does not provide enough preparation for women to advance in the private and industrial sector. I address this below.

In Bahrain, women's education began developing at the beginning of the last century, when the American Mission founded the first girls' school in 1909 with 40 pupils. That milestone was followed by the founding of the government girls' school in 1928, just nine years after the boys' government school. Kuwait followed in Bahrain's footsteps, and founded its first girls' school in 1937. In the UAE and Qatar, this development occurred as late as the 1950s, and in Saudi Arabia, female education commenced in 1960 under the control and guidance of the religious establishment, and thus focused on religious teachings (UNESCWA 2005: 335). As for Oman, schools began to crop up in 1970, when only three boys' schools with a total of 909 students were in operation (Ja'afar 2002: 3).

All the statistics on Gulf education confirm the enormous rise in the number of enrolled students, though the quality and standard of education are still lacking when compared internationally. Furthermore, the GCC states do not apply compulsory education, resulting in a higher illiteracy rate for females than for males. Exceptions to this are in the UAE and Qatar, where illiteracy rates are relatively lower among females than in other GCC countries, as shown in Table 10.1.

Statistics also indicate more women than men at the university level; this, however, may be related to the relatively large number of males seeking education abroad as well as the fact that many males join the military, police, and general workforce immediately after secondary school. Women have a lesser likelihood of doing the same because of traditional cultural mores. Furthermore, women tend to study certain subjects, such as education and topics within the

Table 10.1 Illiteracy average (15–24 years) in the Gulf States, 2005, by percentage

	Females	*Males*	*Both*
Bahrain	15.0	8.1	10.9
Qatar	15.0	18.6	17.5
Kuwait	18.3	15.0	16.5
UAE	18.5	24.0	22.2
Saudi Arabia	29.2	15.4	21.3
Oman	32.8	17.0	24.2

Source: Derived from ESCWA (2005) *Status of Arab Women Report*, Table 5.

humanities, as Table 10.2 shows. This reflects society's expectations that women practice comparatively softer responsibilities than men, such as working among other females in education, health, and social services.

Yet, much progress has been made. By 2003 the number of women students in Bahrain's many schools and educational institutes reached 98,931 in primary schools (50.02 percent of the total), 15,163 at the intermediate level (50.1 percent of the total), and 13,909 at the secondary level (52.5 percent of the total). At the higher education level, 62 percent of all students at the University of Bahrain are female.

Gulf women at work

After the opening of girls' schools, Gulf women began to work as teachers, and then entered other fields, such as nursing, and gradually moved into other professions. In 1957 Kuwaiti women represented only 1.4 percent of the workforce, whereas in 2001 they represented 30.2 percent of it. In Bahrain, the share of women in the workforce in 1971 was 5 percent, rising to 25.7 percent in 2001

Table 10.2 Distribution of students by specialization, 2005, by percentage

	Bahrain		*Kuwait*		*Oman*		*Qatar*		*Saudi Arabia*		*UAE*	
	M	*F*	*M*	*F*	*M*	*F*	*M*	*F*	*M*	*F*	*M*	*F*
Education	23	77	21	79	–	–	9	91	25	75	5	95
Arts and Humanities	24	76	21	79	38	62	12	88	66	34	14	86
Business Law and Social Sciences	42	58	37	63	54	46	23	77	69	31	43	57
Science	28	72	27	73	49	51	21	79	56	44	18	82
Engineering	68	32	51	49	94	9	58	42	99	1	56	44
Health	25	75	27	73	49	51	–	–	61	39	35	65
Other (Agriculture and Unspecified)	62	38	–	–	45	51	63	37	76	24	17	83

Source: Derived from ESCWA (2005) *Status of Arab Women Report*, Table 11.

(Annajjar 2000: 48). Qatari women's participation was 12 percent of the total workforce in 1995, a rise from 6.2 percent in 1986. In 1999, the percentage rose to 40.2 percent (al-Ghanem 2002: 14). In the UAE, women's participation in the labor force rose from 10 percent in 1991 to 13.6 percent in 1998 (Annajjar 2000).

In the private sector, the percentage of women drops visibly. This is due to a lack of qualifications both inside the school and at the workplace because of the reluctance of policymakers to provide training programs for women. As such, Bahraini women, for example, are as few as 4 percent of those employed in the banking sector, and this is only due to separate services for females.

In a 2006 study entitled "Evaluation of the Bahraini Women's Status in the Private Sector" (al-Zayani *et al.* 2007), a sample of 313 private sector female employees in five selected fields and representing 2.5 percent of total women employees were surveyed. The fields covered were industry and textiles, construction, the financial and insurance sector, social and personal services, and tourism and catering. The study revealed that 73.9 percent of the employed women fell into the 19–35 age bracket, and 60.7 percent had university and higher degrees. It also revealed a noticeable drop in the pay scale in the private sector despite high academic qualifications, that is, 25.5 percent of the female employees received monthly salaries below 200 Bahraini Dinars (BD) (U.S. $500), though some had a college degree or higher. Discrimination against the female private sector worker was also evident, as less than 10 percent occupied a high position. The majority of the women surveyed occupied traditional positions, such as secretaries and receptionists. Furthermore, they faced long working hours, a lack of maternity laws, and poor treatment.

Women in industry in Bahrain

The topic of women and industry in Bahrain has not been sufficiently researched. The field warrants attention because though education and training are not at their highest capacity for placing and advancing women in industry, their spread has permitted more women to join the sector.

Since the early 1970s, the industrial sector in Bahrain has been an important contributor to the growth of the gross domestic product (GDP) and to employment opportunities. While the government played a major role in the early stages of industrialization, it subsequently removed itself from involvement in the productive processes through privatization and divesture. The goal in doing so was to strengthen the private sector and promote industrialization. The role of government is now to provide a legal and regulatory framework to assist businesses in competing in the international market.

The number of industrial establishments in Bahrain is estimated at 650, employing nearly 27,000 Bahrainis and valued at $2.7 billion. In 2007, industrial growth rose by 87 percent from the previous year, and the number of industrial companies has increased by 250 percent since 2004. At present, industry contributes nearly 13 percent to Bahrain's GDP. Officials are hoping to increase this figure to 25–30 percent in the year 2025, if future plans are implemented (Fakhro 2008).

One area, located in the industrial zone in Muharraq called Industrial Wharf, will be able to host 500 small, medium, and high technology industries. This alone will result in the employment of nearly 30,000 people when it is finished in five to seven years. Another plan is to obtain 5,000 hectares of land through reclamation in Sitra and Hidd to use for industry. Industrial expansion, however, is up against a potential natural gas shortage in Bahrain, as the country's supply is diminishing. This energy problem could be solved by negotiating with countries with plentiful resources, such as Qatar, Saudi Arabia, or Iran.

The number of female workers at the Ministry of Industry is increasing. Among its 13 directors, five are women and head the following directorates: Foreign Trade, Intellectual Property Rights, Standards and Measurement, Public Relations Information, and Small, Medium, and Traditional Industries.

Author's study

To gain a deeper understanding of Bahraini women at work in the industrial sector, I interviewed CEOs and top management of four of the largest and most important Bahraini industries. Six female employees representing different areas of each company were also queried. Furthermore, I researched a business incubator, which aims to support Bahrain's small and medium business activity. I also examined the textile industry, where thousands of Bahraini women work.

My study tackled the most serious issues facing women in the Gulf, such as equal opportunity, marginalization at work, and the need for a personal status law that regulates marriage contracts and custody of children. The study aimed to identify the difficulties faced by working women in industry that prohibit their participation in administrative positions. The fieldwork provides preliminary information with the goal of creating a more precise picture of the present status of the working woman in the Bahraini industrial sector, with the ultimate aim of finding solutions to the problems women face in it.

In the face-to-face interviews with the female employees, I posed open-ended queries that covered the following topics:

- The difficulties they faced obtaining their job.
- Whether they experience any kind of gender discrimination.
- The attitude of the management toward female employment in regard to training and job promotion.
- Their needs as women and mothers, for example, day care facilities and breastfeeding hours during the six-month nursing period.
- How family law, which promotes equality, will affect their family life and work performance.

Open-ended questions gave respondents the chance to provide their analysis and interpretations on the conditions and status of Bahraini women in the industrial sector. The principal finding of the interviews was that although women are employed in this sector, their numbers are limited, and they are very rarely promoted to professional status. In addition, demands for reform in the workplace are minimally met.

Bahrain National Gas Company (BANAGAS)

Bahrain's involvement with the oil and gas industry started more than seven decades ago, in 1932. Throughout the succeeding 40 years, the gas associated with the production of oil was vented into the atmosphere, as it was perceived largely as a nuisance with little or no commercial value. Then, in the 1970s, major changes occurred as technological developments enabled comprehensive use of this once wasted resource as a feedstock for industry and as fuel for power generation and water desalination. Studies conducted in 1977 ascertained how best to tap the available quantities of associated gas. As a result, BANAGAS company was established in 1979 in Sitra. The primary objective of the company at the time was to optimize utilization of the readily available associated gas by processing it into propane and naphtha. Its other objectives were to make available the residual gas arising from the oil production process for local industrial use and to provide Bahraini nationals with employment and training opportunities.

A vigorous long-term development program was undertaken to train skilled operators to run the plant, which was subsequently extended to provide training to mechanical, electrical, and electronic engineering technicians. Short-term programs were also introduced to meet the immediate needs of the company for other skilled personnel. Annual recruitment of secondary school graduates to follow sponsored technical education courses in Bahrain as in-company training accompanied this program.

Such recruitment and training, which was to continue for a number of years, was initiated for two specific reasons: to ensure rapid Bahrainization without depleting other industries in the country of their trained industrial employees; and to ensure an efficient and highly qualified national workforce. The company also needed staff with professional qualifications, and thus over the years a number of petroleum and gas technology trainees were taken on who would ultimately assume full responsibility for shift operator positions. Some of these trainees undertook their courses at the Gulf Polytechnic in Bahrain, while others were to benefit from the award of BANAGAS scholarships to pursue highest studies either at overseas universities, such as those in Saudi Arabia, the United States, and the United Kingdom, or at Bahrain University (BANAGAS 2006: 16–17). Women's employment at this company is recent; hence few women have benefited from these programs.

The company has developed a range of personal benefits for the workforce, including a savings and loan scheme, a housing loan scheme, medical assistance, life insurance, and social club membership. Today, 380 people work at the company; over 90 percent are Bahrainis, and 28 (or 7.4 percent) are females. Table 10.3 shows the list of female employees who work at the company, where a few form the highest ranks in senior positions. The rest generally work as secretaries, assistants, or trainees.

Table 10.3 Female employees at BANAGAS by specialization, 2009

Department	Grade	Designation
Materials and Management Services	11	Quality Coordinator
Finance	9	Senior Accountant—Financial Accounts
Materials and Management Services	9	Senior Systems Analyst/Programmer
Administration	8	Executive Secretary
Administration	8	Executive Secretary
Finance	8	Accountant—Financial Accounting
Materials and Management Services	8	Assistant—Quality Assurance
Administration	8	Personnel Assistant
Finance	8	Logistics Administrator
Materials and Management Services	7	Document Controller
Administration	7	Senior Secretary
Administration	7	Senior Secretary
Administration	7	Senior Secretary
Administration	7	Senior Secretary
Administration	7	Senior Officer Training
Materials and Management Services	7	Desktop Publishing Officer
Materials and Management Services	6	Help Desk Support Analyst
Finance	6	Account Officer
Public Relations	5	Public Relations Officer—Trainee
Administration	5	Officer Training—Trainee
Administration	5	Telephone Operator
Administration	5	Senior Clerk/Typist
Administration	5	Personnel Clerk
Administration	4	Clerk—Training
Administration	4	Secretary
Administration	4	Typist
Finance	4	Officer Account Payable—Trainee
English and Tech Services	4	Typist

Source: Courtesy of BANAGAS.

The women stressed that the company does not discriminate against them. However, six years ago, the company did not grant female employees housing loans until they negotiated loans equal to what was given male employees. The interviewees agreed that few women are interested in working for this particular company because the work requires them to labor at night or be exposed to gas and heat. They all preferred to work in the administrative sector inside the company's offices.

Gulf Petrochemical Industries Co. (GPIC)

GPIC was established in 1979, and its first project was the construction of a petrochemical complex at Sitra. An area of 60 hectares was reclaimed from the sea for the construction of the ammonia and methanol units, and production started in 1985. The ammonia, urea, and methanol plants have all exceeded 800 days of continuous production.

Training is offered on all levels to both men and women, with staff members continuously involved in courses, seminars, or conferences at GPIC's training center or at other institutions both inside and outside Bahrain. Bahrainis account for 80 percent of GPIC's workforce. The number of employees is around 500, of whom 36 are women, or 7 percent of the total. Most of them work in middle management. Table 10.4 shows that three women work as managers, three work as engineers, one is in senior programming, and five are at the officers level, while the remaining 24 work as accountants and secretaries. The six women interviewed agreed that they do not face any discrimination by the management. It is clear that GPIC has attempted to provide more equitable work conditions for all employees, regardless of gender. In this institution women, albeit in relatively small numbers, have had the chance to move upward in the professional echelons.

Aluminium Bahrain (Alba)

Alba officially opened in 1971 and became the largest modern aluminium smelter in the world when it commissioned its newest reduction line in May 2005, increasing its annual production capacity to more than 830,000 tons per year.

Three thousand and seven employees work at Alba, and women form 90, or 3 percent, of the total. This percentage is the lowest among the companies investigated. One manager explained that the long hours of work as well as the atmosphere of the smelters is not appealing to females, especially married women with children. However, some of the female employees have reached high positions; one is the chief of the medical office, two are civil engineers, and four are IT specialists. Nearly 40 are secretaries and an equal number work in marketing. Some of the women complained that they have to work harder than their male counterparts and become assertive in order to be promoted. This case confirms that female employees in Bahraini industries face discrimination and adverse work conditions, despite training programs available to them as well as their personal efforts to achieve and the success of a few.

Table 10.4 Number of GPIC female employees by specialization, 2009

Management Level	3
Senior Engineers Level	1
Engineers Level	2
Senior Programming Level	1
Officers Level	5
Accountant Level	4
Executive Secretary Level	2
Senior Secretary Level	12
Secretary Level	6
Total number of females working at GPIC	36

Source: Courtesy of GPIC.

The Bahrain Petroleum Company (BAPCo)

The two years that followed the 1932 discovery of oil in Bahrain saw the drilling of wells for production and for observing the reservoir. International competition led to the construction of the Bahrain Refinery and the first Crude Distillation Unit (CDU). The CDU became operational in 1937, and had a capacity of 10,000 barrels a day. Today BAPCo's refinery has a capacity of 260,000 barrels a day.

BAPCo has always had a reputation for training young Bahrainis. In 1954 its workforce had grown to 8,978, 6,720 of whom were natives. BAPCo established a basic school in 1948, which developed into the Apprenticeship Training Scheme, the cornerstone of BAPCo's Bahraini advancement program. In 1957, the program was enhanced to provide a new generation of Bahrainis with the skills required to help them gain faster promotion within the company. The company's scholarship and sponsorship programs currently support more than 150 students in higher education in Bahrain and abroad. Bahraini women are included in these programs.

In addition, BAPCo's Skills for the Workplace initiative commenced in January 2006 in coordination with the Ministry of Labor and the main contracting companies associated with low sulfur diesel production. The aim of this program is to provide training to 600 Bahraini job seekers—both male and female—to develop skills essential for industry and construction and to provide employment opportunities with Bahraini contracting companies.

The number of BAPCo employees is 3,200; women represent 194, or 6 percent of the total, a relatively low ratio for a company established 75 years ago. All of the female interviewees, whose ages ranged from late 20s to 40s, agreed that their jobs are very demanding because of the long hours. Out of 61 managers, only a chemical engineer in charge of planning and development for local markets is female. She complained that she is paid less than her male counterparts. Some of the female employees are senior engineers and senior analysts, but the majority work as secretaries, receptionists, and nurses. Five of those interviewed were married with children, and one was divorced, and all demanded that the company establish a nursery and kindergarten where both male and female parents could place their children during the workday. The case of BAPCo is significant because it represents the most established Bahraini national industry with a long history of employment. This case also clearly shows the slow development in providing equitable conditions for women in the industrial workplace.

Bahrain Business Incubator Center (BBIC)

Establishment of the BBIC in 2003 aimed to support Bahrain's small and medium business activity by accelerating the successful development of entrepreneurial companies via an array of business support resources and services. The BBIC was developed by incubator management, a concept that dates back to the 1960s. It is particularly relevant today for countries like Bahrain, whose infrastructure and economic policies support the development of Small and Medium

Enterprises (SMEs). To add further quality to the initiative, the services of the United Nations Industrial Development Organization (UNIDO) have been used to design and implement the project. The center boasts that a few women have used its facilities to become successful in business, such as in making perfumes and chocolate as well as packaging.

Garment and textile industry

The garment industry took root in the early 1980s, when three factories with a working capital of 307,000 BD ($816,000) opened in the Sitra Industrial Zone. The total labor force was 1,446 Bahrainis, of whom the majority were female. Bahrainis owned two of the factories and a foreign investor owned the third. Their total output came to 7.2 million square meters of fabric, of which $40 million worth was exported. The factories closed in 1985 due to the weak export markets, but they resumed their production in 1987 after the United States allocated a share of its import quota for Bahrain.

By 1996, the number of garment factories rose to 24 with a total workforce of 3,312, of whom 887 were Bahraini women (26 percent)—a significant decrease from the early 1980s due to an increase in hiring foreign labor. In 2001, the number of workers in ready-made garments reached 12,620, of whom 2,840 were Bahraini women (23 percent). Six new textile factories were inaugurated in the mid-1990s, which employed 197 workers, of whom 23 were Bahraini women. By 2001, the number of workers rose to 2,028, including 437 Bahraini women (22 percent). In 2006, 10 textile factories closed, which led to 1,000 Bahraini women losing their jobs. This change in the industry was caused by the end of the quota system as offered by the United States and the application of the Free Trade Agreement.[2]

A field study conducted by Al-Nahdha Women's Society in 2007 on the status of Bahraini women working in the textile industry surveyed 939 female employees working in 20 factories, of whom 18 were administrators. The study showed that the majority faced difficulties at work, including minor injuries for half of them. Some women are speaking out against such treatment. In March 2008, 100 women workers went on strike at the Noble Garment Factory in Askar with a demand for pay raises.

The statistics cited above indicate a newly decreased share of Bahraini women in the garment and textile industry. One reason for this, as mentioned above, is that Bahraini women lack qualifications, since the emphasis in education is on preparing them for the lower echelons of industry. Furthermore, their foreign counterparts are generally more skilled and experienced, exhibit low absenteeism, accept lower pay, and are often favored because they lack awareness of the rules and regulations of Bahrain's labor system.

Policies for women's empowerment

Education and training within industry is highly significant in generating human capital. It is a prerequisite for the success and effectiveness of an efficient professional labor force for both sexes. The number of women joining industry is slowly increasing despite educational and training obstacles. And women are facing further roadblocks in this sector, as the industrial environment exposes women to longer working hours and night shifts during which they often find it difficult to leave their families.

Furthermore, though legislation and its reformist intentions are recognized, it often clashes with tradition, customs, and religion. There is evidence of deviation from the laws, which underpins a lack of confidence in them. Discrimination is further manifested in bureaucratic obstacles, complex procedures, a lack of government services, and insufficient job opportunities and career advancement. These discriminatory obstacles impede women's development and their effective participation in various economic activities, including industry.

In regard to these issues, the women interviewed voiced the following recommendations:

- Adjustment of working hours to fit with their maternal responsibilities.
- Improvement of pay level so as to receive equal pay as their male counterparts.
- Equal opportunity for promotion in executive positions.
- Establishment of daycare facilities in every large industry.

There is also a governmental effort attempting to raise women's status in Bahrain. The Supreme Council for Women, headed by the First Lady, expresses the governmental undertaking. The Council organizes conferences, seminars, and workshops concerning gender equality and creates awareness of this issue among both sexes, especially those with religious leanings who fear that such development will deviate from the true teachings of Islam. But it appears that the application of such an ambitious strategy is not easy and needs more time, a bigger effort, and a political will. What is required is concentrated cooperation between the governmental and the nongovernmental to consolidate efforts for women's empowerment.

Notes

1 Education has also become one of the main channels for professional and social mobilization with regard to urbanization. See the United Nations ESCWA 2005: 331, Table 12.
2 At present the volume of garment export to the United States is around $260 million, about 60 percent of the total export market from Bahrain to the United States.

Bibliography

Annajjar, B. (2000) "Arabian Gulf Women and the Difficulty of Modernization," Presentation at the Beirut Cultural Center. (In Arabic)
Bahrain National Gas Company (BANAGAS) (2006) "Serving Bahrain for 25 Years," BANAGAS.

Fakhro, H (Minister of Industry and Commerce of Bahrain) (2008) Personal interview, Manama, Bahrain, February.

al-Ghanem, K. (2002) "Women and Development in Qatar Society," Presentation at the Supreme Council for Family, Qatar, 21–23 April.

Ja'afar, Y. (2002) "Health Care for Women in Oman," Presentation at the Advisory Forum on Planning an Omani National Strategy for Women, Oman, March 3–5.

Nazir, S. and Tomppert, L. (2005) *Women's Rights in the Middle East and North Africa: Citizenship and Justice*, Freedom House, New York: Rowman & Littlefield.

al-Rumaihi, M. (1984) *Bahrain: Problems of Political and Social Change*, Kuwait: Kadhmeh. (in Arabic)

United Nations Economic and Social Commission for Western Asia (ESCWA) (2005) *Status of Arab Women Report*, New York: The United Nations. (In Arabic)

al-Zayani, A., Abdulla, K., and al-Ajmi, J. (2007) "The Economic Empowerment of Women in Bahrain," Bahrain Competitiveness Council (BCC).

Section V

Gulf industrialization in perspective

11 Gulf industrialization in perspective

Hazem El Beblawi

Introduction

"The Gulf Countries" refers to those Arab states that are members of the Gulf Cooperation Council, or the GCC (Saudi Arabia, Bahrain, Kuwait, Oman, Qatar, and the United Arab Emirates, or UAE). With the exception of Bahrain and Oman, the GCC countries are major oil and gas producers. Saudi Arabia has the largest economy, representing about 50 percent of the GCC's combined gross domestic product (GDP), some 80 percent of its total area, and 70 percent of its population. It also holds about 55 percent of the region's proven oil resources. Moreover, as host to the Holy Islamic Shrines, Saudi Arabia enjoys a traditional cultural influence. Saudi prominence notwithstanding, some small principalities, particularly Dubai in the UAE, exhibit vibrant dynamism as a booming real estate market and a hub for trade and services. Qatar also aspires to play a more visible role; its outspoken *Al Jazeera* network is indicative in this respect.

GCC countries are not only oil-producing countries; they also share among themselves the special characteristic of heavily relying on imported labor. The percentage of expatriates to total population reaches as high as 80 percent or more in the UAE, while the lowest percentage of foreigners is around 20 percent in Oman.

Thanks to the abundance of oil and a low population density, the GCC countries enjoy high per capita income. In fact, some countries in the region rank among the highest per capita worldwide.[1]

Over the last three or four decades, most countries in the region have invested lavishly in large and high-quality physical infrastructure projects, such as roads, ports, airports, electricity, schools, and hospitals. No less generous were governments' expenditures on social welfare, which provided citizens with a wide range of free or low-cost services, such as water, housing, education, and health care. Life expectancy in the GCC increased by almost 10 years to 74 years from 1980 to 2000, and literacy rates increased by 20 percent over the same period. Overall, real economic growth has averaged four percent annually during the last three decades (Fasano and Iqbal 2003). GCC citizens also benefit from the rare privilege of either the absence of taxes or very low tax rates.

Nothing disrupts this peaceful and soft existence except the extremely hot weather and the uncertainty regarding the future, as indeed, the two main economic features of GCC countries—oil, which is nonrenewable, and imported labor—must be addressed if the region is to continue to thrive.[2] Though the weather can reach some 50 degrees Celsius in summer, indoor air-conditioning can help. As for preparing for a post-oil era, the Gulf states hope that a policy of economic diversification in industry will be the appropriate response.

Main features of industry in the Gulf

I do not intend to undertake a detailed analysis of the Gulf's industrialization experience. Rather, the purpose of this paper is to bring to light the major challenges facing the Gulf industrialization model as it heads into the future.

Because the Gulf economies are dominated by oil, it is no surprise that the "Ores and Minerals" and "Government" sectors in Table 11.1 represent more than half of the GDP.

The Ores and Minerals sector is mainly oil and gas production, and the Manufactures sector is basically divided between oil-based and import substitution industries. The oil-based industries, in addition to the extraction of oil and gas, include oil processing refineries and petrochemicals as well as energy-intensive industries such as aluminum. Oil refineries in the Arab world represent about 9 percent of the total world capacity, half of which are in the Gulf area. Saudi Arabia has established two industrial zones for petrochemicals, one in Yanbou on the Red Sea, and the second in Jubayl on the Persian Gulf. Bahrain and the UAE produce aluminum, and Qatar has also embarked on a huge aluminum project, with Oman following suit.

Oil-based industries are usually huge projects that are very modern and highly capital-intensive. They are also export-oriented and enjoy clear high comparative advantage due to the low cost of oil production in the region. They are a gift from nature, turning the region into one of the most conspicuous rentier economies in

Table 11.1 Percentage of GDP by sector in the Gulf

	1995	2000	2005	2006
Commodities	**54.1**	59.3	**64.3**	**65.6**
Agriculture	4.3	3.6	2.3	2.0
Ores Minerals	32.1	39.3	46.4	48.1
Manufactures	9.8	9.7	9.7	9.6
Other	7.9	6.6	5.9	5.9
Services	**44.7**	**39.7**	**34.8**	**33.5**
Government	17.1	14.7	11.9	10.8
Indirect Taxes	**1.1**	**1.0**	**0.9**	**0.9**

Source: The Arab Monetary Fund (2007 and previous issues) *The Arab Joint Economic Report.* Reprinted with permission.

the world and thus affecting the general pattern of economic behavior and the comparative advantage of other potential sectors—the "Dutch Disease." I turn to these concepts below.

Manufacturing industries fall under the heading of import substitution, principally in the areas of food processing and construction materials. Some major international brands find it more expedient to franchise or to form joint ventures with local investors to process their products locally and thus maintain their market share. The local value-added in food processing industries is therefore modest. However, this is not the case with the construction sector. In particular, cement industries use local materials and thus have reasonably high local content and value-added. Cement production has increased substantially in the GCC countries, and there are plans to further increase it in the near future (see Table 11.2). It seems thus that independently from oil, the region enjoys a relative comparative advantage in the cement industry. It must be mentioned, however, that many Western industrialized countries are encouraging the migration of their cement industries because of environmental reasons. Hence the economic benefits from these industries are counterbalanced by high environmental costs.

The oil-based industries' future is, of course, dependant on the availability of oil. Oil will not cease to exist suddenly, but will be gradually phased out over a long period. Most probably, alternative sources of energy will increasingly replace oil, though oil will continue to be used as a valuable raw material for petrochemical industries. Other import substitution industries have very little chance of expanding beyond the needs of the local markets—and their levels of local value are modest, in any case.

It is thus clear that neither oil-based nor import substitution industries have much hope to survive or to expand in a post-oil era. Does this mean that the Gulf countries have up to this point failed to develop a viable industrialization model for the future? If so, why?

Resource-based economies

While the initial thinking was that abundant natural resource endowment is a blessing, more recent writings on the subject emphasize the negative aspects of resource–based economies, usually labeled the "curse of natural resources."

Table 11.2 Productive capacity of Gulf cement industries

	Designed capacity (million tons)		Production (million tons)	
	2004	*2010*	*2004*	*2010*
GCC	42.7	63.9	39.9	56.7
Arab countries	147.5	184.6	112.3	140.7

Source: The Arab Monetary Fund (2006) *The Arab Joint Economic Report*. Reprinted with permission.

The truth is perhaps between these two extremes. Natural resources are neither a pure blessing nor an absolute curse; they can be a definite bonus if well managed.

Negative aspects of resource-based economies can result from a psychological mindset associated with nonearned income and/or an economic distortion of prices, thus disrupting the proper allocation of resources. Resource-based economies can, in fact, favor a rentier mentality and its associated behavior.

I have discussed, in another context, the concept of the rentier state (Beblawi and Luciani 1984). A rentier mentality is incompatible with hard work, discipline, and risk-taking, and it embodies a disconnect in the work–reward relationship. Another negative aspect related to the distortion of natural resources is known as "Dutch Disease." This syndrome was first detected in the Netherlands subsequent to the discovery of natural gas and the windfall of wealth that followed.

Max Corden and Peter Neary first introduced this concept in a 1982 paper (Corden and Neary 1982). The authors divided the economy experiencing such a syndrome into three sectors, two of traded goods and one of nontradable goods—with the first two sectors exporting booming natural resources and the third sector exporting other manufacturing goods. The argument's essence is that the booming resource-based sector will bring about a surge in foreign exchange earnings in such magnitude as to appreciate the local currency. This appreciation can be the result of a general price increase and/or a change in the exchange rate, according to whether the country follows a gold standard or a flexible exchange rate. The appreciation of the exchange rate penalizes other exporting industries and undermines any potential comparative advantage in the rest of the economy. Benefits from the resource-based sector are thus diminished because other opportunities for development are ignored or missed. As such, the economy deepens its reliance on the resource-based industry and denies itself the possibility of developing otherwise competitive industries.

The Gulf states' drama is that oil is not simply another economic activity added to the other existing productive sources within a viable and modern economy, as is the case with the Netherlands or, for that matter, Canada, Australia, and the Scandinavian countries. In the Gulf, the oil sector dominates the economy; it is almost the unique source of wealth.

Contrary to Western oil-producing countries such as the United Kingdom and Norway, oil was discovered in the Gulf countries as they were beginning to establish themselves as nations. The majority of the populations were preindustrial; for the most part, they were poor nomadic tribes constantly moving from place to place looking for pasturage in a sparsely populated landscape. Settled populations were the exception rather than the norm. Faced with such a situation, the first responsibility for the newly independent states was understandably nation-building. The states' prime concern was thus to finance physical infrastructures and provide basic services, leaving economic diversification for the future.

However, today's oil-based and import substitution industries in the Gulf still do not provide the kind of diversification needed for a post-oil era. How has this situation come about?

The original sin: the fallacy of national accounts

The distinction between "income" and "capital" is fundamental to basic economics. Income is a flow concept; it is the recurring flow of goods and services over a period of time and is used to satisfy its earner's needs, both present and future. Income is thus used for consumption and savings. Capital, on the contrary, is a *stock* concept; it is the wealth or assets that exist at a certain moment, and its function is to generate income in the future. Its owner has the obligation to conserve its value and use it to generate income in perpetuity.

From an accounting point of view, income is captured in the *income statement* at the micro level and is an element of the GDP at the macro level. Capital, on the other hand, is a *balance sheet* item. The Gulf states have partially ignored these elementary principles regarding the treatment of oil proceeds by simply considering them as income. As their incomes increased substantially following the rise in oil prices, the Gulf states behaved like rich countries and augmented their consumption enormously. The huge inflow of foreign exchange and the price structure that followed were taken for granted as a proper indication for resource allocation. Oil prices have thus dominated the economy, giving rise to a generalized Dutch Disease.

Various countries outside the Gulf have managed their oil proceeds wisely. Norway is a pioneering example. The third largest oil exporter behind Saudi Arabia and Russia, Norway realized, after some painful experiences, the need to neutralize the impact of oil proceeds on the rest of its economy. The Norwegians thus passed legislation requiring that almost all the revenues from the government-owned oil company, Statoil, be placed in an investment fund to ensure that oil and gas receipts would not distort the economy's price structure and will benefit future generations. As such, the Norwegian economy has succeeded to a large extent in insulating itself from the "oil curse," and it has ensured that actual consumption is confined within the boundaries of the productive capacity of the economy.

The Gulf states have not followed this path. Oil proceeds are still included in their GDP and constitute the principal revenue of the government budget. However, most Gulf states, after an initial period of nation-building, have adopted conscious policies to allocate a portion of their oil revenues to investment funds for future generations.

Gulf investment funds

Thus, though the Gulf states have not subscribed completely to the idea that oil proceeds are *wealth* rather than *income*, they are nevertheless aware that oil proceeds are temporary gifts from nature and that they must build a viable and sustainable economy. Three decades after the discovery of oil, Gulf governments began to manage their wealth more responsibly by looking to the future. Kuwait first envisaged investment in foreign financial markets as a strategy to diversify the economy by opening the Kuwait Investment Office in London in 1953.

Then, in the mid-1970s, Kuwait established an Investment Fund for Future Generations (IFFG) that is also kept outside the government budget.

The Kuwaiti approach was a pragmatic compromise. It did not go so far as to consider oil proceeds as capital assets, but the government has made a point to set aside part of these proceeds in a capital account not to be touched for current expenditures. The returns on these investments are replowed back in the same account and are not included in government budget revenues. Furthermore, the government is not allowed to draw on these funds except in exceptional cases and with special authorization from the parliament. These financial resources proved extremely helpful for the Kuwaiti government during the Iraqi invasion in the early 1990s.

In addition to the IFFG, Kuwait established a number of semi-governmental entities to invest in various sectors inside and outside Kuwait, the most well known among them being the Kuwait Investment Authority (KIA), which now has assets exceeding $200 billion. This investment portfolio has provided Kuwait with handsome returns in amounts that in some years matched oil proceeds. The Iraqi invasion of Kuwait and the subsequent costs of reconstruction depleted a good portion of these funds, but the increase in oil prices in the last few years has helped replenish them, and at present Kuwait is not completely dependent on oil revenues.

Portfolio investment income has thus become as important as oil to Kuwait and, to a lesser degree, to other Gulf states. Most other states in the GCC followed Kuwait's example and have established investment authorities and semi-governmental and private investment companies. Abu Dhabi in the UAE established its investment authority in 1976; it has become one of the largest sovereign funds with total assets now reaching some $875 billion. Dubai, also in the UAE, established its own fund in 2004, and Qatar followed in 2005 (*The Economist* 2008: 62–63).

These financial institutions have become major players in international capital markets. During the recent bank subprime crisis, Gulf investment funds actively participated in rescue packages for many of the troubled banks; KIA and the Abu Dhabi Investment Authority invested in Citigroup to the tune of $3 billion and $2.5 billion, respectively. UBS, the Swiss investment bank, also benefited from Gulf financing during the same crisis.

Hence the Gulf states seem to have realized that their real comparative advantage does not reside in oil *per se* but rather in their accumulated liquid functional assets. Moreover, they all have the prerequisites to play a major role as international financiers.

The question that then arises is whether a country can live solely on the returns of its portfolio investments. History tells us that most international financier centers were usually backed by political, military, and/or economic powers. Finance alone is too vulnerable. For example, London and New York were backed by strong economic and military muscles, and Amsterdam of the seventeenth and eighteenth centuries benefited from a strong maritime force. Even Italian medieval cities such as Venice or Genoa possessed strong armies and naval powers. Perhaps the Vatican is the only financial power without a strong army, but it is backed by the larger global community of faithful adherents and a strong moral authority.

It has been argued in some quarters in Europe and the United States that Sovereign Wealth Funds (SWFs) are politically motivated and often not transparent and thus can create security risks. Two decades ago, the British government under Thatcher forced the Kuwait Investment Office to sell more than half its assets in British Petroleum. More recently, the American authorities rejected the purchase by Dubai Port Authority of a British company (P&O) that serviced a number of United States ports. Some European politicians, such as French President Nicolas Sarkozy, have also indicated their hostility to these funds. Present debate on SWFs casts some doubt on the possibility of relying safely on financial investments as a unique source of income for the Gulf states in a post-oil era. Despite such concerns across the GCC, one location has less need to worry about the future: Dubai.

Dubai exceptionalism

Whereas Abu Dhabi, the UAE's capital, is the federation's largest oil producer, Dubai's oil revenues are modest and their life span is no more than 20 years. Dubai's GDP was estimated in 2006 at $46 billion, of which less than 6 percent was derived from oil and gas. With a population of some 1.5 million, Dubai enjoys one of the highest per capita incomes in the Gulf at around $30,000. Despite its relatively limited natural resources, Dubai is among the fastest-growing economies in the region. Its economic performance over the last few years has been particularly impressive (it has been growing at a sustained rate of 10–13 percent over the last decade), and the prospects for further growth seem promising.

How did Dubai arrive at such success? Could Dubai be a prototype for other Gulf states in a post-oil era?

While Dubai's recent impressive performance might seem quite exceptional, it was actually predestined to achieve such results. History, location, culture, and neighborhood prepared Dubai to become a remarkable achiever. A port at the crossroads of Arabia, Iran, and India, Dubai was poised to be a center of trade as well as a depot for goods for the whole region. For more than two centuries, it performed this role and provided services to its neighbors, particularly India. It has also always been a mercantile town with settled and active Indian and Iranian communities, enjoying the reputation of a free and tolerant metropolis with multicultural populations. In addition, Dubai has always been ruled within a free market framework: traders are kings, and the ruler is the guardian of the merchants' interests. When oil was discovered in Dubai, it came in almost optimum quantities—enough to boost the economy, but not too much to turn it into a rentier economy. Indeed, the oil bonanza that came to its neighbors provided Dubai with vast nearby opportunities to exploit, and Dubai has risen to the task.

With strict adherence to market philosophy, the Dubai authorities have created a friendly environment for investments, with minimal red tape, prompt decisions, and an efficient bureaucracy. First class infrastructure is also available, such as roads, ports, an airport, telecommunications, and electricity. Dubai's development strategy thus seems to be the absorption of the liquidity available in the region and beyond by providing first class services not available locally. Dubai thus provides quality services for high-income strata consumption, such as hotels, beaches, entertainment, shopping, schooling, media, and hospitals. But Dubai is also creating a vibrant financial market. In both cases, the criterion is providing high quality products, or what the ruler of Dubai calls "excellence."

It is also worth mentioning that Dubai realized early that the Gulf's comparative advantage resides in the availability of large liquid assets to better undertake investments with high capital requirements. Dubai thus invested heavily in its airline, Emirates, which entailed huge upfront capital outlays; it soon became one of the more competitive world carriers. Further, Dubai's real estate development is emphasized to the extent that, to a casual visitor, the city gives the impression of a huge workshop with a forest of cranes. Estimates for the increase in demand for housing seem to justify the present real estate boom.

Dubai's skyrocketing real estate as well as its exuberant stock market are signs of success and a vote of confidence. Can Dubai's success be replicated in other places in the region, such as Qatar or Bahrain? Unfortunately for those countries, the strength of Dubai resides in the fact that it came first in an innovative way. It is an exception, and exceptions cannot necessarily lead to norms. Latecomers must invent something different.

Dubai does, however, have a major problem it must address to secure its future—heavy dependence on imported labor. The need for unskilled labor during construction phases is enormous. The assumption is that foreign labor will eventually be reduced and phased out. As a result, Dubai's strategy is to concentrate on clean sectors mainly operated by professionals with limited requirements for massive unskilled labor. Furthermore, the recent financial crisis (2008) showed the extent of Dubai's financial vulnerability. High bank leverage and excessive real estate prices exposed Dubai's financial institutions to serious stress.

What is the situation in the rest of the GCC, and what should its countries do in regard to foreign labor?

Imported labor

While the Arab world at large shows signs of demographic pressure, the Gulf countries are characterized by low population density and a shortage of well-trained and qualified labor.

The total population of the GCC countries, including expatriates, was estimated in 2000 at some 32 million people. Saudi Arabia has the largest population at 22 million, while Bahrain and Qatar have the smallest populations at less than one million each. The expatriate population is only about one-fourth of the total population in Saudi Arabia, but accounts for more than 70 percent of the total in the smaller countries (Fasano and Goyal 2004).

In spite of the high growth in the national population during the past decades, the share of expatriate workers in the labor force has continued to increase. The number of foreign workers rose almost fivefold from 1.1 million in 1970 to 5.2 million in 2000 (*Arab Human Development Report* 2002: 36). Less than a decade later, it is estimated that these numbers have risen to more than 5.5 million. Expatriate workers currently account for 50 percent of employed labor in Saudi Arabia and close to 90 percent in the UAE.

Different job categories in the Gulf include government employees, private sector labor, professionals, skilled, and unskilled labor. For nationals, employment in the government and public sector is implicitly guaranteed. In most GCC countries, more than 60 percent of the national labor force is employed in the public sector, and in Saudi Arabia and Bahrain, the percentage is higher. National women who have entered the labor market in the past decade are also mainly employed in the public sector. Such jobs are the preferred domain of work for nationals, as they usually provide higher wages, job security, social allowances, and generous end-of-service benefits. Moreover, promotion is mainly based on seniority rather than performance. In contrast, expatriates principally work for the nonoil private sector and account, on average, for more than 85 percent of total employed workers in that area (Fasano and Goyal 2004). Paradoxically, both professional jobs and unskilled work are overwhelmingly occupied by expatriates. In these cases, the market is usually more competitive.

Excess in imported labor resulted from two exogenous factors, both of which should be viewed as temporary. The first was the discovery of oil, and the second is the pervasive poverty in adjacent countries. With oil wealth pull and poverty push in the neighborhood, the GCC countries found at their disposal huge numbers of trained, skilled, and unskilled workers looking for better opportunities. Unfortunately for the Gulf, oil is not a permanent source of wealth, and neither is poverty an eternal fate for its neighboring countries.

It is fully understandable that the Gulf countries relied heavily on imported labor in the early phases of their development. However, following this initial phase of nation-building, the countries of the GCC should prepare themselves to return to normality. The depletion of oil wealth and/or the future prosperity of the adjacent countries would render reliance on expatriate labor more and more difficult and expensive. Moreover, the differences between national and expatriate labor is not only confined to cultural background and type of work, but is also manifested in unequal economic rights and privileges. This could be a source of latent discontent in the long-term, as second- and third-generation expatriates will likely be more demanding of equal treatment. Many international institutions are already voicing objections regarding the unequal treatment of foreign labor in the region.

The Gulf countries must thus put forward a more liberal policy toward naturalization of foreign labor, a less protective and paternalistic policy toward nationals, and more egalitarian treatment when it comes to working conditions. These are not easy decisions, as they amount to a renouncement of the rentier mentality. However, difficult decisions must be made after so many years of carefree enjoyment of nature's gifts.

Regional integration

In addition to addressing the problem of foreign labor, the Gulf states may benefit from regional integration.

With the exception of Saudi Arabia and possibly Oman, the Gulf countries are small economies. Economic size is usually measured by GDP, but this is not always a fully adequate measurement. Population is, in many instances, equally important. Sparsely populated with no other resources except oil and gas, the Gulf countries depend heavily on the outside world. It is hence no wonder that the countries of the GCC are highly globalized and export most of their oil while importing almost every other living requirement. Such deep integration in the world economy is a matter of necessity rather than of choice. It is the inevitable consequence of small size.

Integration in the world economy has brought the Gulf countries enormous benefits, promoting them within a few decades from tribal, preindustrial areas into modern consumer societies. The lifestyle and amenities available to citizens in the Gulf during such a short period took Western Europe more than two centuries to attain.

Yet there is a price to pay for such success, particularly in the post-oil era. The long-term political risk of total dependence on the outside world cannot be overemphasized. Renouncing globalization, however, is not only wrong, but also impossible. The risks of extreme globalization can be mitigated by strong regional integration. Historical evidence has shown that rather than acting as a stumbling block, regionalization is a building block to a more healthy globalization—Europe being the most obvious example.

Aware of the benefits of regional integration, particularly for security reasons, the Gulf countries agreed in May 1981 to establish the GCC. This regional arrangement extends over a reasonably wide economic space with a population of some 35 million people and a combined GDP of some $800 billion.

While the GCC countries emphasized coordination in *security* matters in the Council's initial phase, *economic* issues gained increasing importance in later years. Barriers to free movement of goods and services as well as to the mobility of national labor and capital have been largely removed. Prudential regulations and supervision of the banking sector are gradually being harmonized, and stock markets are largely open to all nationals of the GCC. Further, a single common external tariff is now in place, establishing a quasi Gulf customs union.

More ambitious is the commitment to adopt a single Gulf currency by 2012. This last initiative has faced a partial setback with Kuwait's announcement of depegging its currency from the dollar and the subsequent withdrawal of Oman from the negotiations. Indeed, the present decline of the dollar and the *de facto* depreciation of Gulf currencies has brought to the fore differences among Gulf policymakers in regard to the pegging of their currencies to the dollar. Saudi Arabia seems committed to the maintenance of the link, Qatar appears to be less committed, and the Emirates' position is somewhere in between. The recent turmoil in the financial market has added urgency to the issue. Another thorny issue is the countries' varying positions on the candidature of Yemen for the GCC. The Kuwaiti foreign minister announced recently that his country is opposed to the enlargement of the Council at this time.

Opposition to the enlargement of the GCC is understandable in the short-term, as it would mean supporting and eventually subsidizing the poorer Yemen for some time. However, the long-term situation would be very different. While Yemen has few oil resources, it boasts a large population and a promising agricultural potential. This substantial population—provided it is given the proper training and education—could help rectify shortages of labor. Additionally, evidence shows that industrialization, even export-oriented, needs a large home-based market. Such a vast and integrated economic space would establish just this, creating opportunities for viable industrial investments. Thus, in the long-run, the inclusion of Yemen in the GCC would be a source of strength, giving the region more economic vitality and viability.[3]

A similar case can be made for economically integrating the finance-rich Gulf into the wider population-dense Arab world. However, the political landscape in most Arab countries is far from conducive to realizing such a grand scheme. The Gulf countries are too small and lack the political clout needed to assume political leadership in the Arab world. And though investments from the Gulf in the rest of the Arab world have increased substantially over the last few years, those countries must change economically and even more so politically to attract more Gulf finances. This is a dream worth entertaining.

Conclusion

Keynes once said that "in the long-run we are all dead." He wanted to emphasize the importance of immediate problems. This was adequate for Europe of the 1930s, but such advice would be suicidal for the Gulf countries. Oil is their life-blood, yet it is also ephemeral and nonrenewable. Fortunately, the Gulf countries are taking their long-term future seriously.

Oil is wealth, not income. It is true that the Gulf countries have not formally adopted such an approach to their national accounts, yet they are building financial wealth to replace oil wealth. They are also increasingly adjusting their current expenditures in such a way that they do not exceed the income generated from financial investments. More and more, oil proceeds are spent on capital formation—mainly financial portfolios—rather than on consumption.

However, financial wealth alone, without a strong home-based economy, is not risk-free: financially rich but weak countries are an invitation to covetousness. The present debate over Sovereign Wealth Funds is only a prelude to the kind of risks that can arise when financial wealth is not backed by economic or military power. For the time being, these risks are minimal due to the continuous flow of oil to the world economy, giving the Gulf countries a countervailing power against any foreign challenge. In a post-oil era, the Gulf would lose such a defense mechanism and would be left only with moral rights. Historical evidence shows that morality alone, valuable as it is, can be very ineffective against greed.

Most Gulf countries are aware of this risk and recognize the need to diversify their local economies by building strong and viable home-based industries.

Industrialization in the region today, however, is either too oil-dependent or too shallow. Limited population size and a labor shortage are serious obstacles to establishing viable and competitive industries, as is complacency in the face of affluence. Regional economic integration offers the Gulf countries the opportunity of a wider market. Though at first conceived as a security bulwark, the establishment of the GCC proved later to be a wise economic arrangement that overcomes size limitations. In this regard, the enlargement of the GCC to include Yemen represents a long-term strategic advantage; enlarging it further to include the entire Arab world would establish an even more solid base for industrialization. In a post-oil era, the Gulf countries are too small to survive in a globalized world. Regional economic integration is a reasonable price for future security.

In the 1950s and 1960s, the call for Arab nationalism failed because it was triggered by a desire for leadership and domination by the Mashrek. Could this call be revived in the twenty-first century on different grounds? The oil bonanza is a unique opportunity for the Gulf countries as well as for the Arab world as a whole to lay the groundwork for a strong and viable post-oil era economy. The Gulf leaders are now in the driver's seat, and the situation requires imagination and leadership. Will the Arabs seize the opportunity, or will they miss it as they have before? Failing to do so, the oil episode will be remembered in the far future as a midsummer night's dream, blurring fantasy and reality. History will tell.

Notes

1 While it is true that the GCC is a reasonably homogeneous block that shares a common cultural and historical background, differences among its members cannot be ignored. Per capita income ranges from less than $10,000 in Oman to over $30,000 in Qatar and the UAE. The manufacturing industry is far more developed in Saudi Arabia, and the financial sector is more diversified in Bahrain.
2 In some places, though by no means in all, a third element is added to the list of national worries: social discontent. The Arab solution is usually a blend of the stick and the carrot approach, involving some repression coupled with a measure of governmental largesse.
3 The Germans faced a similar situation before the unification of their country at the end of the twentieth century, and today the benefits of its convergence are clear.

Bibliography

The Arab Monetary Fund (2007) *The Arab Joint Economic Report*, The Arab Monetary Fund.
Beblawi, H. and Luciani, G. (eds.) (1984) *The Rentier State*, London: Crome Helm.
Corden, W.M. and Neary, J.P. (1982) "Booming Sector and De-Industrialisation in a Small Open Economy," *The Economic Journal*, 92: 825–848.

Fasano, U. and Goyal, R. (2004) *Emerging Strains in GCC Labor Markets*, International Monetary Fund.

Fasano, U. and Iqbal, Z. (2003) *GCC Countries: From Oil Dependence to Diversification*, International Monetary Fund.

United Nations Development Programme (UNDP) Regional Bureau for Arab States (2002) *The Arab Human Development Report*, Amman: National Press.

12   Industrializing Gulf society

Frances D. Cook and Karen Nielson

Introduction

The Industrial Revolution in the West vastly changed the landscape of not only those economies, but the way those societies functioned. A similar, profound transformation has started in the Arab Gulf, as these countries begin to react to their unprecedented growth and resources. So far, the GCC countries have managed to avoid the seamier underside of globalization and have emerged as some of the most intriguing economic spaces in the world. Furthermore, long viewed as a bastion of Arab tradition, the Gulf now has some of the most visionary and innovative leaders in the Middle East.

In contrast to the United States, for example, Gulf states have cost-free and generally excellent health care for all their citizens. This was an early goal all Gulf states set for themselves, and they are using the current rush of resources to finalize the amazing transformation of health care in the region. In fact, by 2000, Oman was ranked first by the World Health Organization in Health Service Performance and fourth in Best Overall Health Care following France, Italy, and Spain (WHO 2000).

According to the Institute of International Finance, Arab Gulf countries earned $1.5 trillion in oil revenue between 2002 and 2006. This is double the amount made during the previous five-year period, and does not reflect the high oil prices that multiplied all Gulf treasuries many times over. It is expected that the growth rate will reach 8 percent this year, after already reaching 5.2 percent in 2007 (Institute of International Finance 2008). But in addition to huge financial reserves, all GCC countries are coping with challenges, such as a large increase in their youth populations, who will enter the workforce in the next 10 years. In Oman, 42.7 percent of the population is under 14 years of age (CIA 2009a), and the numbers are similar in Saudi Arabia (CIA 2009b). These factors present significant challenges—even danger—but also opportunities for these countries.

Also, and increasingly, each GCC country has set goals and chosen paths to succeed in this globalizing world. As Booz Allen reports, "Although the Middle East is known as a tradition-bound region, its decision-makers are fundamentally progressive. They understand that the world is changing and often recognize when their own institutions must change as well" (Sabbagh *et al.* 2008).

Below, I chronicle some of these positive changes but also point to where attention is still needed in such areas as the economy, education, and employment.

Diversification

It is generally recognized that diversification is critical for an economically successful future. Gulf states, by creating a mixed economy, hope to expand economic opportunity and spread wealth while enhancing stability and reducing their dependence on hydrocarbon income. But a "one size fits all" approach will not work. Oman is building, for example, a service/tourism industry, while other Gulf countries promote the banking, media, or manufacturing sectors that best suit their respective geographical locations and resource base. Yet all have some sort of effort underway that may be broadly called "industrialization."

Trade between the countries remains the lowest regional trade in the world at 10 percent (Middle East North Africa Financial Network 2008). A diversification of services and non-oil exports would create opportunities for trade within the region, instead of competition in the same areas. Also, as GCC states design their modern economic sectors, they must be wary of an overdependence on gas-fueled capital projects. Some projects, currently under construction, have yet to lock in firm gas supplies. As recently as the fall of 2007, I heard project managers discussing either importing coal or developing wind power for industrial projects in the Gulf.[1]

The creation of economic "oasis cities" is another interesting idea currently popular in the region. Reports state that there are over 55 economic cities established or under development in the GCC (Sabbagh *et al.* 2008). The United Arab Emirates has been working on creating them since 1985. Bahrain and Oman are also developing these independent and all-encompassing urban centers, as well as Saudi Arabia, which hopes to create 1.3 million new employment opportunities in six new oasis cities by 2020 (Mouawad 2008). Before the Gulf goes too far down the path of these purpose-built cities, I hope they will examine some of the advantages and disadvantages of similar spaces elsewhere in the region; a visit to the huge mill towns in Egypt's Delta, such as Mahalla al-Kubra, would be instructive.

Booz Allen also reports that

> the emergence of a new regional, diversified economy is a fundamental shift that will affect not just corporate investment, but geopolitical activity as well. The Middle East may be developing a new type of economy, different from any other that has preceded it. It is not patterned on the models of North America and Europe. Instead, if anything, this economy is an attempt to re-create the flourishing, outward-looking Silk Road economy of the Islamic world of the twelfth to fourteenth centuries, when Arab merchants were the world's economic leaders. This phenomenon is being spurred on by a broad group of decision makers – rulers, government officials, bankers, manufacturers, and some outside investors and companies – who are trying

to build a bridge between Middle East culture and its economic potential. They understand that if the region is to thrive, it must build its future on a diversified foundation. They realize, as a result, that they must foster the innate entrepreneurial spirit of their people.

(Sabbagh *et al.* 2008)

I would add that political liberalization is occurring in the Gulf along with bold moves in economic development. It is coming more slowly and in a different manner in each Gulf state, but it is occurring. It will be fascinating to see if Gulf rulers continue to "lead from the front" in this sphere, as they have with economic development.

Education

As the world becomes more global, interconnected, and technological, an educated base from which to draw becomes imperative for the Arab Gulf. The GCC countries have made significant strides toward enrolling children in educational programs from early ages and adding a world language—English—from grade one. These shifts have quickly increased literacy to high levels and have closed the gap in basic education for both sexes. Teachers are also now being trained rather than imported. But reforms are still needed (World Bank 2007).

As we saw with the "Asian Tigers" and, more recently, Ireland, a fundamental building block to economic expansion was an *appropriately* educated workforce. Education in the Gulf needs to focus more on management and technical training, and not on preparing young people to work in the government. The day when the primary employer of educated graduates is the government has passed pretty much everywhere, with the exception of Kuwait, where 90 percent of the country's workers are on the government's payroll (Pollack 2008).

Furthermore, a shift from curricula that rely on rote and nonparticipatory learning to classrooms that promote problem-solving and application of knowledge is still required (Assaad and Roudi-Fahimi 2007: 5). The United Arab Emirates recognizes this need and is working on the issue of primary education with international education consultants. At the heart of this effort is a pilot mentoring program of 37 foreign school principals who mentor two UAE principals each in new methods (Zehr 2008). In addition to continuing reform in primary education, it is also necessary to provide educational opportunities in secondary and post-secondary institutes as well as technical and management training to create a workforce that is ready to take on the opportunities and challenges that await them. A government-private sector partnership in designing training programs for current and future labor markets will be essential in the coming years.

Qatar, long a leader in education in the Gulf, has done an excellent job of recognizing the problem at the tertiary level and has been for some time applying serious resources to education reform. Collaborations with Cornell, Georgetown, Carnegie Mellon, and Texas A&M are well along (Sabbagh *et al.* 2008). Cornell's commitment to education, research, and patient care has been replicated in Doha at the Weill Cornell Medical College in Qatar, where its first class of 16 medical students graduated in 2008 (Sabbagh *et al.* 2008). Qatar has been appropriately "tough" with American institutions who wish to partner with it by insisting with Cornell, for instance, that faculty must be from the Cornell staff—not academics who are baptized "Cornell" and then put on a plane for Doha. That makes a difference, not only in the quality of education offered on the Doha campus, but in Qatar's long-term ties to that prestigious American university. It is important for collaborations such as these to continue to foster growth across cultures and increase the caliber of educational opportunities in the Gulf. I would recommend this insistence on the "real thing" to other Gulf states busy building United States and United Kingdom campuses in the region.

Employment

Population growth in the Middle East and North Africa (MENA) region as a whole has been astonishing. Mortality rates began to decline in the late nineteenth and early twentieth centuries, but the decline in fertility did not occur until the 10-year period between the mid-1960s and early 1970s. The region's population growth rate reached a peak of 3 percent a year around 1980, with a current rate of 2 percent a year. In comparison, the world growth rate peaked at 2 percent decades ago and is currently at 1.2 percent. As a result of these figures, there were nearly 95 million youths between the ages of 15 and 24 in the MENA region in 2005. This number is expected to peak at 100 million by 2035 and then slowly decline (Assaad and Roudi-Fahimi 2007: 1).

The Gulf has some of the highest unemployment rates in the world. Although actual figures are hard to come by, it is estimated that unemployment in Saudi Arabia is at 14 percent, with Oman at 16 percent and Bahrain at 17 percent. The United Arab Emirates, Qatar, and Kuwait all have rates of less than 4.5 percent (Institute of International Finance 2008). The Gulf's very stability can be threatened if meaningful employment is not created quickly for the thousands of young people who enter the job market each year. We have already seen instances of social tensions in states that have too many young people with time on their hands. This is an area to watch specifically to make sure that drugs, radical ideologies and theologies, and other scourges of our times—already present in the Gulf—do not find, among unemployed youth, large numbers of new recruits.

Women

As Arab Gulf countries begin to realize the importance of women in economic development, greater female involvement in all sectors has been evident. For example:

- All member-states of GCC countries, with one exception, have female cabinet ministers—and they are no longer only in "female ministries," but handle portfolios like finance.

- In the Gulf, according to Her Excellency Shaykha Lubna al-Qasimi, the UAE Minister of Economy, women currently form about 25 percent of the workforce, and 4.5 percent own freehold businesses (al-Qasimi 2007).
- Women investors manage investments worth more than $35 billion in the Gulf region (al-Qasimi 2007).
- Women can also be a source of untapped investment capital; it is estimated that Saudi women control approximately $6 billion in untapped bank reserves (al-Ghamdi 2007).
- Oman became the first Arab country to appoint a woman ambassador to the United States in 2006. One-third of Omani civil servants are women, and 13 percent hold senior positions (Oxford Business Group 2007: 5–6).

However, these successes do not tell the full story. The 2002 Arab Human Development Report was a wake-up call, with its detailed account of the uneven and slow pace of the region's development progress (UNDP 2002). Differences between genders were particularly striking as compared to other regions around the world. A broader acceptance of the importance of women for economic development and the industrialization process is still needed for Gulf society to continue to advance. As that understanding deepens, it will discover the many benefits, as I believe Western nations have, of having women in supervisory positions in the workforce (Rosener 1995: 11–12).[2]

Labor and investments

The Gulf, even with its vast monetary resources, has not shown itself to be immune from pitfalls, such as the various "market corrections" in recent years. Though some of these were quite profound, the earlier environment of widespread corruption has greatly abated. However, labor issues—made worse by current inflation pressures—have pushed themselves to the forefront in recent years. Conditions under which Third Country laborers work and live, especially in the region's overheated construction sector, must be improved, and not just "on the books," but in strict enforcement of the international standards the GCC states have committed to honoring. Several serious labor riots in 2007 and 2008 have drawn the world's attention to a genuine need for improvement in this area. Merely expelling activist workers might provide temporary relief, but such a policy is causing long-term damage to the image that the Gulf has worked hard to build in the eyes of the world.

The GCC states (with the exception of Dubai) have also been ineffective at marketing themselves to global investors. The proper marketing skills, advice, strategies, and effort are vital to attract such investment. Instead of hiring three to five public affairs/lobbying firms in the West, the Gulf states should consider engaging marketing pros to do everything from providing an honest assessment of extant "one-stop-shop" investment offices to identifying needed legal reforms to organizing road shows.

Finally, the GCC states need to better understand that potential foreign investors, who are the purveyors of tech transfer, do not make their decisions based solely on a state's model investment code or whether their chief host government interlocutor is a "good guy." They look at land laws; labor regimes; the banking situation and rules for repatriation of capital; the quality of the workforce; the ICT environment; transportation nodes; and perhaps most important of all, the experiences—good and bad—of those foreign investors already on the ground. Working hard to minimize disputes with those foreign companies already committed to a partnership will reap benefits far beyond that particular deal.

Conclusion

This era of industrialization in the Gulf is an unprecedented opportunity for growth and also for reform. GCC states are blessed, by and large, with innovative leaders who not only have vast financial resources, but who understand the region's opportunities and who want to do what is best for their people. I am excited and delighted to have been involved in this region and look forward to watching— along with friends in the Gulf—what the future holds. This is a pivotal moment in the history of the region, and the way ahead is starting to take shape in each GCC state. The transformations will be profound and, I believe, successful.

Notes

1 It is interesting to note that hydrocarbon-based industries—especially liquefied natural gas—often create few jobs for nationals, at least at present, as professional positions are generally highly technical and go to expatriates.
2 Rosener writes: "In 1989, to answer these questions, I conducted a nationwide study of men and women leaders in diverse professions. In particular, I focused on a group of successful women leaders to ascertain how they exercised power, what kind of leadership style they preferred, and what kinds of organizations they worked in. As a basis for comparison, I looked at a similar group of male leaders at the same time. That study formed the basis of my article, 'Ways Women Lead,' which was published in the *Harvard Business Review* in late 1990 and became a lightning rod for debate about gender differences in a management context. I found that women, on average, exhibited and preferred the interactive leadership style, and men the command-and-control leadership style, and that the interactive style is particularly effective in flexible, nonhierarchical organizations of the kind that perform best in a climate of rapid change. My findings did not suggest that one style is better or worse than the other, only that men and women tend to lead differently and that interactive leaders tend to be most successful in nontraditional organizations" (Rosener 1995: 11–12).

Bibliography

Assaad, R. and Roudi-Fahimi, F. (2007) "Youth in the Middle East and North Africa: Demographic Opportunity or Challenge?," *Population Reference Bureau*, April.
Central Intelligence Agency (CIA) (2009a) "Oman," *The World Factbook*. Online HTTP: www.cia.gov/library/publications/the-world-factbook/geos/mu.html (accessed March 24, 2008).

Central Intelligence Agency (CIA) (2009b) "Saudi Arabia," *The World Factbook*. Online HTTP: www.cia.gov/library/publications/the-world-factbook/geos/sa.html (accessed March 24, 2008).

al-Ghamdi, M. (2007) "Breaking Barriers and Building Opportunities," paper presented at Arab International Women's Forum, Dubai, December.

Institute of International Finance, Inc. (2008) "Economic Report: Gulf Cooperation Council Countries," 16 January.

Middle East North Africa Financial Network (2008) "Oman: Unemployment in the Arab World High," Middle East North Africa Financial Network, 11 March.

Mouawad, J. (2008) "The Construction Site Called Saudi Arabia," *The New York Times*, 20 January.

Oxford Business Group (2007) "Emerging Oman 2007," Oxford Business Group, June.

Pollack, D. (2008) "Kuwait's New Political Crisis: Can Democracy Trump Sectarianism?," The Washington Institute for Near East Policy, 25 March.

H.E. al-Qasimi, S. (2007) "How Women Are Empowered Through Business and Entrepreneurship," paper presented at Arab International Women's Forum, Dubai, December.

Rosener, J. (1995) *America's Competitive Secret: Women Managers*, Oxford: Oxford University Press.

Sabbagh, K., Saddi, J. and Shediac, R. (2008) "Oasis Economies," *Booz Allen Hamilton*. Online HTTP: www.boozallen.com/news/39541150?lpid=660614 (accessed March 21, 2008).

United Nations Development Programme (UNDP) Regional Bureau for Arab States (2002) *Arab Human Development Report*, New York: UNDP.

The World Bank (2007) *The Road Not Traveled: Education Reform in the Middle East and North Africa,* Washington, D.C.: The International Bank for Reconstruction and Development.

World Health Organization (WHO) (2000) *World Health Report 2000 - Health Systems: Improving Performance*, Geneva: World Health Organization. Online HTTP: www. who.int/whr/2000/media_centre/press_release/en/ (accessed March 26, 2008).

Zehr, M.A. (2008) "Consultants Help Modernize Arab Schools," *Education Week*, 26 March.

Index

Figures in **Bold**; Tables in Italics

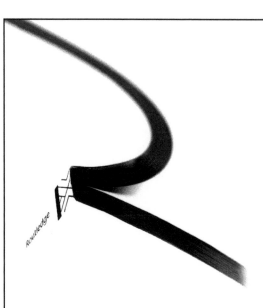

For Product Safety Concerns and Information please contact our EU
representative GPSR@taylorandfrancis.com
Taylor & Francis Verlag GmbH, Kaufingerstraße 24, 80331 München, Germany